DATE DUE

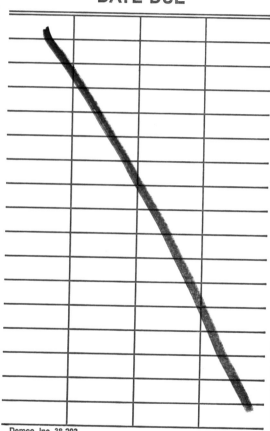

Demco, Inc. 38-293

BEYOND GENDER DIFFERENCES: ADAPTATION TO AGING IN LIFE COURSE PERSPECTIVE

Laurie Russell Hatch

Department of Sociology
University of Kentucky

Jon Hendricks, Editor
SOCIETY AND AGING SERIES

Baywood Publishing Company, Inc.
Amityville, New York

Library of Congress Catalog Number: 99-042083
ISBN: 0-89503-210-4 (cloth : alk. paper)

Library of Congress Cataloging-in-Publication Data

Hatch, Laurie Russell.
   Beyond gender differences : adaptation to aging in life course perspective / Laurie
Russell Hatch.
      p. cm.- - (Society and aging series)
   Includes bibliographical references and index.
   ISBN 0-89503-210-4 (cloth : alk. paper)
   1. Aging- -Social aspects. 2. Aging- -Psychological aspects. 3. Sex role. 4. Adaptability
(Psychology) in old age. 5. Sex differences (Psychology) in old age. 6. Adjustment
(Psychology) in old age. I. Title. II. Series.

HQ1061.H375 1999
305.26- -dc21   99-042083

For Lorraine Russell Hatch

Acknowledgments

This work has benefitted from the contributions and support of many colleagues. I would like to especially thank Larry Burmeister, who reviewed early drafts of the work and provided valuable feedback on matters large and small throughout the process. I am indebted to Joe Hendricks, who has been a most supportive and knowledgeable editor, and with the support of Baywood Publishing, made possible the timely publication of this work. Thanks to Dale Lund and an anonymous reviewer for their careful and insightful reviews. I would also like to thank Margaret Zusky and Christine Smedley for their invaluable editorial advice and assistance at earlier stages in this project. Finally, I would like to express appreciation to colleagues who have participated in dialogues on gender and aging, and who have offered suggestions and support for this project: Marlene Huff, Robynn Pease, Patricia Thompson, Betsy Neale, and Patricia Dyk.

Contents

CHAPTER
1

Introduction

How do we adapt to aging—the gradual changes associated with the aging process, as well as major, sometimes sudden life changes that occur in later life? These questions are of interest to all of us as we grow older and as we are involved with the aging-related experiences of our acquaintances, friends, and loved ones. Not surprisingly, these questions have received a great deal of attention in the field of social gerontology since its origins a half-century ago, and they continue to do so today.

We experience many changes throughout our lives, but older age has been thought to increase our vulnerability to those that challenge our coping skills and diminish our well-being, whether temporarily or for the long-term (Arbuckle and de Vries 1995; Cavan et al. 1949; Elwell and Maltbie-Crannell 1981; Hansson et al. 1986/87; Pearlin and Skaff 1996; Phillips 1957). Older adults who are married or in committed relationships are at increased risk for experiencing the death of their partner. Those who are employed face decisions regarding whether or when to retire, and whether or not to relocate following retirement. Older persons with fewer choices "retire" due to poor health or a lack of employment opportunities. More generally, older age increases our risks for declines in income, health, and independence.

Although every change over the lifespan suggests both gains and losses (Baltes 1987), research on aging has focused predominantly on the latter (Tornstam 1992). From the scant evidence available thus far, we know that gains can also accompany aging. Some creative abilities apparently increase with age, such as imagining new and diverse uses for familiar objects (Horn 1982). John Horn suggests that older adults differ from younger ones "in having somewhat more flexible access to stored information" (1982:268). The adage embodied in "wisdom of the elders" also has found empirical support. Evidence suggests that older adults possess a more fully-elaborated knowledge system than younger adults, which can help them deal with problems of everyday life as well as those that emerge in novel situations (see Baltes 1987). Thus, it seems possible that for some facets of aging, later life *enhances* rather than detracts from our adaptive

1

abilities. With Betty Friedan's book, *The Fountain of Age* (1993), and other popular works emphasizing positive aspects of aging (e.g., Heilbrun 1997), these possibilities may become known more widely.

GENDER DIFFERENCES IN ADAPTATION TO AGING

Questions surrounding adaptation to aging, and how adaptation can best be achieved, have been of central concern in gerontology. Early gerontologists asked whether adaptation was facilitated if people slowly but surely withdrew from their social roles as they grew older—or whether it was more desirable, for both individuals and society more broadly, if older people remained active and involved. More recently, questions of adaptation have focused on individuals' access to economic, health, and social resources, and have asked how differing levels and types of resources impact adaptation to aging.

Over the years, gender differences have been invoked in the answers to these questions. Women and men have been thought to follow different—and unequal—pathways in adapting to older age. Depending upon the explanation at hand and the specific dimension of adaptation under consideration, one or the other gender has been portrayed as adapting more effectively or encountering greater difficulties in the aging process.

Consider the following quotes:

> As a group, and compared to both older women and younger men, (older men) are more likely to have fewer financial liabilities and more assets, enjoy good health unhindered by disability, and experience few distressing "turning points" or "life events" in this age of the life span . . . later life for older men presents fewer troubles (Thompson 1994:9).

> Required to adjust to many role shifts . . . a woman is more likely than a man to be flexible and to be able to cope with life changes. She is also more likely to have same-gender friends upon whom she can depend for social support (Markson 1995:266).

Adaptation to aging is considered a cumulative process, but gerontologists also have examined how well women and men adapt to specific life events in older age. Two of these, in particular, have been focal points for theory and research: the death of a spouse and retirement from paid labor. These events obviously encompass very different experiences and cannot be equated in how they impact individuals' lives and well-being. However, gerontologists have considered spousal bereavement and retirement the two central life events of older age, requiring extensive adaptive efforts for those who experience them. For each of these events, debate has centered on whether women fare better or worse than men.

Consider these pairs of quotes:

On adaptation to the death of a spouse

Problems of adjusting to the loss of a spouse are often worse for a woman than
for a man (Aiken 1995:213).

Widowhood has markedly greater adverse impact upon older men losing a
wife than upon older wives losing a husband (Cohler 1991:316).

On adaptation to retirement from paid labor

Current studies suggest that women are more likely than men to experience
retirement as a stressful life event . . . and to take longer to adapt to the
retirement transition (Szinovacz 1983:105).

The primary commitment of most women is to family and home . . . One may
argue that because work is relatively less significant in their lives—an unsub-
stantiated argument—women are more likely than men to be positive about
retirement" (Antonovsky et al. 1990:62).

These selections are representative of the scholarly controversies that have
surrounded gender differences in later life.

The tendency to frame the aging experience along gender dichotomies is
not limited to scholarly works. For example, students in my aging classes overwhelmingly believe that retirement from paid labor is a more difficult experience
for men than it is for women. Anecdotal evidence is offered about male relatives
who fell ill shortly after their retirement or who lost their zest for life after leaving
the world of paid work. On the other hand, most of the students believe that
women are impacted minimally if at all by retirement from paid labor. A subsequent chapter of this book examines retirement in depth. For now, I will simply
note that the research evidence does not support these commonly-held assumptions about gender differences in adaptation to retirement.

AIMS OF THE BOOK

This book examines adaptation to aging in light of the theoretical explanations and empirical evidence bearing on gender differences. A number of controversies surrounding gender and aging are addressed. For example, do women
and men become more similar to one another as they grow older, and does "gender
role androgyny" promote successful aging? Is it true that retirement is more
stressful for men than it is for women, or is the reverse more likely? Which gender
copes better when a spouse dies? Are women or men more dependent on others
as they grow older?

A central aim of this book is to challenge these questions as well as the
answers they have typically evoked. Gender is central to our identities,

experiences, and life chances,[1] but of course is not the sole influence. I wish to show how a life course perspective is useful in moving beyond this simple, often misleading dichotomy. A life course perspective focuses attention on important dimensions of differentiation and inequality which help to shape human lives—race, ethnicity, social class, age and birth cohort, as well as gender and sexuality. A life course perspective places these interlocking dimensions in social and historical context, encompassing our personal histories as well as the societal context in which we live. In this way, similarities as well as differences between women's and men's adaptation can be identified across space and time, and the life course factors underlying these similarities and differences can be analyzed.

The conceptual and theoretical framework for this project is presented in the following chapter. Why is a focus on gender differences problematic? I review the two theoretical approaches to gender differences that have been used most widely in social gerontology—traditional gender role theory and explanations focusing on women's and men's access to resources. Gender role theory has been vigorously critiqued in the fields of gender studies and women's studies, but retains a strong presence in gerontology. On the other hand, access to social, economic, and health resources is essential to consider in how people adapt to aging, but this approach provides only a partial answer. A life course perspective incorporates this piece of the puzzle, placing women's and men's access to resources in social and historical context. The chapter outlines essential features of a life course framework, including the contributions of this perspective as well as its limitations as a theory. In order to explicitly identify central sources of similarity and difference in the life course, I describe a "multi-level life course model" which is used as a heuristic framework throughout the book.

In the chapters that follow, I examine adaptation to aging as a broad and cumulative process (Chapter 3) and the two life events that have been thought to pose the greatest challenges to adaptation in older age: the death of a spouse (Chapter 4) and retirement (Chapter 5). Each of these three chapters is designed to address these questions: How have theories of gender difference been used to explain adaptation in this realm of experience? To what degree have gender differences been documented in the relevant empirical literature, and are the reported findings supportive of gender difference theories? How and why does a life course perspective provide a more satisfactory framework for understanding women's and men's adaptation to aging, and their adaptation to later-life events in particular?

---

[1] The term life chances derives from Max Weber, who described "the typical chances for a supply of goods, external living conditions, and personal life experiences" (1946:180). Thus, life chances refer to "the probability of experiencing events, circumstances, or opportunities that enhance or diminish the quality of life" (Rothman 1993:14).

In the concluding chapter, I examine the theoretical underpinnings for the life course approach utilized in this book, and suggest theoretical linkages that can be made with this approach. In response to the critique that the life course perspective is atheoretical, I argue that this is a strength of the approach rather than a limitation. The life course perspective provides a flexible conceptual framework which can be integrated effectively with a wide range of theoretical perspectives. I address how two theoretical perspectives—symbolic interactionism and political economy—can provide effective linkages with a life course approach. This final chapter concludes by considering how adaptation to aging can be framed to focus more fully on lifelong processes and challenges, rather than on particular life events which are assumed to be stressful. Instead of being stressful, some life events may offer respite from chronic strains. Consideration of lifelong processes and the context for life events is consistent with the life course perspective advanced in this book.

CHAPTER
2

Putting Gender in Life Course Context

Growing old in the United States is very different for women than for men.
Older Women's League (1999)

Much research attests to the Older Women's League assertion. We know that women in the United States and other advanced industrialized countries are at greater risk than men for developing chronic, but nonfatal, illnesses as they grow older. On the other hand, men are more susceptible than women to life-threatening health problems, and they do not live as long on average (Crimmins, Hayward, and Saito 1996; Verbrugge 1989). Due to gender differences in life expectancies and the fact that women typically marry men who are several years older than themselves, women face greater risks than men for spousal bereavement (Blom 1991; Morgan, Megbolugbe, and Rasmussen 1996). Because older women are more likely than older men to remain single following widowhood or divorce, they are also more likely to live alone (Krivo and Mutchler 1989). Living alone, in turn, is linked with a range of other outcomes in older age, including poverty (Zsembik 1993), greater use of health services (Cafferata 1987), and residence in a nursing home or other long-term care institution (Ford et al. 1990; Greene and Ondrich 1990).

The study of gender differences in aging does not rest with women's and men's relative risks for nursing home residence, poverty, bereavement, and so forth. Rather, the central question has been: Who *adapts better* to aging—women or men? This question begs its converse, which has been phrased in stark, unequivocal terms: Who *suffers more* from aging—women or men? (e.g., Stroebe and Stroebe 1983). From the information above, one might conclude that men suffer more than women from the effects of aging because they do not live as long on average. On the other hand, although women have greater life expectancies, their quality of life may be compromised. As will be evident in this book, this is only one interpretation that has been proposed for gender differences in adaptation to aging.

Adaptation to aging has been assessed by a wide range of indicators, including participation in social networks, quality of interpersonal relationships, mental health and coping, subjective well-being (morale, happiness, life satisfaction),

7

and physical health. What may be considered the ultimate measure of adaptation—how long people live—also has been part of this discussion. On some measures, women may seem advantaged relative to men; on others, the reverse may seem to be the case. However, conclusions to be drawn about differences in women's and men's adaptation to aging depend not only upon the dimension of adaptation under consideration. Even when the focus is narrowed to a specified dimension, researchers often have reached varying if not contradictory conclusions.

A focus on gender differences is useful in some limited ways. Rather than assuming a homogeneous aging experience, gender is recognized as an important influence in people's lives. Focusing on gender differences also can help bring to light assumptions that are held about gender which might otherwise remain implicit (e.g., Antonovsky et al. 1990:62).

Like other dichotomies, however, a focus on gender differences is over-simplified and can yield misleading conclusions.[1] At a minimum, such a focus neglects or ignores altogether other realms of experience and hierarchies of privilege that shape people's lives in addition to gender, including race, ethnicity, social class, sexuality, and age. A focus on gender difference also ignores the *intersections or linkages* between these sources of heterogeneity and diversity. For example, gender differences in labor force participation historically have been more evident among white, middle-class Americans. Although paid labor—and, hence, retirement from that labor—traditionally has been considered more pertinent to men's lives than to women's, this assumption ignores the fact that some groups of women have always worked in the labor force (Kessler-Harris 1981), especially poor and working-class women and women of color (Glenn 1985; Jones 1985).

Furthermore, a focus on gender differences primarily has been a focus on *individuals* (e.g., Deaux and Kite 1987). The social and historical context for those differences is seldom given much attention—to the degree that such differences are "real," and not merely artifacts of the researchers' conceptualization or methodology.

This chapter lays the groundwork for moving beyond gender differences to a life course perspective on adaptation to aging. In the following section, I address the methodological and conceptual limitations of studies which focus on gender differences, and discuss why minimizing or ignoring gender differences also is problematic. In subsequent sections of the chapter, I review two widely-used

---

[1] In the preface to her book *Deceptive Distinctions* (1988), Cynthia Epstein selected this appropriate quote from Stephen Jay Gould, which also has relevance here:

Since the world is so full of a number of things, . . . we must categorize and simplify in order to comprehend. But the reduction of complexity entails a great danger, since the line between enlightening epitome and vulgarized distortion is so fine. Dichotomy is the usual pathway to vulgarization (Gould 1984, as cited in Epstein 1988).

theoretical perspectives on gender differences, and present an alternative life course approach.

CRITIQUES OF GENDER DIFFERENCE STUDIES

Critiques of gender difference studies are not new, by any means. As early as 1910, Helen Thompson Wooley examined the extant evidence on sex differences in intelligence, and concluded that disparities between men's and women's intellectual, sensory, and motor abilities were generally small and inconsistent. Wooley also critiqued the biases underlying these investigations, arguing "There is perhaps no field aspiring to be scientific where flagrant personal bias, logic martyred in the cause of supporting a prejudice, unfounded assertions, and even sentimental rot and drivel, have run riot to such an extent as here" (quoted in Deaux and Kite 1987:93). One need not look far to find examples of blatantly biased "scientific studies" conducted by researchers of the time, many of whom were endeavoring to "prove" the inferiority of women (see Deaux and Kite 1987) or of African Americans (see Thomas and Sillen 1991). Standardized tests for measuring intelligence subsequently were developed in this emerging field of research, but "the quest for sex differences in mental abilities persisted" (Deaux and Kite 1987:94).

Over half a century later, Eleanor Maccoby and Carol Jacklin (1974) reviewed more than 2,000 studies of sex differences in intelligence, personality, and behavior, most of which were published after 1966. Based upon their review, Maccoby and Jacklin concluded that many beliefs about sex differences were not supported empirically, or had not yet received adequate research attention. The few areas of difference that they believed *did* hold up empirically (greater verbal ability among girls; greater aggression and greater quantitative and visual-spatial abilities among boys) were challenged by subsequent reviewers of this body of research (Block 1976; Epstein 1988; Frodi, Macaulay, and Thome 1977).

These critiques addressed a broad range of issues, but focused primarily on the small magnitude of difference reported in many of the studies, and the fact that many were based on small, nonrepresentative samples. Concerns were also raised about the generalizability of results provided by controlled laboratory studies. Noting these and other limitations of sex difference studies, Cynthia Epstein asks, "How can an effort to summarize findings of studies on sex differences be valuable if the research on which it is based is impaired to begin with?" (1988:81).

By the late 1990s the terms "gender" and "gender differences" largely replaced "sex" and "sex differences." This change in terminology resulted from increased acceptance among scholars that gender is socially constructed. It is commonly accepted among social scientists today that "sex" refers to biologically-based categories of female and male, while gender refers to what people "make" of these sex categories (e.g., Thompson 1994; Turner 1994). The terms are not as clear-cut and mutually exclusive as this commonly-accepted definition implies, however. For example, the biological criteria used to determine sex categories must be socially agreed upon. For this reason, Suzanne Kessler and Wendy McKenna (1978) argue that *both* gender and sex are socially constructed. Furthermore, the sex-category placement indicated by one biological criterion sometimes diverges from that indicated by another one. For some individuals, for example, the physical appearance of genitalia indicates membership in one sex category, while chromosomal typing indicates the other category. It is also possible for people to identify themselves (and to be identified by others) as members of one sex, in contradiction to the agreed-upon biological criteria for placement in that category (for example, transsexuals) (West and Zimmerman 1987). (A social constructionist approach to gender will be reviewed in greater detail shortly.)

Although the newer terminology has become convention in the social science literature, many studies continue to reflect older conceptualizations. What was termed a "sex difference" in the 1970s and 80s now is commonly called a gender difference, apart from debates or niceties of distinction regarding social and/or biological processes that may give rise to those differences. Furthermore, despite extensive critiques of gender difference (formerly sex difference) studies, a continuing stream of research focuses upon dichotomized comparisons of women and men (or of girls and boys). Similar critiques have continued to be raised about these studies, including the typically small size of reported gender differences and the neglect of within-gender variation (for reviews and critiques, see Eagly 1987; Epstein 1988; Fausto-Sterling 1992; Hare-Mustin and Maracek 1990a, 1990b; Howard and Hollander 1997; Lips 1988; Riger 1992; Thompson 1993; Turner 1994; Winstead, Derlega, and Rose 1997).

It is also worth pointing out that reviews of gender difference research are based primarily upon published reports. Given the bias toward publishing "positive findings"—non-findings generally are non-publishable—one must also consider the potentially huge number of unpublished studies languishing in researchers' filing cabinets and desk drawers, which have failed to document a gender difference of any size.

Are Gender Difference Studies Fundamentally Flawed?

Some feminist writers have asserted that a focus on gender differences (formerly "sex differences") is fundamentally flawed, beyond methodological concerns. Kay Deaux and Mary Kite contend that the term sex differences in itself suggests "the conclusions that are often sought" (1987:92), calling to mind the adage that everything looks like a nail when one is holding a hammer. Since dichotomous thinking is prevalent in contemporary Western society (and found cross-culturally in many, if not most social groups) (see Deaux and Kite 1987; Epstein 1988), it can also be argued that researchers who focus on gender differences are helping to fortify overly-simplified, biased views of the social world (and that researchers are not exempt from such biases). The problem of exaggerating gender differences has been termed "alpha bias" (Hare-Mustin and Maracek 1990b).

The significance of alpha bias extends beyond scholarly works. Feminists and others have emphasized that scientific frameworks are not value-free and that they carry political implications. Findings from gender difference studies have long been used to justify women's subordinate positions in society and men's dominant ones (Epstein 1988). Cynthia Fuchs Epstein notes that findings of childhood gender differences—however small these measured differences may be—have been used as a springboard to explain the unequal social positions of adult women and men. For example, findings that boys are more aggressive than girls have been used to justify why men have greater social and political power than women (e.g., Goldberg 1974).[2] Physical differences between males and females, such as size and strength, also have been used to justify social inequalities (see Lambert 1978). "Small biological differences are turned into bigger physical differences which themselves are turned into the gambits of social, political and ideological power play" (Cockburn 1983:204).

In the process, important information about the *context* for reported gender differences are ignored or obscured. For example, findings of gender differences in aggression are contingent upon specific features of the situation in which aggression may be displayed or encouraged. They are also contingent upon how aggression is conceptualized and measured (see Eagly 1987; Frieze et al. 1978; Frodi et al. 1977).

For aggression as well as virtually all measured behaviors, attitudes, and beliefs, research shows that girls and boys and women and men are not polar opposites. Great variation has been found within gender groups, on most if not all outcome variables of interest (see Ferree and Hess 1987). This is true even where presumably incontrovertible gender differences are concerned, such as size and strength. Furthermore, using physical differences which differentiate women and men *on average* to justify inequitable social arrangements ignores the fact that people's physical qualities may be irrelevant to those social arrangements. Judith Lorber points out that men's "supposed greater strength rationalizes the gendered division of work even when it is machinery that does the actual physical labor" (1994:49).

In sum, feminist writers have charged that studies which focus on gender differences are misleading, if not inherently biased, and that findings from these studies have been distorted to justify inequitable and oppressive social arrangements. This does not mean, however, that taking the *opposite* approach—

---

[2] Epstein points out that findings of childhood differences in verbal skills have not been used analogously. If such were the case, findings of greater verbal abilities among girls relative to boys would be used to justify why women should become politicians.

minimizing differences between women and men and emphasizing their similarities—is necessarily unbiased or emancipatory.

Minimizing or ignoring differences between women and men can be as biased as approaches which overemphasize differences. This problem has been termed "beta bias," in contrast to the alpha bias of approaches which exaggerate difference (Hare-Mustin and Maracek 1990b). Using men's experience or all-male samples to draw generalizations about human development, personality, or behavior illustrates beta bias. Hare-Mustin and Maracek point out that this source of bias was common in scientific theory and research until recent decades.

Beta bias also is evident when disparities between women's and men's resources and power are ignored. Gender-neutral approaches have dominated scholarship in family studies, even in areas where power and resources are clearly salient, such as housework and family violence (Thompson and Walker 1995). To understand these rather surprising patterns, Thompson and Walker note that the family systems approach has dominated the research literature. Applied to family violence, this approach has focused primarily on the transmission of violence across generations and the involvement of both spouses in marital violence, overlooking gender differences in the frequency and severity of violence in the family. More generally, family systems theory concentrates more upon generation as a focal point of study and neglects issues of power *within* generations, such as whether daughters are afforded resources and autonomy equal to those afforded to sons, or whether mothers' power in the family is equal to that of fathers. "By regarding all members of a generation as equal interacting participants in the family system, systems theories put forward a neutered representation of family life" (Hare-Mustin and Maracek 1990b:36).[3]

It is not only family systems theory and research which reflects beta bias. Traditional gender role theory, which I review in detail below, encompasses *both* forms of bias. Alpha bias is reflected in the assumption of dichotomous, non-overlapping gender roles (exaggeration of attitudinal and behavioral differences). Beta bias is reflected in the assumption that gender roles are complementary and equal (minimizing or ignoring power differences). Some permutations of role theory appear to ignore gender altogether, but further inspection reveals otherwise. For example, the "retirement role" has been presented as gender-neutral (e.g., Richardson and Kilty 1991), but closer examination reveals that this role has been based upon a stereotypic "male model" of experience (Calasanti 1996; George, Fillenbaum, and Palmore 1984; Gratton and Haug 1983; Matthews and Brown 1988). Rarely are women used as the stereotypic model for human experience. (Research on spousal bereavement probably comes closest to woman-centered beta bias in social gerontology.)

---

[3] Hare-Mustin and Maracek reference Judith Libow (1985) for this point.

Beta bias is reflected in social policies as well as the research literature. For example, the Social Security program is based upon a "male model" (especially, a white, middle-class male model) of work, which presumes lengthy and continuous labor-force history, and ignores the unpaid family caregiving typically performed by women.[4] And gender neutral social policies such as no-fault divorce ignore the fact that women typically have fewer economic resources at their command than the men to whom they were married—a fact reflected in women's increased risks for poverty following divorce (Arendell and Estes 1991; Duncan and Hoffman 1985; Older Women's League 1999).

Thus, ignoring or minimizing gender differences is not the answer to the problems posed by approaches which exaggerate differences. Furthermore, not all feminists agree that gender distinctions are necessarily invidious for women. Although a number of gender difference theories can be seen as rationalizing or justifying gender inequalities, others explicitly reflect feminist issues and concerns. Carol Gilligan (1982), for example, argues that women and men develop different moral orientations toward justice, responsibility, and nurturance, which shape their identities and their relationships with others.[5] Men are oriented toward rights and rules, while women are the "more caring sex," emphasizing fairness and responsibility to others. In contrast to Freud, Piaget, and Kohlberg, who portrayed women's moral development as weaker than men's, in Gilligan's schema these differences are affirming of women and their contributions in society.

Some feminist scholars agree with Gilligan "that affirming difference affirms women's value and special nature" (see Hare-Mustin and Maracek 1990b:52). Feminist rebuttals to this affirmation of difference make an argument which I believe is persuasive: by valorizing women's "special nature"—which derives from and is linked with their subordinate status in society—the status quo is further legitimized and strengthened (see Hare-Mustin and Maracek 1990b), a problem shared with approaches which are antithetical to feminist concerns and goals. Furthermore, valorizing women's "special nature" dichotomizes women and men, and invariably neglects within-gender variation. These problems are shared with other gender difference theories.

THEORIES OF GENDER DIFFERENCE

Without doubt, role theory has dominated the conceptualization and study of gender. Despite extensive published critiques (e.g., Lopata and Thorne 1978;

---

[4] This issue is addressed in greater detail in the chapter on retirement.

[5] Gilligan does not specify the mechanisms by which these gendered orientations are developed (e.g., via socialization or some combination of socialization and biology), but suggests that they are entrenched in our psyches.

Stacey and Thorne 1985; West and Zimmerman 1987), traditional gender role theory remains popular in the social sciences and in social gerontology in particular. Because traditional gender role theory and its "parent" theory of structural functionalism retain an important presence in the literatures examined in this book, it is important to take a close look at this approach. This section summarizes and critiques this theory of gender difference, as well as an opposing but also widely utilized approach, which focuses upon women's and men's access to socioeconomic resources.

Gender Roles and the Legacy of Functionalism

Broadly, gender roles refer to

> those expected attitudes and behaviors which a society associates with each sex. These include the rights and responsibilities that are normative for the sexes in a given society (Lindsey 1997:3).

There is more to the gender role approach than this broad definition, however. "Traditional gender role theory" is largely traceable to functionalism, specifically Talcott Parsons' analytic approach (Parsons 1954, 1955; Parsons and Bales 1955). This influential sociological theory had its heydey in the 1950s and 60s, but Parsons' legacy continues in sociology and related fields of study (Glenn 1987), including social gerontology (Marshall 1994).

Briefly, functionalism is a theory of consensus, meaning that shared norms and values are considered the bedrock of societal order (as opposed to perspectives which view the social order as reflecting the dominance of powerful groups). Components within society, including institutions of education, religion, the economy, the polity, the family, and so forth, are viewed as fulfilling different functions, helping to maintain societal stability and equilibrium. These components are interconnected with one another; changes in one component generate changes in others. From this perspective, social change is likely to be disruptive unless it is gradual, allowing the components to re-equilibrate.[6]

The functionalist approach to gender lies in its explication of the family and its functions. In contrast to traditional societies, where the family fulfills multiple essential functions including economic production, Parsons argued that the family in modern society specializes narrowly in socioemotional functions—socialization of children and the emotional support and nurturance of family members. Just as is true for the larger societal system, according to Parsons, the family system requires a division of labor to operate efficiently and remain in

---

[6] Miriam Johnson provides an interesting feminist rebuttal to some of the criticisms levelled against Parsons. She argues that Parsons's approach should not be interpreted as upholding the status quo, as many feminist and other critics have claimed—"for Parsons was in fact a celebrant of progressive change" (1989:107).

equilibrium. Tasks within the family are allocated on the basis of gender and age. Those related to the primary socioemotional functions of the family unit are assumed by women. In contrast, men's primary responsibilities are considered instrumental—providing economic support to the family and linking the family with outside institutions via men's occupations and involvement in public life.

Parsons argued that this division into separate but complementary roles helps to promote harmony within the family unit. Because the number of status-giving roles is limited to only one family member—the husband, by virtue of his occupational role—competition for status between the marital partners is eliminated. Furthermore, the status of the family in the community is "relatively definite and unequivocal" (Parsons 1955:326), since the family's status derives from the occupational role of one rather than both marital partners. To Parsons, this is a further function of distinct family roles: "There is much evidence that this relative definiteness of status is an important factor in psychological security" (although such evidence is not cited.) Parsons dispensed with employed married women by stating that, at most, these women have "a job" rather than "a career." Similarly, he viewed men's involvement in housework, child care, and other "internal affairs of the household" (p. 325) as minor in comparison to their breadwinning role.

Parsons considered this division of tasks functional for the larger society as well as the family unit—stable and efficient family units fulfill the functions of reproduction and socialization required for societal maintenance and stability. At the same time, he believed that this "utilitarian division of labor" (p. 325) creates strains within families because women are stymied in their ability to achieve equality with their husbands in the socially-valued realm of occupations. However, Parsons argued that the marital relationship itself is based upon mutuality and equality of the wife and husband, rather than a pattern of "superordination-subordination" (p. 327).

In Parsons's framework, two sets of mechanisms structure individuals' personality systems, such that they become compatible with the functional requisites of social systems. Socialization is the process by which individuals internalize the shared norms and values of society and develop the skills needed for their assigned roles. The other process is social control—the interpersonal and institutional mechanisms used to reduce sources of strain and deviance and enforce conformity with norms and values (Parsons 1954; Parsons and Bales 1955). However, socialization processes have been emphasized by Parsons and subsequent gender role scholars, with little attention paid to mechanisms of social control.

Flaws in the Traditional Gender Role Approach

Functionalist thinking about gender has had an enduring impact in the social sciences (Ferree 1990). The functionalist approach is evidenced in part by the widespread use of role language—"the male role" "the female role," "gender roles," and "gender role socialization" (Glenn 1987:353). The presumed nature and content of these roles often corresponds to Parsons's depictions. It is not difficult to find contemporary works which characterize women's and men's roles as dichotomous and complementary, with women's roles considered primarily socioemotional and family-centered, and men's roles considered primarily instrumental (e.g., Barer 1994; Cohler 1991; Gradman 1994; Rawlins 1992).

The traditional gender role approach is problematic for many reasons, both conceptual and empirical. Looking first at the content of "traditional gender roles," it is clear that Parsons' thesis reflects "cultural and historical myopia" (Epstein 1988:108). The phenomenon of women devoting themselves to mother-hood is culturally and historically specific, and is also specific to women in particular social class and racial-ethnic groups. "What Parsons implied to be universally true appeared to hold only for middle-class women in the 1940's and 1950's" (Epstein 1988:109). More accurately, these patterns applied primarily to white, middle-class women in Western societies (see Glenn 1985; Miller and Garrison 1982).

Furthermore, in contrast to the functionalist claim that families and other small groups function most efficiently when different individuals take responsibility for socioemotional and instrumental tasks (thereby justifying "traditional gender roles"), researchers have found that these tasks are not incompatible. The same individual can provide both socioemotional and instrumental leadership in a group (Meeker and Weitzell-O'Neill 1985). This dichotomy also ignores the activities of homemakers which could be defined as instrumental (for example, providing linkages between the familial "private sphere" and the "public sphere" through involvement in parent-teacher associations or volunteer activities), or which oc-cupy a hazy line between "expressive" and "instrumental" tasks (for example, buying, preparing, and serving food) (Glenn 1987:352).

A further central criticism of the traditional gender role approach is that it is fundamentally static (Connell 1985; Epstein 1988). This is shown clearly among writers who characterize women's and men's roles much as Parsons did in the 1950s. However, this shortcoming also is evident in arguments which stress that significant changes have occurred in women's and men's roles. R.W. Connell (1985) argues that from a role perspective, change is something that *happens to* gender roles, coming from external social forces. For example, changes in the economy have been cited as producing changes in women's roles. Lacking a mechanism to link social-historical change and individual behavior, role theorists are trapped into generalizing about social norms "and then using the frozen descriptions as boxes into which to pack the events of people's lives. . . . The logic of role analysis forces role theorists to reify sex roles" (Connell 1985:263).

A parallel argument is made by Cynthia Fuchs Epstein in her critique of gender role theories:

Only rarely has research located the specific gatekeepers and mechanisms responsible for assigning "sex roles," and thus creating the clustered combinations of statuses that feed the stereotypes of what is regarded as "normal" behavior. These patterns have been ascribed to custom and tradition, to prior forces, to early socialization, to conditioning of men and women, to natural preferences and desires emanating from their different capacities and interests, and to patriarchy as a general system. Some believed that a search for origins was futile in this case, and that it was sufficient to identify many practices as "institutionalized"—socially embedded (1988:117).

The underpinnings for the bulk of gender role research are even vaguer than Epstein's characterization. In 1978, Helena Lopata and Barrie Thorne pointed out that "sex role" was used as a catchall term. The same is true today. Like its earlier sex role counterpart, "gender role" is used to refer to "everything from structural disadvantage to implied personality traits" (Ferree 1990:867).

Whether defined as structural disadvantage, personality traits, natural preferences, or some other phenomena, the central focus of gender role study has been on *individuals,* rather than features of the society in which people live or contextual elements of the situations in which they interact (Risman 1987; Stacey and Thorne 1985). This seems paradoxical, in that *changes* in gender roles usually are viewed as coming from forces external to individuals, such as changes in the economy. These social structural forces tend to be invoked in vague terms, however. The central focus of concern has been on how gender roles are or can be linked with a range of interests, attitudes, skills, and behaviors for girls and boys, women and men. Thus, gender role explanations typically neglect the sociopolitical context of women's and men's lives and depoliticize their interpersonal relationships.

I believe these critiques have merit and are valid for many if not most incarnations of gender role theory. However, it is important to point out that some scholars have worked to address a number of these shortcomings. For example, Ralph Turner and Doug Abbott (1990) have endeavored to identify sources of gender role change and the conditions which facilitate or hinder such change. Some scholars have argued that "traditional" gender roles may be more applicable to today's older adults than to younger age groups (e.g., Solomon and Szwabo 1994) or that gender roles change across an individual's life course (e.g., Wilson 1995). Furthermore, some writers who take a gender role approach disagree that women's and men's roles are equal and complementary. Their arguments will be addressed shortly.

An insurmountable limitation shared by all versions of gender role theory is that gender is conceptualized as a *master identity* which cuts across situations. In contrast, a role is a *situated identity*—"assumed and relinquished as the situation demands" (West and Zimmerman 1987:128). West and Zimmerman point out that

> Unlike most roles, such as "nurse," "doctor," and "patient" or "professor" and "student," gender has no specific site or organizational context. Moreover, many roles are already gender marked, so that special qualifiers—such as "female doctor" or "male nurse"—must be added to exceptions to the rule . . . Conceptualizing gender as a role makes it difficult to assess its influence on other roles and reduces its explanatory usefulness in discussions of power and inequality[7] (pp. 128-129).

The same treatment has not extended to other social statuses. Some years ago, Helena Lopata and Barrie Thorne observed the unique way in which gender has been conceptualized in terms of specific roles: "It is significant that sociologists do not use the terms 'class roles' or 'race roles' " (1978:719).

Structural Explanations: Gender Differences in Resources

An evident alternative to role-based explanations for gender differences is to focus on the *structural positions* of women and men in society, specifically their access to socioeconomic resources and power. In contrast to gender role explanations, a structural approach does not assume that women and men are socialized to hold different orientations toward family, paid work, and so forth, or that their personalities and interests are intrinsically different. Rather, individuals are assumed to be influenced similarly by the opportunities available to them in society, and by the constraints that impinge upon them. When women's or men's social structural positions change, bringing changes in their access to resources, their attitudes and behaviors are also expected to change (e.g., Blau 1977).

Rosabeth Moss Kanter's *Men and Women of the Corporation* (1977) is a classic structuralist study of gender. Her study of employees in a large corporation found that more women than men emphasized family life over their careers, showed little interest in promotions at work, and fantasized about vacations and leaving their jobs. Gender role theorists would interpret these findings as reflecting traditional gender role socialization and the primacy of family over career roles for women. However, most of the women in the corporation held dead-end jobs as secretaries and clerks, with little chance for promotion, while men were more likely to be managers or to have jobs offering upward mobility to management. Kanter shows convincingly that men in dead-end jobs hold the same attitudes toward work and achievement as women in dead-end jobs, emphasizing family life and socializing over their careers. Conversely, both women and men

---

[7] West and Zimmerman cite an unpublished manuscript by Barrie Thorne for this point.

are committed to their careers and express aspirations for promotion when their jobs offer opportunities for promotion.

In addition to examining structures of opportunity and power that are available (or unavailable) to women and men as workers, Kanter also examines the impact of sex ratios on workplace dynamics. She argues that when women (or members of any group) are under-represented, they are likely to be "tokenized"— perceived and treated as stereotyped symbols of their group, rather than as unique individuals. Other structuralist theorists have focused more broadly on sex ratios in society, and how imbalanced ratios impact women's power in public life and in interpersonal relationships (Guttentag and Secord 1983; South and Trent 1988). A few social gerontologists have considered how women's and men's adaptation to aging may be impacted by skewed sex ratios (these efforts are examined in Chapters 3 and 4). However, this type of structural approach is less common than resource-based explanations for gender differences.

Limitations of Resource Explanations

Kanter's approach delineates structural elements of the workplace environment and how these elements impact women's and men's attitudes and behaviors at work. Other writers utilizing a structural explanation for gender differences (whether explicitly or implicitly) tend to focus more simply on whether women have access to more or less of a particular valued resource (income, social ties, health) compared to men (e.g., Fischer and Oliker 1983; Hatch 1992; Markson 1995; Schulz 1995). Differential levels of resources are then linked with attitudinal and behavioral outcomes. For example, Elizabeth Markson states "if older women were no more likely to brave financial strain than men, there would be no significant gender differences in their sense of mastery and psychological distress" (1995:270).

Resource explanations for gender differences move beyond a primary concern with individuals' personality traits and dispositions, and are more satisfactory than gender role approaches in my view, but they provide only a partial picture of women's and men's lives. The locus of concern has remained more often with individuals (i.e., a focus on individuals' incomes, health, social ties, and so forth) than on the social institutions and processes in society which give rise to unequal distributions of resources, and which help to maintain (or potentially challenge) these inequalities.

This need not be the case. A number of sociological theories take individuals' structural positions and control over resources in society as the locus of concern, and ground these in social and historical context. Some structural theories based upon Marxian ideas, for example, create a view of social structure

> as the distribution of resources among actors who use their respective resources in social encounters and, in the process, reproduce social structure

and its attendant distribution of resources. Thus, structure *is* the symbolic, material, and political resources that actors have in their encounters; and, as they employ these resources to their advantage, they reproduce the structure of their social relations because they sustain their respective shares of resources (Turner 1991:490-491).

In contrast to most uses of a generic "resource explanation" for gender differences in aging, Marxian analysts locate human actors and their control over resources within particular societies at particular points in time. Socialist feminists also do so, focusing more specifically on issues which are pertinent to women's lives, such as reproduction (e.g., Hartmann 1981; Mitchell 1971).[8]

Blending the Gender Role and Resource Explanations: Gender Roles as Structured Inequality

In their "pure form," traditional gender role and resource explanations focus on differing phenomena. The former focuses on differences in women's and men's internalized traits and dispositions, while the latter emphasizes differences in their access to valued resources in society. The explanations also suggest differing responses to gender inequalities. The former suggests relatively enduring characteristics over the course of an individual's lifetime, and inequalities typically are not a matter of concern—gender roles tend to be viewed as complementary and equal. The latter suggests that equivalent access to resources will produce equivalent outcomes for women and men.

In practice, these explanations often are used in combination with one another. Gender role socialization is thought to shape women's and men's paid work and family experiences, which in turn influence the economic resources available to them (e.g., Umberson, Wortman, and Kessler 1992). Gender differences in social resources also are often attributed to traditional gender roles. In particular, women's presumed socio-emotional specialization is thought to enhance their relationships with family and friends and to provide health-protecting benefits to them (Rawlins 1992; Weiss 1983).

Some scholars make a more explicit connection between gender roles and social inequality. In this approach, gender differences in health, economic and other resources stem from the stratification of gender roles (e.g., Lipman-Blumen 1984). Walter Gove (1972) and Jessie Bernard ([1972] 1978) exemplify this perspective. These writers have argued that women's health suffers when they are married, but that marriage enhances men's health due to inequalities structured into the institution of marriage. Inequalities in the family derive from men's economic and political dominance in society at large. This approach is superior to

---

[8] For a socialist feminist approach to aging, see Calasanti and Zajicek (1993).

role explanations which ignore gendered inequalities, but, in my view, continues to fall short of the mark.

Whether separate or combined, gender role and resource explanations share some of the same limitations. Both types of approaches tend to focus on dichotomized gender comparisons and neglect sources of variation within gender groups. Both focus primarily on the individual and neglect broader social structures and processes. Both also present a relatively static picture of gender. As they are typically utilized, gender role and resource explanations also tend to be ahistorical, not only with respect to the societal context for human lives, but also the personal histories of the individuals involved.

SOCIAL CONSTRUCTION OF GENDER

Although questions concerning the etiology of gender are far from settled, many contemporary feminist scholars agree that gender is socially constructed (e.g., Britton 1997; Dellinger and Williams 1997; Hare-Mustin and Maracek 1990a; Lorber 1994; Lorber and Farrell 1991; West and Zimmerman 1987). From this perspective, gender differences are acknowledged but are not deterministic. Rather, gender differences must be considered within the social and temporal *contexts* in which they appear. Power relations are of particular interest, as these are evidenced in interpersonal interactions (West and Zimmerman 1987) and within larger social institutions and structures (Lorber 1994).

Candace West and Don Zimmerman's article "Doing Gender" (1987) has become a classic micro-level social constructivist statement on gender, focusing on face-to-face interactions between individuals. To West and Zimmerman, "a person's gender is not simply an aspect of what one is, but, more fundamentally, it is something that one *does*, and does recurrently, in interaction with others" (p. 140). From this perspective, gender is not a property of *individuals*— embedded within our biologies, psychologies, or social roles. Rather, gender is an emergent property of social interaction, which varies across different interactional settings.

One of the examples that West and Zimmerman cite as an illustration of "doing gender" is taken from Cahill (1986:176):

> The following interaction occurred on a preschool playground. A 55-month-old boy (D) was attempting to unfasten the clasp of a necklace when a preschool aide walked over to him.
>
> A: Do you want to put that on?
> D: No. It's for girls.
>
> A: You don't have to be a girl to wear things around your neck. Kings wear things around their neck. You could pretend you're a king.
> D: I'm not a king. I'm a boy.

"Doing gender" involves innumerable everyday interactions, such as a man taking a woman's arm to guide her across the street—and the woman "consenting to be guided and not initiating such behavior with a man" (West and Zimmerman 1987:135). To West and Zimmerman, doing gender is essentially unavoidable, since "in virtually any situation, one's sex category [identification as female or male] can be relevant, and one's performance as an incumbent of that category can be subjected to evaluation" (p. 145).

In some settings, doing gender can *challenge* prevailing social expectations—for example, individuals whose appearance or behavior does not provide clear signals to others concerning whether they are female or male. Challenge also comes when a person's sex category is unambiguous, but the behavior is inconsistent with prevailing expectations for that category—women who do not take the arm proffered by a male companion, for example, or men who do not proffer their arm, despite their female companions' expectations that they will do so. West and Zimmerman note that "If we fail to do gender appropriately, we as individuals . . . may be called to account (for our character, motives, and predispositions)" (p. 146). On the other hand, "If we do gender appropriately, we simultaneously sustain, reproduce, and render legitimate the institutional arrangements that are based on sex category" (p. 146).

West and Zimmerman, along with other social constructionists, work to avoid the deterministic underpinnings of previous theories of gender by focusing on individuals' own interpretations of their experiences and situations, rather than imposing the researchers' definitions of what these may involve. This approach is consistent with Myra Marx Ferree and Beth Hess' (1987) characterization of a feminist approach—"beginning from and remaining true to personal experience. . . . Resistance, ambivalence, conflict, and struggle are key concepts for feminist theory and methodology because of the centrality of the distinction between what is and what ought to be" (p. 14). Individual women and men are active participants in creating and interpreting their social worlds. In Ferree and Hess' words, "people do not always become what they are expected to be" (p. 14). At the same time, those who desire to resist oppression confront a limited range of choices. Structures of opportunity and constraint are not the same for all women or for all men, nor do they remain static across time.

West and Zimmerman claim that viewing gender as "an achieved property of situated conduct" focuses our attention not only upon the interactional realm, but ultimately, institutional arenas as well (1987:126). Their focus is clearly on the former, however, and it is here where these writers have made important contributions. For West and Zimmerman, it is face-to-face interaction—the "doing" of gender—which helps to maintain institutions in society. Apart from making some general claims, the authors say little about the broader social structure.

Judith Lorber's attempt to provide clarity to the concept of gender addresses this issue. Lorber also takes a social constructionist position, but she emphasizes that gender encompasses more than interpersonal relations. Lorber agrees that gender is constructed in social interaction, but more than this, gender is *built into* the social institutions of society—ideology, family, economy, and politics—"and is also an entity in and of itself" (Lorber 1994:1). In Lorber's approach, gender reflects "a process of social construction, a system of social stratification, and an institution that structures every aspect of our lives because of its embeddedness in the family, the workplace, and the state, as well as in sexuality, language and culture" (1994:5). In sum, *gender is a social institution.*

Although it is undoubtedly the case that debates will continue to surround the conceptualization of gender, I find Lorber's effort a helpful advance. In particular, she calls attention to the multiple dimensions encompassed in the social construction of gender, and emphasizes that gender must be studied in cultural and historical context. Lorber does not wish to merely document the ways in which gender is institutionalized in society, but, rather, to challenge its presumed "naturalness" and inevitability. "Gender has changed in the past and will change in the future, but without deliberate restructuring it will not necessarily change in the direction of greater equality between women and men" (Lorber 1994:5).

THE LIFE COURSE PERSPECTIVE

Many writers agree that the context for observed gender differences must be considered, particularly those who emphasize that gender is socially constructed (Epstein 1988; Lorber 1994; Stacey and Thorne 1985; Thompson and Walker 1995). Although such statements often are made without much discussion of what the context for gender might encompass, some explicit models have been proposed. For example, Kay Deaux and Brenda Major (1987) offer a contextual model which focuses upon interactants' expectations concerning gender, their self-identities, and situational cues. Deaux and Major note that interchanges between individuals often are reflective of prior histories of interaction, but their micro-level model does not extend to the larger social and historical context in which social interaction takes place.

Gerontologists have contributed to the development of a conceptual framework which links women's and men's lives with the broader social and historical context in which they live.[9] This framework, the life course perspective, is not inconsistent with recent attempts to refine the understanding of gender, including West and Zimmerman's micro-level perspective on "doing gender" and Lorber's multidimensional conceptualization of gender. Rather, the perspective can usefully inform (and be informed by) a wide variety of explanatory frameworks. The life course perspective acknowledges the importance of women's and men's

---

[9] Versions of the life course perspective are utilized in a wide range of fields including sociology, psychology, economics, history, family studies, and gerontology.

access to resources. However, in contrast to a generic "resource explanation," the life course perspective explicitly identifies potential sources of similarity in women's and men's lives as well as sources of difference, encompassing multiple levels of human experience.

At a micro or individual level, prior histories of experience are key to understanding women's and men's current circumstances, and together the past and present "stake a claim on the future" (Allen and Pickett 1987:518). Personal histories—past, present, and future—are embedded in social-historical time and space. "Each life is punctuated in diverse and unique ways by idiosyncratic events and experiences" (Allen and Chin-Sang 1990:735), but some events and experiences are shared in common with others of the same birth cohort—an age group travelling through history together (Hareven 1978). Portions of one's personal biography also are shared in common with others who occupy similar social structural positions. Gender is a fundamental stratifier of people's lives, but, of course, it is not the only one. Gender interlocks with other hierarchies of inequality, including race, ethnicity, social class, sexual orientation, and age, which together help to determine individuals' social locations. Finally, large-scale events such as World War II or the Great Depression shape the direction and content of human lives, as do the social institutions and policies in place at a given place and point in time.

I will discuss more fully each of the levels of experience which comprise the framework used in this book, after describing the origins and development of the life course approach. It is important to emphasize at the outset, however, that these contextual layers cannot be understood adequately in isolation from one another. For example, mental and physical health are considered part of one's personal biography, but health status is linked with one's social location: those with greater socioeconomic resources tend to have better health, fewer disabilities, and lower risks for mortality (Crimmins et al. 1996; Schoenbaum and Waidmann 1997; Smith and Waitzman 1994). A major economic recession is consequential for all segments of society, but its effects on individuals and their families will vary according to a person's age when the event occurred, aspects of her or his personal biography (including prior life events and histories of experience, patterns of coping, and so forth), and access to valued resources in society. Nor do systems of inequality remain static over an individual's lifetime. As societies change over time, so too do opportunity structures (Stoller and Gibson 1994).

Origins and Development of the Life Course Perspective

The life course perspective has a lengthy history and multidisciplinary roots, including contributions from life history analysis, life span psychology, age stratification theory, and the demographic concept of age cohort (Elder 1978; Hareven 1980). Not surprisingly, then, there is no single "theory of the life course" (George 1996). One of the distinctions that can be made among life course approaches is that some versions take the individual as the primary unit of analysis, while others focus primarily upon family development and change.

Life Course Approach to Individual Biographies and Social Change

A focus on the individual life course and social change can be traced to the early Chicago school of sociology. Following from W.I. Thomas and Florian Znaniecki's landmark work, *The Polish Peasant in Europe and America*, originally published in 1918, sociologists gathered rich and detailed life history data from diaries, letters, and other personal documents to examine intersections between individual biographies and social change. The use of qualitative data requiring researchers' subjective interpretations fell out of favor after World War II, when the "new positivism" gained ascendancy in the social sciences (Elder 1985).

Interest in linking individual biographies with social history flagged until the 1960s (Elder 1985), at which point a life course approach emerged from researchers in several social science disciplines, notably Norman Ryder in sociology (1965), K. Warner Schaie in psychology (1965), and Richard Easterlin in economics (1961). While their substantive topics for research differed, each of these scholars recognized "the joint significance of age, period, and cohort"[10] in linking individual lives with social change (O'Rand 1996:230). The use of qualitative data drawn from individual life histories subsequently regained popularity and sophisticated quantitative techniques also began to be developed and applied to life course research (Elder 1985).

As will be elaborated in the pages to come, the model advanced in this book is consistent with this approach to life course study, focusing on individual life histories embedded in a broader socio-historical context. The book draws upon results from quantitative as well as qualitative studies to explore life course dimensions of individuals' adaptation to aging and to life events in older age.

Life Course Approach to Family Structure and Dynamics

Other versions of the life course perspective take the family as the primary unit of analysis rather than the individual. The life course approach improves upon earlier theories of family change and development, termed the "family life cycle theory" and the "family developmental approach" (Glick 1977; Hill 1968a, 1968b, 1970; Hill and Rodgers 1964; Rodgers 1973). Most versions of these theories postulated that a "typical family" passes through successive critical stages during its life span, beginning with engagement and marriage and continuing to successive stages of "birth of children, children leaving home, the 'postchildren'

---

[10]The terms period and cohort will be discussed shortly.

or 'empty nest' period, and ultimate dissolution of the marriage through death of one of the spouses" (Glick 1977:5).

The life course approach overcomes many of the limitations associated with stage models of family development. In contrast to the "static snapshots" of families provided by stage models (Elder 1978:18), a life course perspective focuses upon transitions, timing, and multiple career lines, giving "fluidity and color" to family life (Allen and Pickett 1987:518). The ahistorical approach of stage models is replaced by an explicit focus upon the socio-historical context in which families are located. Also, in contrast to the normative approach embodied in most versions of the family life cycle and developmental approaches, which focused upon heterosexual, intact marriages, the life course approach considers variations in family histories and structures, as well as variations in the timing of life events (Allen and Pickett 1987; Elder 1978; Hareven 1980).

Linkages between Individual and Family Development

Since the lives of individuals are intertwined with families, it seems most useful to consider individual and family development simultaneously, focusing upon intersections between "individual time," "family time," and "historical time" (Hareven 1978:1). On the other hand, Susan Watkins (1980) points out that the life courses of individuals typically diverge from those of families, with differing beginning and ending points, differing life stages and transitions, and so forth. Watkins argues that for methodological reasons, researchers must select either the individual or the family as the primary unit of analysis.

Such a selection (or, in contradiction to Watkins's position, the decision to focus explicitly upon linkages between the life courses of individuals and families) depends upon the theoretical and research goals at hand. In this book, I have elected to focus on individuals as the primary "units of analysis" to understand sources of gender similarities and differences in adaptation to aging. This does not mean, however, that family life is omitted from consideration. Just as birth cohort and membership in social hierarchies shape the direction and content of individuals' lives, as do large-scale social events and the social institutions in place at a given point in time, so too are family-related events and dynamics important for the life course of individuals. Here, family is defined broadly to encompass non-traditional families (e.g., cohabiting heterosexual couples, homosexual couples), as well as traditional family forms. However, attention to the former is limited by the fact that relatively little scholarship has been conducted on non-traditional families in later life.

A MULTI-LEVEL LIFE COURSE MODEL

Taking a life course perspective, we can examine the context for aging in terms of multiple levels of experience. The following discussion builds upon and extends the life course framework of Eleanor Stoller and Rose Campbell Gibson (1994), which I believe is useful to delineate key components of this broad and complex perspective. For purposes of this discussion, I term this heuristic framework a "multi-level life course model." All life course approaches encompass multiple layers of social phenomena, but their features are not always systematically demarcated. The aim of the following discussion is to disentangle and identify explicitly the classes of experience encompassed by the life course approach taken in this book. The model begins with the level of personal biographies and concludes with the larger societal context. Intermediate levels of experience are captured by group membership, including social hierarchies of privilege which help to determine the resources that are available to different segments of society and membership in particular birth cohorts.

Personal Histories

At a micro or individual level, we enter older age with differing personal histories of experience. Personal biographies encompass the events we have experienced during our lifetimes, our personal characteristics (including personality, intelligence, health, and other personal resources),[11] and the patterns of coping and adaptation we have developed throughout our lives. Some life course researchers include additional biographical elements such as "biological and psychological vulnerabilities," and "motivational structures" (see Folkman 1991).

Clearly, personal biographies can encompass a vast range of phenomena. Within this contextual layer, the greatest attention has been on events experienced over the life course.

Life Events

According to Linda George (1989:243), life events are "identifiable, discrete changes in life patterns that disrupt usual behaviors and can threaten or challenge

---

[11]In their life course framework, Stoller and Gibson (1994) combine individuals' personal biographies with their membership in social hierarchies of privilege. Stoller and Gibson define personal attributes as "characteristics of individuals that determine their positions in systems of inequality" (p. 4); these characteristics include race and gender. The authors consider economic security an adaptive resource available to individuals, which derives from their membership in social hierarchies of privilege.

Personal biographies are closely connected with membership in hierarchies of privilege. Indeed, all levels of the life course framework are interconnected. However, I think that it is helpful for conceptual purposes to distinguish these levels of analysis. Some important life events and aspects of individuals' personalities and coping patterns are shared with others of similar social locations. Other components of personal biographies are shared with members of the same birth cohort (but who differ in terms of their social locations), and some components are unique to the individuals concerned. Social class, race-ethnicity, age, gender, and sexuality—and their intersections—are important features of personal biography, but, as noted by Stoller and Gibson, they also determine one's position in systems of inequality (or "social location"). Taking a social constructionist position, these elements are more fully reflections of social definitions and social relationships, grounded in place and time, than characteristics of individuals.

personal well-being." All types of major life events can be stressful, but events considered undesirable are more closely linked with illness than those considered desirable (see Tausig 1986). Examples of life events commonly investigated include changes in marital status, birth of a child, serious illness of a family member or experienced by oneself, retirement, and significant changes in financial status (Tausig 1986). Events such as these act as "anchors" for future life events, helping to determine whether, when, and how particular events will occur in the future. Life events are assumed to have an identifiable time of onset (George 1989), but are expected to vary widely in their duration—the "waiting times or spells between a change in state" (Elder 1985:32)—and in their intensity or importance.

Transitions

Life events which involve shifts in a person's social identity are termed *transitions* (for example, entry into or exit from the labor force, entry into parenthood or grandparenthood, remarriage). Some of these transitions are self-initiated (an individual's entry into the labor force). "Counter-transitions" are brought about by the life changes of other persons (parenthood can lead to grandparenthood) (Hägestad 1988).

Trajectories

Life events including transitions can serve as important turning points in people's lives, modifying their life trajectories. A trajectory is "a pathway defined by the aging process or by movement across the age structure" (Elder 1985:31). More simply, trajectories reflect long-term patterns of stability and change (George 1993), which are described by a sequence of life events.

The potential impact of life events on trajectories can be understood by considering: 1) the nature of the event—its intensity, duration, and so forth; 2) the resources, beliefs, and experiences that individuals bring to the situation; 3) how the event is defined; and 4) resulting lines of adaptation taken by individuals, selected from available options (Elder 1985). According to Glen Elder, the first three factors influence a person's mode of adaptation, but the latter serves to connect events with the flow of the life course. "Lines of adaptation represent a process of constructing the life course. The same event or transition followed by different adaptations can lead to very different trajectories" (Elder 1985:35).

Life course trajectories are intertwined. Numerous studies have examined linkages between women's marriage, childbearing, and labor force participation (Bennett, Bloom, and Miller 1995; Griffith, Koo, and Suchindran 1985; Koo and Janowitz 1983; Leibowitz and Klerman 1995). Each of these trajectories is defined by a series of life events (changes in marital status; one or more births;

entrances and exits from the labor force) which can impact events that occur within the flow of the other trajectories. Together, these trajectories help to determine women's earnings in the labor force and their economic resources in old age (Elder 1985; Moen 1995).

The Concept of Timing:
Contested Terrain in the Life Course Perspective

Life course scholars agree that the timing of life events is important to consider, as well as the sequencing or order of those events. However, there is some controversy concerning how and why timing is important. Examination of this controversy can help to clarify how age is socially constructed and institutionalized in society.

The "normative approach" to life events is linked with the functionalist perspective (Passuth and Bengtson 1988), and is widely accepted in the life course literature (see Settersten and Hägestad 1996). This approach assumes that age norms regulate the timing and sequence of events in the life course. The timing of life events is considered important in part because humans desire predictability in their lives—"a sense of what lies ahead" (Hägestad 1988:405). Through the transmission of age norms via socialization and other processes, individuals come to believe that certain events should occur at given points in their lives, which can be anticipated or planned. Life course scholars have argued that events which take place "off-time" hinder individuals' coping and disrupt the subsequent flow of events in their lives. Furthermore, social support is more likely to be provided when events occur "on-time," in keeping with age-based norms, while off-time events can bring social disapproval (Neugarten, Moore, and Lowe 1965). On-time events can also provide social support by virtue of the fact that age peers are experiencing similar life events at similar points in the life course—"others who are in the same boat at the same time can provide preparation and support" (Hägestad 1988:405).

Some writers have questioned the degree to which life events are regulated by social norms. They argue that although individuals perceive age deadlines for various life events, violation of those deadlines does not necessarily bring personal distress or social punishment (Lashbrook 1996; Settersten and Hägestad 1996). For example, Richard Settersten and Gunhild Hägestad (1996) found that most respondents associated age deadlines with various family transitions (leaving home, marriage, parenthood, etc.). However, "missed deadlines" were not considered problematic for either women or men, or for their families. Settersten and Hägestad conclude that cultural thinking about family-related timetables is "relatively loose and flexible" (p. 187).

Anne Foner (1996) suggests that such flexibility may reflect a weakening of age norms in contemporary society, or it may reflect variations in social class, ethnicity, and other contexts. It is difficult to assess whether age norms have changed over time because researchers have tended "to equate socio-cultural norms with statistical frequency" (i.e., the numbers of persons experiencing a particular life event at a particular age) (Marini 1984), rather than to test such norms empirically. Those who have done so have tended to consider age norms in a broad societal context, rather than within specific communities or interaction settings (Lawrence 1996).

An exception to this pattern is found in Barbara Lawrence's study of age norms in work organizations. Lawrence distinguishes analytically between age norms, which she defines as "widely shared judgments of the standard or typical ages of individuals holding a role or status within a given context" (1996:209) and age norm sanctions—rewards and punishments associated with norm conformity or deviation. Managers in three large organizations were asked their judgments of the typical age for incumbents of their career level. Age norms were more consistent and more widely shared in the two work organizations with low rates of turnover among their employees than they were in the organization with higher rates of employee turnover. The study did not directly assess sanctions for deviations from age norms, but many of the respondents themselves "deviated" from the age norms which they had identified. According to Foner (1996), these results may provide additional evidence of flexibility in age structuring, in that many of the managers' own ages did not accord with those they had judged as typical for incumbents of their career level.

This study identified a contextual feature of organizations which appeared to influence the managers' judgments concerning age—the degree of stability in the organization's employment. Lawrence suggests that the size of the organization also may influence age norms: judgments in large organizations may change more slowly than in small organizations.

Lawrence's call to study age norms within specific contexts is promising, but I believe that research in this area can be enhanced by considering conceptual advances in the study of gender discussed earlier in the chapter. Specifically, judgments and expectations concerning age can usefully be viewed as the products of social interaction, which occurs within particular situational contexts. Just as face-to-face interaction can help to maintain expectations concerning gender (the "doing" of gender), so too can social interaction maintain expectations concerning age. Using Candace West and Don Zimmerman's (1987) language, we can speak of "doing age" (see also West and Fenstermaker 1995).[12] Expectations concerning age also can be challenged through social interaction. Admonitions to

---

[12]Candace West and Sarah Fenstermaker draw on the authors' earlier work on reconceptualizing gender to develop "further implications of this perspective for the relationships among gender, race, and class" (1995:8). Age is an additional basis of social difference which can be usefully incorporated with West and Fenstermaker's social constructionist approach to "doing difference" in interactional settings.

"act your age" can be met with compliance, or they may be ignored or resisted. The latter can help to create new shared meanings concerning age.

This approach provides greater conceptual clarity than a focus on age norms, which implies consensus and stability of meanings and which relies upon hazy mechanisms of norm transmission. A social constructionist approach emphasizes the potential fluidity in meanings concerning age, including variations across interactional contexts and changes across time. Sanctions for behavior defined as inappropriate are part of the interactional context, as are (rewarding) sanctions for behavior defined as appropriate. This does not mean that structural elements of the situation are unimportant—for example, the size and stability of a work organization may well impact the meanings workers come to share concerning appropriate ages for promotion, as Lawrence (1996) suggests. In sum, the timing of life events is a matter for empirical investigation, rather than assuming homogenous meanings concerning "on-time" and "off-time" events and their presumed effects on individuals.

Implications for Conceptualizing Age

The foregoing discussion has focused on meanings of age which are defined and acted upon in the interactional realm. Formal age rules also impact the timing of life events—for example, laws specify the ages at which people can drive, vote, drink alcohol, marry, and so forth. Borrowing again from advances in the conceptualization of gender, the social construction of age can be seen as multidimensional. Judith Lorber was quoted earlier that gender reflects "a process of social construction, a system of social stratification, and an institution that structures every aspect of our lives because of its embeddedness in the family, the workplace, and the state, as well as in sexuality, language and culture" (1994:5). A similar argument can be made for age. Like gender, age also is a social institution. Age is socially constructed through interaction, serves as a mechanism of social stratification, and is embedded in the social world, including family life, the workplace, and the state (for example, through age-related social policies and programs). Subsequent chapters of this book will explore these facets. However, to understand gender and age fully, the linkages between these and other social phenomena must be considered.

Social Location and Membership in Social Groups

Many features of our personal biographies are unique to ourselves. Some features are shared in common with others of similar "social location." Age, gender, race-ethnicity, social class, and sexual orientation reflect social hierarchies of privilege, and help to determine the life chances available to us over our lifetimes (Dressel 1988; Stoller and Gibson 1994). As much as possible, dimensions of social location should be viewed in terms of their intersections, moving beyond gender (or age or race or class) dichotomies. Taking these factors into consideration means more than simply "adding up" different dimensions of disadvantage.

This issue is exemplified by the concept of double jeopardy, which gained wide use in the gerontological literature (e.g., Aiken 1989; Ferraro 1987, 1989a; Jackson, Kolody, and Wood 1982; Thorson 1995). Initially used to refer to the situations of older African Americans, who face challenges from both racism and ageism (Talley and Kaplan 1956, as cited in Jackson 1985), double jeopardy subsequently was applied to additional racial-ethnic minority groups (e.g., Bengtson and Morgan 1987). The jeopardy thesis was also extended to further sources of discrimination. Triple jeopardy suggests a third source of oppression— for example, being old, African American, and female. Older African American women who are poor have been described as facing quadruple jeopardy (Jackson 1985).

As it has come to be used, the jeopardy thesis implies that sources of oppression and disadvantage can simply be "added on," without considering the unique social locations of the groups involved. Each form of discrimination is treated as if it exerted "a single, direct, and independent effect" (King 1988:47), calling to mind a simple mathematical formula: ageism plus racism plus sexism equals triple jeopardy. Rather, the *intersections* between these forms of oppression must be considered. For example, African American women experience the intersection of racism and sexism, and, often, classism. Their situations are "qualitatively, not quantitatively, different from those of white women," and also qualitatively different from the situations of African American men (Dressell 1988:178).[13] This means that an interactive rather than an additive model must be employed (King 1988).

Household composition, marital and family circumstances, and other social ties also help to determine life chances. Although these groups are not defined as parameters of social location, I believe that they can be incorporated usefully within this level of life course analysis. To illustrate: Within racial-ethnic groups, married women and men are better-off economically than unmarried persons (Hardy and Hazelrigg 1993; Harrington Meyer 1990). Risks of poverty among unmarried persons are reduced when they share a household with others (Waehrer and Crystal 1995; Zsembik 1993). Older adults who are married or who live with others also use fewer health services and are less likely to be admitted to nursing homes or other long-term care institutions (Cafferata 1987; Ford et al. 1990; Wolinsky and Johnson 1992). In addition, studies have documented the importance of supportive relationships for mental and physical health (Baldassare, Rosenfield, and Rook 1984; Chappell and Badger 1989; Lin and Ensel 1989; Lin, Woelfel, and Light 1985). Subsequent chapters will examine how individuals'

---

[13]Paula Dressel cites Linda Burnham (1985) for this point.

social locations and their membership in social groups (specifically, families and households) impact adaptation to aging.

Birth Cohort

The experience of aging also is shaped by our membership in particular birth cohorts. "Because historical conditions change, and because newly emerging conditions impinge on successive cohorts at different ages, each cohort is thus somewhat different from those that preceded it and from those that follow" (Pearlin and Skaff 1996:244). A birth cohort can encompass any designated time span, but a five to ten year span is conventional. Despite this conventional usage, the question remains, "What makes a cohort a cohort?" (Rosow 1978). Some researchers identify cohorts in terms of their relationship to unique historical events. For example, Glen Elder and his colleagues compared a cohort of Americans who experienced the Great Depression as adolescents with a cohort who were young children during the Depression (Elder, Downey, and Cross 1986; Elder and Rockwell 1979). Pearlin and Skaff (1996) argue that a need also exists to identify more subtle historical contexts which may distinguish particular cohorts.

The recognition that cohorts face differing historical conditions raises an additional criticism of the double jeopardy thesis discussed above. Although racial inequalities are unlikely to change greatly in the near future (e.g., Hess 1986; Torres-Gil 1986; Watson 1986), some of the findings which support the jeopardy thesis may be cohort-specific. Older racial-ethnic minorities in the future will face a different social and political environment compared to cohorts of the past (Jackson 1985; Stoller and Gibson 1994). According to Jacquelyne Jackson, double jeopardy implies that race *per se* is the central issue in adaptation to aging, rather than the status of these groups and their access to resources, which are subject to change over time.

The relative size of a birth cohort also has implications for its aging. The cohort of Americans born between 1931 and 1940 was smaller than those that preceded it or the ones that followed it. As a consequence, this cohort—now in their late 50s to late 60s—faced less competition for employment and educational opportunities. Eleanor Stoller and Rose Gibson (1994) point out that the smaller size of this cohort also brings potential difficulties. Fewer siblings means that fewer family members may be available to assist elderly parents when they become ill or frail.

Societal Context

At the broadest level, aging is experienced within a given social-historical context. "Period effects" are ever-present, since they reflect the effects of societal circumstances at a particular moment. These include large-scale events such as wars or major economic depressions, and the social policies and institutions in place at a given point in history.

Period effects can have far-reaching consequences throughout society, but they are seldom uniform. In other words, period effects interact with other influences on the aging experience. For example, economic losses experienced during the Depression brought differing consequences for working-class and middle-class families. Many families in both social class groups suffered substantially reduced incomes during the Depression, but working-class families had fewer savings and economic assets on which to draw compared to middle-class families (Elder 1974).

While period effects refer to a particular moment or slice in time, the occurrence of a large-scale event such as the Great Depression or the implementation of a social policy such as Social Security also brings long-term consequences. For example, economic problems experienced during the Depression continued to plague many working-class families into the postwar period. (In contrast, middle-class families were better able to regain their pre-Depression income, and many did so within a few years) (Elder 1974). Studies also have documented long-term effects of the Depression experience into older age, impacting the health and well-being of today's elderly cohorts (Elder and Liker 1982; Elder and Rockwell 1979).

Because the age at which an event is experienced is consequential, enduring "period effects" often translate into cohort differences.[14] Glen Elder and Richard Rockwell (1979) examined long-term effects of the Great Depression among men who were born in 1920-21 and men who were born in 1928-29. Although developmental problems resulting from Depression hardships were observed for both cohorts, the consequences were more adverse and more persistent for men who were young children at the time of the Depression compared to those who experienced the Depression as adolescents. Elder and Rockwell argue that economic deprivation produced more adverse consequences for the younger cohort due to their earlier developmental stage when economic strains in the family were experienced and their total dependence upon family support, which was "made unpredictable and insufficient by the stress of survival requirements" (Elder and Rockwell 1979:250).

In sum, a life course perspective recognizes explicitly that life experiences are interconnected, both within individuals' personal histories and within the broader social-historical context. Gender is interwoven throughout these layers of experience.

Glen Elder's research on children of the Depression helps to illustrate this point. His longitudinal study (1974) of a cohort born in 1920-21 in Oakland,

---

[14]In other words, cohorts effects are essentially interactions between age and period effects (see Watkins 1980).

California found that economic pressures brought by the Depression had differential impacts on girls and boys. In general, boys' psychosocial development was impacted more negatively by the Depression experience compared to that of girls. However, gender differences were not uniform, but were linked with the children's birth cohort, the class standing of their families prior to the Depression, and the degree to which their families suffered economic deprivation during the Depression. (Many middle-class as well as working-class families suffered significant economic losses during the Depression. In Elder's research, economic deprivation was defined as income loss greater than 34%.) The sample was comprised of white children, most of whom had Protestant, native born parents.

Elder shows how economic strains experienced by families in the Depression impacted these children's lives and future life chances. Adolescent children often took on adult responsibilities when their families experienced economic stress during the Depression. Daughters frequently took on additional responsibilities in the household, especially in larger families. (Some adolescent daughters also took paid jobs.) Elder reports that family responsibilities encouraged stronger attachments between the girls and their mothers. Due to bonds with their mothers and limited educational opportunities, the girls from deprived families were more strongly oriented toward achievement through marriage, and less likely than girls in non-deprived families to achieve through education and workforce participation. In deprived families of the middle-class, in particular, the girls were likely to marry early and become full-time homemakers. This pattern is linked with economic dependencies on husbands, and, often, with greatly reduced income when the spouse dies or in the event of divorce (Arendell and Estes 1991). On the other hand, middle-class women who had experienced economic strains as adolescents showed greater psychological resilience in mid-life than women of their cohort who had not suffered Depression-era deprivation (Elder and Liker 1982).

Both short-term and long-term effects of the Depression experience also were found for boys. Adolescent sons often took on paid work when their families experienced economic hardships, a pattern found among middle-class as well as working-class families. Elder argues that sons in these households developed relatively weak ties to both of their parents due to their freedom from parental supervision (brought by the sons' employment) and due to unemployed fathers' loss of status in the home. As adolescents, these boys manifested greater difficulties in their social relationships compared to girls and compared to boys in non-deprived households. Furthermore, having interrupted their education to go to work, many of the boys in deprived households were unable to complete their formal education. This experience apparently did not impact the boys' occupational aspirations, however. Social class origins were linked more strongly with the boys' aspirations than the experience of economic deprivation. In fact, "as 20-year-olds, the economically deprived showed greater vocational certainty or crystallization than the nondeprived in both social strata, and were more likely to establish a stable career line at an early age" (Elder and Rockwell 1979:282). By middle-age, the educational handicaps of the deprived group were largely overcome through their workforce participation. The adult years also brought increased psychosocial health for these men.

In these studies, Elder and his colleagues trace sources of similarity and difference in the life pathways of women and men who experienced the Great Depression during their early years. A common conclusion, which I will examine more fully in the next chapter, is that the experience of economic deprivation in early life does not produce uniformly negative outcomes for adaptation in mid-life or older age. This is not to say that economic stresses in early life are necessarily beneficial, either. "Neither a privileged life nor one of unrelenting deprivation assures the inner resources for successful aging" (Elder and Liker 1982:267). Rather, the experience of deprivation must be placed in context. Both the short-term and the long-term consequences of Depression-era deprivation were less harmful for children of the middle-class than they were for working-class children. Furthermore, as noted earlier, Elder and Rockwell's study of boys (1979) found that adverse psychosocial consequences of the Depression were less severe for the cohort who were adolescents during this period, compared to the cohort who experienced the Depression as young children.

CRITICISMS OF THE LIFE COURSE PERSPECTIVE

The strength of the life course perspective lies in the explicit recognition of multiple, interlocking dimensions of human experience. The perspective locates individuals and groups in time and space, discouraging simple—and simplistic—comparisons and conclusions.

The scope and complexity of the life course perspective are seen as its central limitations. The approach has been criticized as too vague and too broad, seeming "to have left little out" (Watkins 1980:182). Patricia Passuth and Vern Bengtson (1988) argue that in its current form, the life course perspective has little explanatory power as a theory.

I agree with this latter criticism. The life course perspective is not a theory, in the sense of comprising a set of integrated assumptions and providing an interpretation of how and why events are connected to each other.[15] However, I believe that this is not a limitation but a strength of the perspective. The life course perspective provides a valuable framework for conceptualizing research and interpreting findings, which can be integrated fruitfully with diverse theoretical perspectives (e.g., Elder, George, and Shanahan 1996; George 1996; Pearlin and Skaff 1966), including social constructionist approaches.

---

[15]However, researchers using a life course perspective can and do generate testable hypotheses (e.g., Elder and Rockwell 1979), and some explicitly utilize theoretical frameworks such as symbolic interactionism as the basis for their life course research (e.g., Allen and Chin-Sang 1990).

What does it mean to use a life course perspective? The term "life course" is used so widely that it has come to refer to virtually any research on adulthood and aging (Passuth and Bengtson 1988). In my view, using a life course perspective requires consideration of the levels of analysis discussed in the foregoing section and sensitivity to intersections within and between these levels. It is not possible—either conceptually or methodologically—to consider all facets of the life course perspective simultaneously.[16] Depending upon the research question at hand, some dimensions of the perspective constitute the focal points for study. Other dimensions can be used to help interpret results derived from the study and to raise issues for further investigation. Life course studies which illustrate these features are highlighted in succeeding chapters.

Given its lengthy history and multidisciplinary roots, it is not surprising that diverse versions of the life course approach have been developed (see Marshall 1994). I have focused especially on sociological approaches to the life course. "Life span theory" has an extensive history in psychology (see Baltes 1987), as do life course approaches in family studies.

Thus, some critiques of the life course perspective are more relevant to some versions of the perspective than to others. The observation has been made that the life course perspective is essentially functionalist due to an emphasis on the role of norms in shaping behavior (Passuth and Bengtson 1988). This point is made, in particular, to the assumption that life events are normatively prescribed, and that events which occur "off-time" disrupt the life course and impede adaptation. However, while the timing thesis has been accepted in much of the life course literature, some contemporary scholars question this thesis (Pearlin and Skaff 1996; Settersten and Hägestad 1996).

Both the timing thesis and the traditional gender role approach have roots in functionalist theory; similar criticisms can be raised for both. The argument has been made in this chapter that functionalist assumptions are not integral to a life course approach. Subsequent chapters will take this argument further, showing how the life course perspective can be strengthened by eliminating vestigial elements of Parsonsian functionalism.

CONCLUSION

Despite extensive critiques of approaches which dichotomize gender and neglect within-gender variation, a continuing stream of studies focus on gender differences (see Fausto-Sterling 1992; Hare-Mustin and Maracek 1990a, 1990b; Thompson 1993). Although this pattern is not exclusive to the field of aging, newer conceptualizations of gender have made few discernable inroads to date among gerontologists (see Ray 1996).

---

[16]Most notably, it is virtually impossible to disentangle age, period, and cohort effects in a single study (see Kovach and Knapp 1989).

Estes, Binney, and Culbertson (1992) argue that the field of aging is vulnerable to such lags because a clear disciplinary perspective in gerontology has not yet been developed, and also because a framework for truly interdisciplinary work has not yet been accomplished. As a consequence, paradigm shifts evidenced in sociology and other disciplines have not followed smoothly into the field of gerontology. "What should be a strength of gerontology—its multi-disciplinary focus—has become a weakness instead, reflected in the 'tokenization of gerontology' in traditional disciplines, and 'the Balkanization of specialized gerontology programs' with respect to other, established disciplines" (Estes et al. 1992:50).

Although the field of gerontology has lagged in adopting newer conceptualizations of gender, gerontologists have made important contributions to the development of a life course perspective which can provide a valuable tool for gender studies. A life course perspective helps to explicate sources of similarity as well as diversity between women and men, and also helps to identify sources of similarity and diversity *within* gender groups. Thus, the effective use of a life course perspective can avoid the pitfalls of both alpha bias (exaggerating gender differences) and beta bias (ignoring or minimizing gender differences).

By using a multi-level life course model as a heuristic device, some central sources of gender similarity and difference can be identified. However, it is essential to consider intersections between—and among—the levels of social phenomena identified in the model. Doing so will help us to avoid an additive approach to studying gender, in which patterns relevant to gender are simply "added" to patterns linked with other social phenomena.

Furthermore, by incorporating a social constructionist approach, dimensions of gender difference and similarity are not rigidified. Rather, understandings and (re)creations of gender vary across interactional contexts, which are linked with additional, interlocking dimensions of identity and differentiation, including race-ethnicity, social class, sexual orientation, and age. These interactional contexts, in turn, are linked with temporal and structural changes in the broader societal context.

The following chapter examines the theoretical explanations and research evidence bearing on gender differences in adaptation to aging, then turns toward a life course perspective.

CHAPTER
3

Adaptation to Aging

Broadly speaking, adaptation involves adjustments on the part of the individual to new or changed circumstances, including physical, psychological, and social changes. These adjustments involve processes internal to the individual, such as assimilating new information about the environment, as well as external processes, such as responding to changes in the environment. Age-related changes can be gradual or sudden, small or large, deriving primarily from within the individual, from the environment, or, most frequently, from intersections between these.

Studies of adaptation to aging reflect these diverse foci. Some researchers consider adaptation as part of the individual's personality (Turner 1982), while others focus on the role of the environment (George 1980). Some researchers focus more on *processes* of adapting to change, such as how individuals cope with a stressful life event (Wortman, Silver, and Kessler 1993), while others examine outcomes that are presumed to follow from these processes (Arbuckle and de Vries 1995). This latter approach, focusing on outcomes of individuals' adaptive efforts, has been the more commonly pursued research avenue.

Most frequently, the outcome of the adaptation process is conceptualized as an "intrapsychic evaluation of general life quality" (George 1987:5). This is true whether adaptation is considered primarily in terms of intrinsic processes and changes or primarily as extrinsic to the individual. Not surprisingly then, the measures used most commonly to assess adaptation rely on respondents' subjective evaluations—their expressed life satisfaction and happiness, perceived health status, and the like. The reliance on these measures derives partly from the assumption that individuals' subjective assessments are reflective of their objective circumstances—that a "certain parallelism exists between the subjective and objective world" (Baltes and Baltes 1990:6). However, people in quite diverse life circumstances often express strikingly similar assessments of their situations—for example, those with low incomes and poor health often report relatively high levels of life satisfaction, comparable to those who are better circumstanced (see Bearon 1989). Paul Baltes and Margaret Baltes (1990) argue that a reliance on subjective measures is suspect for this reason—humans are able to use various psychological mechanisms to adapt to adverse circumstances, distorting reality in the process.

This argument is less compelling if one subscribes to the view, as I do, that reality is itself socially constructed. When we speak of reality being distorted, we must ask, whose reality is it? The use of subjective measures thus can also be traced to the assumption that "the perceiving self ought to be the litmus test for the quality of life" (Baltes and Baltes 1990:6). Nonetheless, I agree with Baltes and Baltes and other writers (e.g., George 1980) who advocate that multiple measures, both "subjective" and "objective," be utilized to assess adaptation. This call derives in part from the difficulty of disentangling objective and subjective phenomena. Assessments of physical, psychological, and social functioning are classified as objective measures of adaptation (Baltes and Baltes 1990; George 1987), but all of these rely to some degree upon the perceptions of the evaluator. Length of life may be the only truly "objective" measure of adaptation.

In addition, the use of multiple measures can provide a fuller understanding of adaptation. A multicriteria approach is supported by the finding that differing measures of adaptation are positively associated with one another (for example, greater functional health is associated with greater life satisfaction), but their associations are typically rather small in magnitude (Baltes and Baltes 1990). Thus, the measures apparently tap somewhat differing dimensions of the broad umbrella concept that is termed adaptation.

TRADITIONAL FOCUS ON THE INDIVIDUAL

As the preceding discussion suggests, gerontologists' concerns with adaptation has meant that the *individual* has been the primary focus of study. Outcome variables of interest, as well as the factors which predict those outcomes, have been located primarily at the individual level rather than at the macro or societal level. This is true even among sociologists, whose discipline stresses broad social structures and processes. Social structural variables have been considered, but these are treated primarily as resources available to individuals, in the form of health, income, and social relationships. Victor Marshall (1994) argues that until fairly recently, the causes or antecedents of these resources were largely unexplored; to do so would shift the focus from the social psychological level toward the social structural level.[1] Contemporary gerontologists increasingly are pursuing such examination, by exploring the political economy of aging (e.g., Minkler and Estes 1991, 1999), considering how feminist theories may be applied to aging

---

[1] Age stratification theory was developed after the disengagement and activity theories of aging (to be discussed shortly) were formalized and critiqued, "enabling aging theory to turn a corner" (Estes et al. 1992). Unlike the earlier theories, age stratification theory focuses upon the social structural rather than the individual level of analysis. Attention is placed upon the status of older persons in society rather than their adaptation to aging. However, like disengagement and activity theories, age stratification theory is essentially structural-functionalist in its focus on social roles (Marshall 1994).

issues (e.g., Calasanti 1992; Ray 1996), and by placing aging in life course perspective.

AIMS OF THE CHAPTER

Although individuals' assessments of their health and well-being have been the most commonly used measures of adaptation, theories of adaptation to aging have derived primarily from scholars' judgments of the qualities and outcomes which constitute adaptive or successful aging. Women and men have been thought to travel different pathways to successful aging. Nearly always, one gender is portrayed as faring better or suffering more than the other. Often (but not always), women are viewed as adapting more successfully to older age, while men are thought to suffer more.

My central aims in this chapter are to explore the reasoning behind these proposed gender differences, to examine whether these theoretical conjectures have been supported in empirical research, and to show why a life course perspective provides a better tool for understanding women's and men's adaptation to aging. In the process, I analyze the adequacy of theories and measures of adaptation, beyond their gendered components.

Adaptation is examined here primarily in terms of older women's and men's adjustments to life changes and events, as opposed to developmental or maturational changes (e.g., Labouvie-Vief 1985). This is admittedly a thin line at times, but is useful in excluding perspectives that focus primarily on internal processes, or those that do not specifically consider issues relevant to later life. Thus, most of the theoretical perspectives and empirical studies that fall within the area of developmental psychology are not considered here, particularly those that deal with cognitive, memory, and personality development. Beyond the fact that it would not be possible to address adequately the myriad of perspectives and studies that deal with "adaptation" in all of its forms, as a sociologist I am especially interested in approaches that deal with intersections between individuals and their social environment—both at the micro level of individuals and small groups, as well as at the macro, societal level. Because social gerontology is inherently multidisciplinary, this plan does not exclude contributions from disciplines in addition to sociology, including psychology, economics, family studies, and other fields of inquiry. Contributions from anthropologists also are incorporated (e.g., Hewlett 1997; Lamphere 1997), but cross-national and cross-cultural comparisons are not a feature of this work. The focus for this investigation primarily is the United States, for which the greatest amount of information currently is available concerning adaptation to aging.

Plan of the Chapter

Theories of adaptation to aging are first reviewed. As I will show, Parsonsian assumptions about traditional gender roles were incorporated in the earliest theoretical formulations and continue to be reflected in contemporary explanations for gender differences in adaptation to aging. This is so despite an explicit rejection of the early adaptation theories in which gender role assumptions were embedded and despite a general lack of empirical evidence to support these assumptions.

I then examine the empirical record on adaptation to aging, focusing on the most commonly-investigated dimensions—social relationships, physical health and mortality, and mental health and coping, including individuals' evaluations of their well-being. I evaluate each of these dimensions with respect to its adequacy as a measure of adaptation in older age, and findings of gender differences are reviewed. This review will show that for most dimensions, older persons do not differ greatly from their younger counterparts, suggesting that "adaptation to aging" is not as problematic as has been generally assumed. The review also shows that conclusions concerning gender differences in adaptation depend upon the specific dimension of adaptation under consideration. Findings of gender differences also are often contradictory and the magnitude of difference generally is rather small (conclusions also reached by other reviews of gender difference research) (Epstein 1988; Fausto-Sterling 1992; Lips 1988; Maccoby and Jacklin 1974; Nielsen 1990). Thus, in addition to serious conceptual limitations, most of the hypothesized gender differences in adaptation to aging have not found strong empirical support.

I next examine some attempts to explain adaptation to aging which incorporate gender, but which do not rest with dichotomized gender comparisons. One of these concerns androgyny and aging. I review this controversy, along with several related arguments. Although these arguments are laudable in their attempts to move beyond dichotomous comparisons between women and men, most of them consider only limited sources of diversity which impact women's and men's lives and neglect the social and historical context for aging.

A life course perspective helps to provide these vital missing pieces. In the final section of the chapter, I summarize and discuss research findings which are relevant to a life course approach to adaptation, using the multi-level model discussed in the previous chapter as an organizing framework. I also show how the results from life course studies challenge central assumptions embedded in gender-difference explanations.

THE CLASSICAL THEORIES OF ADAPTATION TO AGING: PASSING ON THE SEX ROLE LEGACY

A focus on the individual and how women and men adapt to aging can be seen as a legacy of the Kansas City Studies (Marshall 1994). This series of studies spawned the two major theories of social gerontology of the 1960s and 70s, disengagement theory and activity theory.[2] Undertaken by a multidisciplinary team of researchers at the University of Chicago, these studies were conducted from 1942 to 1962. During this period, over a thousand Kansas City residents age forty and older were interviewed, with some respondents interviewed a number of times over a six-year span. Kansas City was chosen as the research site due to its presumed typicality as an American city. Only healthy, economically secure persons were included as respondents in the study (Marshall 1994). The purpose of these selections was to focus on "normal" aging, but as Victor Marshall points out, neither social class or race-ethnicity were prominent in these considerations. Furthermore, although studying the environment for aging was an initial purpose in selecting Kansas City as the research site, the theoretical and research foci centered upon the individual.

Another major study of the period, the first Duke Longitudinal Study (1956-1976), incorporated the disengagement and activity theories of aging, along with continuity theory (Marshall 1994). Activity theory was developed as a rebuttal to disengagement theory, but theorists in both camps agreed that traditional gender roles produce gender differences in adaptation to aging. Advocates of continuity theory disagreed with central tenets advanced in both of the earlier theoretical approaches, but did not challenge the traditional gender role assumptions embedded in those approaches.

Disengagement Theory

Disengagement theory was the first "truly explicit, truly multidisciplinary, and truly influential theory" of social gerontology (Achenbaum and Bengtson 1994:756). It was also the first, probably the only, grand theory of social gerontology, attempting to incorporate all levels of analysis. This is understandable, given that disengagement theory drew heavily from Parsons's grand theory of structural functionalism (see Chapter 2). Although central functionalist assumptions were retained, examinations of disengagement theory nonetheless focused almost exclusively on individual-level outcomes (Marshall 1994).

Formulated by Elaine Cumming and William Henry (1961; see also Cumming et al. 1960), disengagement theory proposes that a mutual withdrawal of the older person and society is a normal and inevitable part of the aging process. Because death becomes more expected with old age, progressive withdrawal paves the way for this "total disengagement." Social withdrawal is evidenced by decreased levels of interaction with others and by changes in types of interaction. Relationships which revolve around (men's) instrumental activities become unimportant, according to Cumming and Henry, since the elderly have a decreased

---

[2] Elements of these perspectives existed prior to the Kansas City Studies, however.

desire to feel needed. Thus, psychological withdrawal is key to the disengagement process. With older age, personality changes bring decreased involvement with others and increased involvement with oneself.

From this perspective, disengagement is considered functional for society as well as for the aging individual. The process prepares society for the replacement of the individual, and in the occupational sphere, frees up positions for younger workers. At the same time, disengagement is considered necessary for individuals' successful adaptation to aging. The progressive withdrawal from social roles and responsibilities helps individuals to adjust to progressive decrements in their abilities, and helps to prepare them for the ultimate disengagement— withdrawal from life itself.

Men and women are thought to follow different pathways to this total disengagement. Drawing directly from Parsons, Cumming and Henry asserted that "because the central role of men in American society is instrumental, and the central role of women is socio-emotional, the process of disengagement will differ between men and women" (1961:212). More specifically, men's (presumed) central life task is to provide economically for the family, while women's revolves around reducing tension among family members and reinforcing family values and norms. Thus, men's disengagement revolves primarily around their withdrawal from paid work and other roles in the public sphere. Women's disengagement comes primarily from role losses in the private sphere of home and family, disengaging partially from their central role when their children leave home, and completely from it when their spouse dies.

Cumming and Henry argued that role disengagement typically produces a period of crisis and loss of morale for both women and men, reflecting "disequilibrium between personal readiness for withdrawal and the demands or opportunities presented by the social structure" (see Tissue 1968:513). Ultimately, however, problems of disengagement are resolved with increasing age, when ego changes have eventuated in "preoccupations with inner states and to the narcissism of the very old" (Cumming and Henry 1961:215). Temporary solutions are available in the interim. Recreational groups or temporary part-time employment can address retired men's instrumental needs, for example, while widowed peers can provide socio-emotional support to women. Subsequent chapters on bereavement and retirement elaborate these arguments, but I will note here that Cumming and Henry believed that problems of disengagement, although short-term, were more severe for men than for women. This is so, they argued, because men lose status when they relinquish their breadwinning role, while women's status is largely unaffected by the loss of their central role as wife: "Widows are given enough consideration in this society to compensate for loss of status" (1961:216).

It is not clear whether Cumming and Henry believed that widowed women's status is higher than that of retired men, or that women's status is lower relative to men's regardless of employment or marital circumstances, and doesn't change much when they are widowed. Beyond this rather confusing (and untested) assumption, Cumming and Henry's own data do not support their contention that men have a more difficult time in the disengagement process. To develop their disengagement propositions, Cumming and Henry analyzed data from a subset of the Kansas City Studies described above. Inspection of the data presented reveals that for three of the four identified stages of the "disengagement process," the women showed *lower levels* of morale than the men. (However, we cannot say that women fared worse than men over the course of the so-called "disengagement process," since there are no data on respondents' morale prior to this process.) On what basis, then, did Cumming and Henry conclude that disengagement is more difficult for men than women?

Furthermore, Cumming and Henry ignored the problems of women who do not become widowed, or those of men who never retire. If disengagement is essential to successful aging, but can only occur when women's and men's "central roles" are given up, what happens to older women who face the ultimate disengagement of death without having relinquished their role as wife? What about women who never marry, who thus never engage in the "central role" of wife? Are they better or worse off than married women who never become widowed? And what happens to men who never withdraw from their primary role of breadwinner,[3] or have "disengaged" from it prematurely due to poor health, unemployment, or job layoffs? Beyond the problems associated with conceptualizing gender in terms of roles, which I addressed in the previous chapter, Cumming and Henry raised many unanswered questions about gender differences in the disengagement process.

Contemporary readers may see these questions as taking pot shots at work that was written decades ago, and which has since been refuted in the gerontology literature. I think it is important to raise these sorts of questions now. Although serious criticisms were leveled at disengagement theory from the moment it appeared in print (e.g., Maddox 1963; Reichard, Livson, and Petersen 1962; Tobin and Neugarten 1961), Cumming and Henry's assumptions about gender did not figure prominently in these debates—and to my knowledge, never have. Even Arlie Hochschild's influential critique of disengagement theory published in 1975 did not say much about its gendered assumptions, though at the end of the article Hochschild explores how gender role ideology may differentiate groups of men (for example, she states that some men will attach more importance to being a breadwinner than will other men and that this will affect their disengagement process). A further and more important reason for casting a critical eye on the gendered assumptions embedded in disengagement theory is that they were passed on to subsequent theoretical perspectives in gerontology. Parsonsian

---

[3] Cumming takes up this issue in her 1963 revision, explaining that the perspective does not consider "non-modal" cases, such as men who work past the age of retirement.

gender role assumptions survived more or less intact, and, as I will show, continue to emerge in contemporary research on aging. Furthermore, although subsequent theories no longer prescribed disengagement as the route to successful aging, retirement and spousal bereavement continued to be seen as crises, with the importance and the severity of crisis differing for men and women.

Critiques of disengagement theory focused on the presumed inevitability and universality of disengagement, the "assumed functionality" of disengagement, especially for individuals, and the theory's failure to consider the role of personality (see Atchley 1971:476). Researchers reported that for a number of societies, including the United States, elders' engagement in social roles was more common than disengagement, and psychological engagement was found to enhance rather than detract from elders' well-being (e.g., Havighurst, Neugarten, and Tobin 1968; Shanas et al. 1968). However, Arlie Hochschild (1975) demonstrates that the perspective is inherently unfalsifiable: because Cumming and Henry stated that there would be variations in the "form" and "timing" of disengagement, but did not specify these, potential counter-evidence could be re-interpreted as providing support for the perspective. Despite subsequent independent revisions of the theory by Cumming (1963) and Henry (1965),[4] and despite some attempts to resuscitate it (e.g., Holloway and Youngblood 1985/86), disengagement theory faded away by the early 1970s.

Activity Theory

Cumming and Henry contrasted their perspective with the "implicit theory" that was subsequently formalized by other writers as activity theory (Havighurst et al. 1968; Lemon, Bengtson, and Peterson 1972).[5] During the late 1960s and early 70s, disengagement and activity theorists were the central contenders in the

---

[4] Subsequent to these and other critiques, Cumming and Henry each made independent revisions to the theory. In the initial formulation, the disengagement process could be "initiated by the individual or by others in the situation" (Cumming and Henry 1961:14). By 1963, Elaine Cumming no longer viewed societal pressures as sufficient to initiate disengagement, and she focused on the role of innate biological and personality characteristics. However, she continued to invoke socialization as the key to understanding gender differences in disengagement. Specifically, Cumming characterized men as less prepared to accommodate themselves to disengagement processes, due to the instrumental nature of their previous roles. For both men and women, the socioemotional roles remaining to them take on added significance in providing esteem and approval from others, as well as "a minimum of stimulation" (p. 383). Thus, Cumming emphasized that differential disengagement helps individuals adapt to aging, a point taken up by activity theorists. For his part, William Henry (1965) wished to modify disengagement theory to reflect a *decreased* emphasis on intrinsic processes, since this implied that disengagement was inevitable and universal, two central critiques of the original formulation (e.g., Maddox 1964).

[5] Works which presaged activity theory were published in 1949 by Cavan, Burgess, Havighurst, and Goldhamer, and in 1953 by Havighurst and Albrecht.

social psychology of aging, elaborating and testing perspectives which essentially mirrored one another. In fact, the debate between these theories eventuated in the rejection of both of them (Marshall 1994).

Rather than prescribing social and psychological withdrawal as the key to successful aging, activity theorists argued the reverse, just as their moniker implies. Barring health limitations, older people "are the same as middle aged people, with essentially the same psychological and social needs" (Havighurst et al. 1968:161). In the activity framework, decreased social interaction in old age is caused by societal withdrawal from the individual, against the wishes of most older persons. Retirement and the death of one's spouse or friends are given as examples of important social roles and activities that older people are forced to relinquish. Optimal aging is achieved by staying active and resisting the contraction of one's social world: Older persons should maintain the roles and activities of middle age for as long as possible, and they should find effective substitutes for those that are lost. These need not be exact substitutes, however: "Retirees can find nonjob roles that meet many of the same needs that jobs did, and widows can find alternative sources of intimacy even if they cannot find new husbands" (see Atchley 1994:367).

Note that role losses continued to be gender-typed, just as they were in disengagement theory. Retirement was again portrayed as the greatest challenge to men's adaptation, and widowhood to women's. Zena Smith Blau (1973) argued that men experience greater difficulties than women in the adaptation process due to losing their breadwinning status and the "invidious implication" that society is better off when they retire (p. 32). Blau also claimed that retirement is more isolating for men than widowhood is for women.

These parallels between activity and disengagement theories are not surprising, given that both have roots in structural-functionalism. Both of these theories prescribe what is "functional" for individuals' adaptation to aging, and see social roles as the mechanisms whereby adaptation is facilitated or impeded. Furthermore, the theories assume that the enactment or relinquishing of social roles helps to maintain the larger society.

Some of the charges leveled against disengagement theory were met by activity theorists. In particular, Robert Havighurst and his colleagues acknowledged the value judgements implied by their "theory of optimum aging" (1968:162), and suggested that the prescription for activity may be more applicable to modern Western societies. Certainly, there is a widespread assumption in Western societies, the United States in particular, that social activity is "good for you," and the more the better. This relationship has been characterized as the most central theorem of the activity perspective (Longino and Kart 1982): "The greater the frequency of activity, the greater one's life satisfaction" (Lemon et al. 1972:515). That this assumption is held widely by researchers who do not call themselves activity theorists is reflected in the vast body of research on social activity and subjective well-being.

Many studies do indicate that social activity is positively and significantly related to subjective well-being (see Okun et al. 1984), but these associations often are rather modest in magnitude and depend greatly upon the source and type of activity under consideration. For example, contrary to activity theory, some types of formal activities have been found to *reduce* rather than promote life satisfaction in later life, and solitary activities do not hinder life satisfaction (Longino and Kart 1982). Although elders' well-being is enhanced when they interact frequently with their friends, similar salutary effects have not been found for their interactions with adult children and other kin (e.g., Glenn and McLanahan 1981; Keith 1983; Lee and Ellithorpe 1982). On the other hand, Russell Ward and his colleagues found that well-being *is* enhanced when elders believe they see their children "frequently enough" (Ward, Sherman, and LaGory 1984). It is *meaningful interaction* with others that is key, not simply activity (Longino and Kart 1982). (I return to this point in evaluating social interaction as a measure of adaptation.)

Although activity theory has enjoyed more empirical support than disengagement theory (Marshall 1994), this conclusion can be drawn only for a rather loose conceptualization of the theory. Attempts to formalize it have not produced strong evidence (Marshall 1994), and these attempts at formalization have not escaped the charge most often leveled against activity theory—that it is too simplistic (Hendricks and Hendricks 1986).

A recent attempt to refine activity theory examines the impact of social activities on self-esteem, rather than the traditional focus on activities and well-being. Donald Reitzes and his colleagues hypothesize that self-esteem will increase when individuals participate extensively in activities associated with various roles: parent, spouse, co-worker, friend, and extended relative (Reitzes, Mutran, and Verrill 1995). Their reasoning is that role-related activities provide opportunities to obtain confirmation from others about one's role performance, and hence can enhance feelings of self-esteem. The researchers also hypothesize that role-related activities may be more important to women's self-esteem than to men's. The rationale for this hypothesized gender difference is drawn directly from traditional gender role theory: activities with others should be more important to women because "female-gender norms stress emotional and affective relationships." In contrast, "male-gender norms may stress social status, formal activities, and the instrumental outcomes of role occupancy" (p. 264). Hence, activities with others may be less important to men's self-esteem. In sum, role-related activities are expected to enhance self-esteem for both men and women, but these effects are expected to be stronger for women.

Only minimal support was found for the research expectations. None of the five role-related activities predicted men's self-esteem. Only two types of role activities predicted women's self-esteem (activities with relatives and activities with co-workers). Furthermore, when respondents were asked about their levels of commitment to these various roles, women's commitment to their jobs was as high as that reported by men, and married men reported a *higher level* of commitment to the role of spouse than did married women. These findings are in opposition to traditional gender role theory. More consistent with the theory, women expressed higher commitment to the roles of friend and parent than did men.

Examination of other studies shows that the gender differences proposed by activity theorists have not been borne out in empirical research. For example, in one of the original examinations of activity theory, Robert Havighurst and his colleagues (1968) compared the affect and life satisfaction of men and women at different ages. For both men and women, the researchers reported a pattern of decreasing activity with older ages and concomitant declines in well-being. (This pattern is counter to disengagement theory, which suggests that decreasing activity is beneficial to individuals as they age.) Inspection of their published data does not reveal any pattern of gender differences for these variables, or for any of the other variables that were examined. The researchers themselves do not address this question in any detail in this particular work.[6] Nonetheless, some subsequent activity theorists, Zena Smith Blau (1973) in particular, argued that men had greater difficulty in adapting to aging than women due to differences in their primary roles.

Most tests of activity theory and disengagement theory simply ignored the gender role assumptions embedded in these perspectives. The recent work of Donald Reitzes and his colleagues is an exception to this pattern. Largely unexamined and unchallenged, traditional gender role assumptions were passed on to subsequent theories of aging and to applications of those theories.

Continuity Theory

This would seem to be less the case for continuity theory, which stresses diversity across individuals. Prior to its identification as a theory (with this term used in a loose sense), variations in individuals' personalities and lifestyles often were used post-hoc to question the generalizability of the disengagement and activity perspectives (e.g., Havighurst et al. 1968; Keith 1977; Knapp 1977). Although the initial statements concerning continuity were just as prescriptive as the disengagement and activity theorists had offered (maximum continuity in individuals' life patterns was advocated for "good adjustment") (Rosow 1963:216), subsequent writers took a more neutral stance, attempting to describe rather than prescribe (e.g., Atchley 1989).

---

[6] Although Robert Havighurst and his co-authors did not tie activity theory explicitly to gender roles in their 1968 publication, a co-authored work published the following year referred to employment as men's major role in life and wifehood/motherhood as women's major roles (Neugarten and Havighurst 1969:140). Other activity theorists have made explicit links between traditional gender roles and adaptation to aging (e.g., Blau 1973; Reitzes et al. 1995).

This theory of adaptation emphasizes that many of the patterns established earlier in a person's life are likely to continue as she or he grows older (Covey 1981). Coping strategies, ways of interacting with others, and personality traits, including one's sense of self, tend to show continuity over time (Atchley 1972; Fox 1981/82; Rosenmayr 1981). In this sense, continuity theory is similar to activity theory, in that the latter views older persons as having the same needs as middle-aged people (Fox 1981/82). However, in contrast to activity theory, the continuity framework does not view all middle-age or older people as having the same needs.

Continuity need not be equated with lack of change. Robert Atchley (1994), in particular, has asserted that continuity should be viewed in the context of continuous adult development. He argues that by mid-life individuals have fairly clear ideas about their adaptive strengths and weaknesses, and that they use these ideas in making choices. Thus, in adapting to change, people tend to use strategies that have proved useful in the past. Furthermore, to the degree that change occurs in earlier periods of one's life, change itself should be viewed as reflecting continuity (Atchley 1989).

Not everyone has the same ability or resources to continue in valued social roles (Hendricks and Hendricks 1986). Those with greater socioeconomic resources may be better able than others to continue in their social roles, if they so desire (for example, professionals generally are better able than other types of workers to continue their work beyond retirement). In addition, Herbert Covey (1981) stresses that the sociocultural context is important in encouraging or discouraging older people to continue in their long-term social roles (Covey 1981).

Empirical tests of the continuity perspective are rather limited. Most of these studies are based on cross-sectional or short-term longitudinal data, making it difficult to assess whether or not observed patterns were developed earlier in respondents' lives (e.g., Fox 1981/82). The perspective also has been criticized as overly broad (Covey 1981). However, it has shown greater lasting power than the disengagement or activity theories (Marshall 1994).

In fact, as is evident from the above discussion, many aspects of continuity theory are consistent with the life course perspective. While the latter does not restrict itself to issues of continuity (and thus is even broader in scope than continuity theory), both emphasize the importance of considering what has gone before in individuals' lives, with past experiences serving as anchor points for future ones. Furthermore, although the life course perspective is much more explicit about the historical and socio-cultural context for aging and the need to consider this context to understand individuals' lives, the two perspectives are not in disagreement on this point (e.g., Covey 1981).

Gender is not addressed explicitly in continuity theory. Rather, the theory is presented in gender-neutral terms. Some continuity theorists have come close to rejecting the assumption that women and men adapt differently to aging due to traditional gender roles, but, in my review of the literature, have not addressed the issue head on. For example, Judith Fox (1981/82) notes that many older persons have multiple roles and are likely to maintain their self-identity despite the disruption or loss of a particular role. Although she cites widowhood as an example of one such role loss (for which women have been seen as vulnerable to losses in self-identity), Fox couches her discussion in gender-neutral terms. Similarly, Virginia Richardson and Keith Kilty (1991) argue that continuity theorists reject the centrality of occupational identity assumed by role theorists. Richardson and Kilty do not say so, but the assumption that occupations are central to one's identity has been made primarily for men. A rejection of this assumption implies, then, a rejection of traditional gender roles. However, this rejection has not been made explicit.

In fact, continuity scholars have invoked traditional gender roles to account for observed (or expected) gender differences in aging, just as writers in previous (and subsequent) theoretical traditions have done. For example, Robert Atchley, a prominent continuity theorist, states that bereaved men are less likely than women to experience problems when the spouse role is lost, due to differences in traditional male and female roles (1994). However, as I will show in this and subsequent chapters, gender roles rarely have been examined empirically in studies of adaptation to aging. When gender differences are found, traditional gender roles are used as a post-hoc explanation to account for them.

Summing Up the Classical Theories

The triad of disengagement, activity, and continuity theories are the best-known of the early perspectives in social gerontology. Although the first two claim few adherents today, components of activity theory continue as the basis for many contemporary studies of aging (for example, John Kelly's edited volume, *Activity and Aging: Staying Involved in Later Life*) (1993).

The limitations of disengagement and activity theories, in particular, are obvious—overly broad, overly simplistic, and overly prescriptive—but they have had considerable impact in shaping the study of aging. Although continuity theory also has been criticized as overly broad (Covey 1981), and is limited in its explication of the context for aging, this approach has continued as a viable perspective (Marshall 1994).

Disengagement theorists, drawing directly from Parsonsian structural-functionalism, were explicit in their assumptions concerning gender roles and how these should differentiate women's and men's adaptation to aging. Although activity theory was presented as a direct challenge to disengagement theory, assumptions concerning gender roles were not questioned. Activity theorists who addressed issues of gender agreed with their disengagement colleagues that men should have a more difficult time adapting to aging than women and that traditional roles hold the key to these gender differences. With their focus on multiple pathways to adaptation, continuity theorists would seem most likely to challenge the assumption that traditional gender roles play a central role in how we adapt to aging, but, in fact, these assumptions rarely have been noted, much less challenged.

Consideration of these early theories helps us to understand current debates about gender differences in aging. The theories reflect the origins of these debates, which continue to draw upon traditional gender roles to propose or explain gender differences in adaptation to aging. This is so despite recognition that older women and men often differ in their access to economic and other resources, which in turn are predictive of health and well-being. Furthermore, traditional gender roles have been used to explain *divergent* sets of findings. In some studies, they are used to used explain why older men "suffer more" than older women; in others, they are used to explain the reverse—why women have greater difficulties in aging than men. An in-depth look at the twists and turns that traditional gender role explanations have taken is provided below and in subsequent chapters focusing on adaptation to the death of a spouse and adaptation to retirement.

EXPLANATIONS FOR GENDER DIFFERENCES IN ADAPTATION TO AGING

As discussed in the previous chapter, most explanations for gender differences in adaptation to aging fall into two general categories. The first draws on traditional gender role theory to explain why women or men should experience greater problems as they age. Typically, these explanations assume that gender differences in aging reflect the enduring effects of early socialization into gender roles, although this assumption is not always made explicit. The second broad category of explanation focuses on women's and men's economic, health, and other resources. From this latter framework, gender differences in adaptation to aging reflect differences in women's and men's access to valued resources, rather than differences in their personalities or other internalized characteristics.

Gender Role Explanations

It is fascinating to find that there is no clear consensus whether socialization into traditional gender roles should be helpful or harmful in adapting to aging. For example, Ruth Barer (1994) argues that women fare better than men in adapting to problems of aging. This is due in part, she says, to the fact that women live longer than men and hence have more time to adjust to their losses. But she also invokes gender role socialization. Barer states that women's socialization "to domesticity and family responsibilities" benefits them in later life, by affording "greater role continuity in their late life activities and relationships" (p. 39).

Other writers also have argued that traditional gender roles are advantageous to women's adaptation, but they posit a quite different avenue by which this occurs. According to this argument, women's adaptation to aging is enhanced because they experience greater role changes than men—not greater continuity. Hence, women develop a greater flexibility to changes which occur with aging (e.g., Kline 1975; Markson 1995; Stevens 1995). According to Chrysee Kline (1975), for example,

> it appears that the impact of socialization on American women creates *impermanence* in the form of role loss and repeated adjustment to change in the life situation—and that this socialization process facilitates adjustment of women to old age (p. 489).

The flip side of this gender difference argument is that women fare worse than men in adapting to aging. Some writers taking this viewpoint have argued that women do, in fact, experience more life changes and role transitions than men, but that this is stressful rather than beneficial (e.g., Szinovacz and Washo 1992). Women also are thought to be more involved than men in the life events of friends and loved ones—including providing care to those who are ill or otherwise require assistance—which produces stress in women's lives. Gender role socialization is invoked for this argument as well. In this view, women are more vulnerable to these sources of stress because they have been socialized to be more aware of social relationships and to be more sensitive toward them (Kessler and McLeod 1984; Szinovacz and Washo 1992; see also Miller 1990). For example, Ronald Kessler and Jane McLeod argue that "This sense of responsibility for the life events of loved ones could lead women to report more of these events and to experience these events as more distressing" (1984:621). In addition, the health and economic costs of providing care to others are thought to hinder women's adaptation at all ages, but especially so in later life, when multiple life events are likely to be experienced in close proximity to one another, such as retirement, widowhood, and geographic relocation (Szinovacz and Washo 1992).

Resource Explanations

An alternative explanation for better or poorer adaptation on the part of women or men lies in the economic, health, and social resources that are available to them, as opposed to differences in their personalities, attitudes, or values. Financial strain has been linked with poorer adaptation on the part of older women relative to older men (Markson 1995, Morgan 1986; see also Feinson 1987). Women's difficulties in aging also have been attributed to their greater risks for chronic illnesses (Crimmins et al. 1996). On the other hand, women's social resources—their relationships with family and friends—are thought to help buffer the stresses associated with life changes, providing women with adaptive advantages over men (Ferraro 1989b; Rawlins 1992). Thus, women are thought to have greater access than men to some resources which help them adapt to life changes, but less access to other resources.

Although a resource-based explanation for gender differences in adaptation makes common sense, it is limited in important ways. This chapter will demonstrate that we cannot a posit a simple one-to-one correspondence between economic or other resources and adaptation outcomes. Nor can we assume that gender differences reported for women and men as aggregate categories are applicable to women and men in particular racial-ethnic groups, social classes, or birth cohorts.

Blended Explanations

As noted in the previous chapter, gender role and resource explanations also have been combined to explain gender differences in adaptation to aging. This blending of approaches is especially apparent where women's and men's social resources are concerned, which have bearing on their physical and mental health. Traditional gender roles are believed to produce greater social resources for women, which in turn are thought to help them adapt to changes and losses in older age (e.g., Barer 1994; Rowe and Kahn 1987). In contrast, men's presumed specialization in instrumental rather than socioemotional roles is thought to limit their social resources and render them vulnerable to physical and mental health problems as they grow older (e.g., Rawlins 1992; Weiss 1983; Wortman et al. 1993).

DIMENSIONS OF ADAPTATION AND THE EMPIRICAL RECORD ON GENDER DIFFERENCES

To what degree are these theoretical perspectives on gender differences supported in the empirical literature? In order to address this question, it is necessary to consider a range of processes and outcomes thought to reflect adaptation to aging; gender differences may be observed for some of these dimensions but not for others. Those that have figured prominently in the gerontological literature are:

- social relationships
- mental health (including subjective well-being) and coping
- physical health and mortality

Depending upon the model under consideration, any of these dimensions can be considered *outcomes* of individuals' adaptive efforts, or (with the obvious exception of mortality) as *resources* which help to predict their adaptation. In some studies, for example, respondents who interact frequently with friends and family members are thought to show greater social functioning, and hence better adaptation, compared to those who report low levels of interaction (e.g., Elwell and Maltbie-Crannell 1981). (I will discuss why frequent interaction is not necessarily reflective of better adaptation.) In other studies, adaptation is conceptualized in terms of physical or mental health, and social relationships are examined in terms of how they influence health outcomes (Baldassare et al. 1984; Wortman et al. 1993). In these studies, social relationships are considered a resource which individuals may draw upon in times of illness or which may help them to remain healthy. Thus, when we evaluate gender differences in adaptation, we are also evaluating differences in women's and men's health and social resources.

In the following section, I examine the empirical record concerning each of these dimensions, assessing their adequacy as measures of adaptation to aging and examining findings of gender differences in later life. Of interest is whether the findings support the gender role or resource explanations (or a blended explanation) for gender differences. That is, do gender differences reported for a facet of adaptation disappear when differences in women's and men's economic, health, or other resources are taken into consideration (supporting the resource argument)? Or, do findings of gender differences in adaptation remain fairly constant, despite the application of such controls (possibly supporting the gender role argument)? I have noted that gender roles seldom have been assessed directly in these studies, but rather inferred ex post facto.

Social Relationships

Scientific interest in social relationships and adaptation has a long history, traceable to Durkheim's theory of anomie ([1897] 1951). Writers who equate social relationships with adaptation have assumed that people are better integrated into society, and hence better adapted, when they interact frequently with others (e.g., Elwell and Maltbie-Crannell 1981; Lowenthal and Haven 1968). These assumptions, consistent with the activity theory of adaptation, are shared by many who do not identify themselves as activity theorists. Social scientists and policymakers, as well as health care personnel who work with older persons, often assume that elders who live alone or who have no family members are poorly adapted, and hence in need of aid (see Chappell and Badger 1989).

It is true that such persons are at greater risk for nursing home admission when they become ill (Freedman 1996; Steinbach 1992), but living alone or lacking family members does not necessarily translate into isolation or poor health (Chappell and Badger 1989). Furthermore, in contrast to commonly-held assumptions about aging, older persons are no more likely than younger ones to report that they feel lonely (Creecy, Berg, and Wright 1985). In fact, no significant differences have been found in the size of older adults' support networks compared to those of younger adults (Antonucci 1991).

Studies have shown that mere quantity of interaction or social network size is not predictive of health and well-being (Antonucci 1991; Chappell and Badger 1989; Larson, Zuzanek, and Mannell 1985). Rather, the perceived quality of interaction is what is important. Having intimate and supportive relations with others enhances elders' (and others') well-being (Baldassare et al. 1984; Chappell and Badger 1989; Hays et al. 1998; Lowenthal and Haven 1968). This can be a matter of having just one person in whom to confide.

Beyond the direct benefits that confidants can provide, social relationships can affect health and well-being indirectly. Supportive relationships with others may buffer the negative effects of stressful life events by counteracting or reducing these effects (Chappell 1995; Jackson and Antonucci 1992; Lin, Woelfel, and Light 1985; Lin and Ensel 1989). In this buffering model, the benefits of social support "kick in" when stressful life events are experienced.

Social ties are not always beneficial, however, whether intimate or more distant. David Morgan states that "negative aspects of relationships may be at least as important as their supportive aspects," especially when a stressful life event is experienced (1989:101) (see also Eckenrode and Wethington 1990; Ingersoll-Dayton, Morgan, and Antonucci 1997; La Gaipa 1990; Okun and Keith 1998). In Morgan's study, almost 40 percent of all the relationships mentioned by a group of older widows were negative, with family members receiving more negative mentions than friends. Another study found that negative aspects of social relationships exerted stronger effects on psychological well-being than did positive aspects of those relationships (Rook 1984). The connections between social support, health, and well-being are complex, and researchers are continuing their efforts to unravel these connections (e.g., Bosworth and Schaie 1997; Fernandez, Mutran, and Reitzes 1998; Hays et al. 1998; Ingersoll-Dayton et al. 1997; Okun and Keith 1998).

Gender Differences in Social Relationships

In addition to the fact that quantity of interaction seldom predicts well-being (and hence is of questionable validity as a measure of adaptation), findings of gender differences have varied greatly on these quantitative dimensions. Some studies have found that men have a larger network of friendships than women (Booth 1972; Pihlblad and Adams 1972; Powers and Bultena 1976). Others (more frequently) have found the reverse (Akiyama, Elliott, and Antonucci 1996; Antonucci and Akiyama 1987a; Depner and Ingersoll 1982; Reitzes, Mutran, and Fernandez 1996). Findings have also varied concerning whether men have more (Powers and Bultena 1976) or less (Fischer and Oliker 1983) frequent contact with friends—or whether women and men have about the same rates of social interaction (Antonucci and Akiyami 1987a; Booth 1972; Kohen 1983; Petrowsky 1976). Men also may be more (Babchuk and Booth 1969; Young and Glasgow

1998), less (Keith 1983), or equally (Booth 1972; Depner and Ingersoll 1982) involved in voluntary organizations compared to women.

Measurement variation makes it very difficult to draw conclusions about gender differences on any of these dimensions.[7] For example, since women attend religious services more frequently than men, and are more active than men in other religious activities (Cutler and Danigelis 1993; deVaus and McAllister 1987; Taylor 1986), women's scores on measures of organizational involvement are likely to be higher when religious activities are included.

Measures of the quality or intimacy of relationships have produced more consistent reports of gender differences than have measures of the quantity of interaction. This pattern is helpful for this review, given the fact that qualitative measures also produce more consistent associations with health and well-being. Many writers have concluded that women have richer, more intimate relationships than men (Adams 1994; Booth 1972; Brehm 1992; Caldwell and Peplau 1982; Keith 1983; Kohen 1983; Peters et al. 1987; Powers and Bultena 1976; Rawlins 1992; Rubin 1985; Williams 1985; Wright 1989; Wright and Scanlon 1991). Women are more likely than men to have same-sex confidants—their mothers, sisters, and friends—and to have more than one confidant (Babchuk and Anderson 1989; Lin, Woelfel, and Dumin 1986; Oliker 1989). This finding extends to married as well as unmarried women—"(married) women's expectations for friendship are not always completely satisfied by their husbands or their couple friendships" (Rawlins 1992:172). Men of all ages also tend to rely on women for emotional intimacy (but see Akiyama et al. 1996). Unmarried men often name a woman as confidant (Lin et al. 1986; Rubin 1985), but this pattern doubtless is more characteristic of heterosexual men (e.g., see Lee 1990). Married men typically name their spouse as their primary or sole confidant (Antonucci and Akiyama 1987a; Keith et al. 1984; Lin et al. 1986; Rubin 1985).

This pattern has important implications for aging among married men because they may lose their primary or sole source of emotional intimacy when their spouse dies. Compared to men who are widowed, women who lose their spouse are more likely to report having one or more close friends (Kohen 1983; Lowenthal and Haven 1968; Strain and Chappell 1982).

Gender differences also have been reported in same-sex friendships as women and men grow older. Roberto and Kimboko (1989) found that women are more likely than men to report continuity in their friendships over the life course, remaining emotionally close to friends made at younger ages. Along parallel lines,

---

[7] For example, contact may be specified as in-person (Baldassare et al. 1984), or may encompass telephone and mail contacts (Harel and Deimling 1984). Some studies focus on contacts with all family members (Morgan 1984a) or specific types of kin (O'Bryant 1988); others include friends, neighbors, and co-workers (Babchuk and Anderson 1989). The time period in which contacts are assessed also varies, from daily or weekly contact (Chappell and Badger 1989) to other units of measurement (Wolinsky and Johnson 1992).

Scott Swain (1989) suggests that men may have fewer opportunities for intimate same-sex friendships as they grow older. He hypothesizes that college may be more conducive than job and career settings for maintaining friendships among (heterosexual) men.[8] In his study, Swain found that college men develop close friendships with one another, but that their intimacy is expressed mainly by activities such as exchanging favors, joking, touching, and doing things together. He argues that men simply express intimacy differently than women, through shared activities rather than verbal expressions. Verbal intimacy (such as expressing personal weaknesses to a confidant) is constrained by men's fears of violating cultural norms for male behavior.

Karen Walker's research (1994) challenges these conclusions. From her study of men and women age twenty-four to forty-eight, Walker found that "When men and women discuss friendship they emphasize the behavior that corresponds to their cultural notions of what men and women are like. Men focus on shared activities, and women focus on shared feelings" (pp. 246-247). However, when questioned about specific relationships with their friends, men revealed that they share feelings *more* than the literature indicates, and more than they themselves initially reported. In contrast, women's discussions of specific friendships showed that they shared their feelings *less* than the literature indicates, and less than they had initially reported. Walker concludes that "the notions that women share intimate feelings whereas men share activities in their friendships are more accurately viewed as cultural ideologies than as observable gender differences in behavior" (p. 246).

Walker also found social class variations in friendships which do not follow the gender difference patterns reported in the literature. Employed middle-class women said that they were sometimes reluctant to share their feelings with friends. On the other hand, working-class men "report regularly sharing feelings and discussing personal problems" (p. 247).

Theoretical Implications

Empirical evidence suggests that heterosexual men are more vulnerable than women to losses in their intimate relationships as they grow older, especially studies showing that widowers often lose their primary—or only—confidant. Some writers have linked this pattern with men's shorter life expectancies (Lowenthal and Haven 1968; Weiss 1983). Lawrence Weiss, for example, refers to the "lethal aspects of the lack of disclosure" for men (1983:148). Other writers have argued more generally that intimate relationships are unimportant to men, or that their capacity for emotional intimacy is limited (Candy 1977; Lowenthal and

---

[8] Although Swain does not say so, his hypotheses and findings are more applicable to heterosexual men than they are to homosexual men. Emotional intimacy between partners is an important element of enduring gay relationships (Lee 1990).

Robinson 1976; Powers and Bultena 1976; Rubin 1985; see also Keith et al. 1984; Strain and Chappell 1982). These findings and interpretations are in line with the predictions of traditional gender role theorists.

Scott Swain (1989) disagrees that men lack the capacity or desire for intimacy. He suggests that men simply express intimacy differently than women. Further, by hypothesizing that college provides a more favorable context for men's same-sex friendships than the workplace, Swain questions the notion of a fixed gender role.[9] On the other hand, his conclusion that men express intimacy in same-sex friendships through shared activities is consistent with the instrumental/expressive dichotomy proposed by traditional gender role theorists.

The study by Karen Walker (1994), discussed above, produced results which directly challenge the view that women develop intimate relationships with one another, while men engage in "male bonding" instrumental activities with one another. Her findings concerning social class also reinforce the importance of considering contextual variations in men's and women's friendships.

Walker's study is provocative, challenging gender difference patterns which have been widely accepted in the literature. She does not focus specifically on friendships of older adults, however, or how friendships may aid adaptation to aging. Later in the chapter, I discuss an exemplar of life course research which examines friendships among older cohorts of men who served in World War II or the Korean War. Furthermore, Walker's results do not preclude the oft-reported finding that married men rely primarily upon their spouses for emotional intimacy and support. This issue is taken up in the following chapter on women's and men's adaptation to spousal bereavement.

Mental Health and Coping

Measures of mental health are the most commonly used measures of adaptation to aging, especially measures of subjective well-being. Mental health encompasses psychological and emotional states, including morale, happiness, and life satisfaction (e.g., Mastekaasa 1992), mental and personality disorders (Aneshensel, Rutter, and Lachenbruch 1991), and psychological distress (Zautra, Reich, and Newsom 1995). Coping, or the things that people do to prevent, avoid, or control distress (Pearlin and Schooler 1978), obviously is connected with mental health: better mental health can produce as well as reflect effective coping strategies. Coping captures more of the *process* of adaptation than the other dimensions examined here, which are treated either as outcomes of adaptation processes or as resources which help to predict adaptation.

---

[9] Other evidence also suggests that expressions of intimacy vary across interaction settings (Adams 1994; Caldwell and Peplau 1982; Kaye and Applegate 1994).

Few, if any, differences have been found in the types of coping strategies used by older persons compared to younger ones (Costa, Zonderman, and McCrae 1991). Also, contrary to popular belief, many (though not all) studies have failed to document a relationship between psychological distress and older age (see Hendricks and Turner 1995). In fact, some studies have found that psychological disorders are more prevalent among younger than older age groups (e.g., Feinson 1990). Furthermore, when asked to evaluate their own mental health, older adults report generally high levels of happiness and satisfaction with their lives (Baur and Okun 1983; Stolar, MacEntee, and Hill 1995). These findings challenge commonly-held notions concerning the aging process.

Gender Differences in Mental Health

The general consensus is that women have greater psychological impairment than men (Feinson 1987; Gove 1972; Gove and Tudor 1973; Lin et al. 1986; Mirowsky and Ross 1996). However, a different picture emerges when the measures used in these studies are examined. The likelihood of a gender difference—and the direction of that difference—hinges upon the items that are included in mental health measures.

When specific categories of psychological impairment are examined, we find that women report greater distress than men and more depressive symptoms, but that men are more likely to evidence antisocial personality disorders, including drug and alcohol abuse (Aneshensel et al. 1991; Lennon 1987). Because depressive symptomatology is more commonly included in measures of mental health than the personality disorders more often associated with men (e.g., Atchley 1976a; Gallagher et al. 1983; Gore and Mangione 1983; Mirowsky and Ross 1996), women typically show poorer mental health.

Gender differences in depression and other types of psychological impairment apparently are less pronounced among older adults than they are among younger persons (Feinson 1987; George 1992; Srole and Fischer 1980; Weissman and Myers 1978). In a cross-sectional study, Marjorie Feinson (1987) considered the full range of DSM-III and affective disorders in her examination of fifteen community surveys. Her findings revealed smaller gender differences in psychological impairments and reports of distress among respondents sixty-five and older than among younger age groups. Longitudinal studies also suggest that differences in women's and men's levels of psychological impairment may grow smaller as they grow older. However, differing patterns of convergence have been reported. In one study, symptoms of psychological impairment declined among both women and men as they grew older, but declined more quickly among women (Srole and Fischer 1980). In another longitudinal study, symptoms among women declined, while those for men increased (Weissman and Myers 1978). Furthermore, older women and men often report similar levels of well-being when they are asked to evaluate their own happiness, satisfaction with their lives, and the like (Antonucci and Akiyama 1987a; Doyle and Forehand 1984).

Gender Differences in Coping

Effective coping strategies derive from the psychological, social, and socio-economic resources that are available to people (Conway 1985/86; Costa et al. 1991; Pearlin and Schooler 1978). According to Leonard Pearlin and Carmi Schooler, men are more likely than women to have psychological attributes which help them to reduce life stresses, and men are also more likely to utilize stress-reducing strategies. Coping strategies used more often by women than by men (such as ignoring a problem) were found to produce *more* rather than less stress. However, access to material resources was clearly implicated. Those with higher income and greater education were more likely to display the coping mechanisms identified as more effective by the researchers. Apparent links between gender and effective coping strategies could be explained by the men's greater income, a possibility the researchers do not pursue.

Theoretical Implications

Similar questions concerning gender differences arise from studies of mental health and those focusing on coping. Findings that women and men are susceptible to different mental health disorders (e.g., Aneshensel et al. 1991) often are interpreted as reflecting gender roles. Rather than internalizing conflict and becoming depressed, as women are thought to do, men are characterized as "acting out" the conflict (Loring and Powell 1988). The antisocial personality disorders (including substance abuse) which men are more likely to exhibit are considered representative of acting-out behaviors.

Parallel findings have come from studies of coping. Leonard Pearlin and Carmi Schooler (1978) report that women are more likely than men to ignore problems (similar to "internalizing conflict"). Similarly, Dolores Gallagher and her colleagues (1989) conclude that widowers are somewhat more likely than widows to use the "action oriented" (presumably masculine) coping strategy of keeping busy, while widows are more likely to use the (presumably feminine) "self-talk" strategy.

While it may be tempting to interpret such findings in terms of traditional gender roles—women as more passive (internalizing conflict, becoming depressed, trying to ignore problems or engaging in "self-talk") and men as more active (acting out as well as acting on their problems)—material resources play an important role. Those with greater economic resources tend to have better health and more effective coping strategies (Gass 1989; Umberson et al. 1992). Considering women's greater risks for economic hardships and chronic illnesses, it would be surprising if women's scores for depression were *not* greater than men's.

The finding that gender differences in depression and other forms of psychological impairment are less pronounced among older populations has generated diverse interpretations. Marjorie Feinson's (1987) suggested explanations draw upon both gender role and resource theories of gender differences. According to Feinson, women may face greater demands from work and family responsibilities when they are younger, generating higher levels of stress and psychological impairment. When women are older, these demands abate, producing higher levels of well-being and narrowing the gender gap in mental health. Although this interpretation may be considered "structural" in the sense that younger women are seen as lacking the resources needed to meet the demands they face, Feinson connects this argument with a gender role explanation. That is, women's and men's roles are seen as growing more similar in older age, when men have retired and women's responsibilities for childrearing have ended. (The gender role androgyny and aging thesis is discussed more fully in a subsequent section of this chapter.) According to Feinson, greater similarity in roles may produce greater congruence in women's and men's mental health. Alternatively, Feinson proposes that retirement may produce a loss of status and decreased sense of control among older men, eventuating in higher levels of impairment. "Thus, (men's) rates of impairment rise to the level of similarly powerless females, again producing little or no gender differences" (p. 710). Finally, Feinson suggests that women may accumulate more effective coping strategies during their lifetimes (a suggestion which contrasts with the conclusions reached by Pearlin and Schooler, who reported poorer coping strategies among women), which eventuate in higher levels of mental health for them. In older age, women's mental health levels thus approximate those of men. These are diverse interpretations which could but apparently have not been tested empirically.

Physical Health and Mortality

Physical health also is commonly used to assess adaptation to aging; mortality is the ultimate indicator. Measures of physical health are diverse, including chronic and acute illnesses, levels and types of functioning or disability, as well as respondents' assessments of their health. The latter often is measured globally (e.g., "Generally speaking, would you rate your present health as excellent, good, fair, or poor?"). Although these global self-assessments confound mental and physical health dimensions, they do correlate (modestly) with more specific health measures (Engle and Graney 1985/86; Herzog 1989).

While it is true that physical health problems and disabilities are more common in later life (e.g., German 1995), old age should not be equated with poor health and dependency (Rowe and Kahn 1997; Stahl and Feller 1990). There is a great deal of diversity within the older population, as well as among younger age groups (Spitze and Logan 1992; Rowe and Kahn 1997; Stahl and Feller 1990). This section of the chapter focuses on gender differences—comparing women as a group to men as a group—but a life course perspective emphasizes the importance of considering sources of diversity within the older population for all dimensions of adaptation.

Gender Differences in Physical Health and Mortality

The most prominent gender-linked health difference in most societies is the fact that women live longer on average than men (Rahman et al. 1994). In the U.S., women can expect to live nearly 80 years, or seven years longer than men. Women who reach the age of sixty-five can expect to live an additional nineteen years, or four years more than men of the same age (U.S. Bureau of the Census 1996a, Table 3-1).[10] We do not yet know why women live longer than men. Possible explanations include genetic and hormonal influences, and the greater tendency among men to engage in risky behaviors such as smoking, drinking, driving, and violence (Nathanson 1990; Wingard 1984). Men thus may be seen as adapting more poorly to aging, in that they are more susceptible to death.

In contrast, women are subject to more illness (morbidity) than men (Johnson and Wolinsky 1994; Verbrugge 1990). They report poorer overall health and more acute and chronic conditions than men, though fewer injuries (Crimmins et al. 1996; Thompson et al. 1984). Women also report more disability days, especially more days in bed. This gender difference continues after pregnancy-related days are omitted. However, employed women do not report taking more sick days from work than employed men (Wingard 1984).

Among older adults, women are more likely than men to suffer from debilitating chronic illnesses (Verbrugge 1989). Due in large part to the types and severity of illnesses they are prone to develop, older women also typically have greater mobility limitations than older men, and greater difficulties performing various personal care activities such as bathing. Fewer chronic illnesses afflict older men, but they are at greater risk than older women for life-threatening health problems, including cancer, injuries, and heart diseases (Crimmins et al. 1996; Verbrugge 1985, 1990).

Lois Verbrugge (1990) argues that women's greater morbidity in later life reflects social factors. Those she identifies include psychosocial factors (such as feelings of self-esteem and mastery, which favor men on average), women's lower rates of employment, and their engagement in less physically demanding leisure activities. Her research reveals that "controlling for a wide array of social factors makes sex differences in health narrow and often vanish statistically" (1990:175).

[10]Life expectancies are lower for racial-ethnic minorities than for whites, within gender groups. For example, African American women have a life expectancy at birth of 73.8 years, compared to 79.6 years for white women. The figures for African American men and white men are 64.6 and 72.9 years, respectively. All figures are for persons born in 1991 (U.S. Bureau of the Census 1996a, Table 3-1).

To enhance older women's health, Verbrugge advocates women's involvement in productive roles (such as employment) and increased aerobic activity.

An interesting alternative explanation for gender differences in morbidity among older adults is proposed by Omar Rahman and colleagues (1994). Noting that men have higher mortality rates than women, these writers suggest that gender differences in the incidence of ill health may reflect a selection effect. "Even if males and females have the same incidence of poor/ill health over their lifetime, the cumulative effect of higher male mortality rates will lead to an increasing gender gap in health status between men and women with age" (p. 464). In other words, "the 'sick' men will die off, leaving behind a relatively more robust group of older males" (p. 464). Since women have lower mortality rates, those who are in poor health are more likely to remain alive, compared to men of similar age and health status. Thus, gender differences in morbidity in later life, which seem to favor men over women, may actually reflect a selection effect resulting from higher male mortality.

Theoretical Implications

It has been suggested that gender differences in reporting account for women's greater morbidity at all ages (Lewis and Lewis 1977; Phillips and Segal 1969). Writers making this suggestion have reasoned that women may be more willing to talk about illness, more likely to perceive illness symptoms, or more compliant in following physicians' advice to take bed rest. These explanations are consistent with a traditional gender role perspective, which stresses women's perceptiveness and compliance. However, other studies show that women's greater morbidity cannot be explained by reporting behavior (Elwell and Maltbie-Crannell 1981; Wingard 1984). In fact, among women and men with similar levels of illness, women tend to be more optimistic about their health (Ferraro 1985/86).

From a structural perspective, greater equivalence in women's and men's activities should produce greater equivalence in their rates of morbidity and mortality. For example, according to Lois Verbrugge (1990), equal rates of employment and equal levels of physically demanding activities would help to reduce gender disparities in morbidity. Similarly, gender gaps in mortality should narrow if more women engage in the "risky behaviors" which have been identified as contributing to lower life expectancies among men (Nathanson 1990; Wingard 1984)—or if men reduce their rates of smoking, drinking, driving, and violence.

Evaluating the Empirical Record

The main purpose of this review has been to evaluate studies of gender differences in adaptation to aging. Some broader conclusions concerning adaptation also can be reached. First and foremost, it is quite difficult to evaluate what "adaptation to aging" actually involves. The term itself is inherently value-laden. But even if we grant that the perceptions of the individuals involved should be used as the litmus test for their quality of life (a perspective consistent with a social constructionist approach), there are a number of difficulties associated with this area of study.

This review has shown that not all of the measures used to assess adaptation are particularly good ones. Measures of social functioning that rely on the quantity of interaction or the size of a person's social network are especially suspect. It is also important to consider that not all social relationships are supportive, and that some can be harmful to an individual's health and well-being (Bankoff 1983; Krause and Jay 1991; Morgan 1989). Other dimensions of adaptation correlate positively with one another (Baltes and Baltes 1990), suggesting a degree of reliability across the measures.[11] Those in better physical health tend to have better mental health, for example, and tend to report greater life satisfaction, morale, happiness, and the like (Levkoff, Cleary, and Wetle 1987; Rozzini et al. 1988).

A further broad conclusion is that researchers have focused far more on presumed *outcomes* (or predictors) of the adaptation process, rather than adaptation *processes* (studies of coping are an exception).[12] Because of the relative lack of attention to process, and also because longitudinal studies are not as prevalent as cross-sectional studies, it is difficult to evaluate unique dimensions of adaptation in the later years, as compared with adaptation at earlier points in the life course.

In fact, the evidence suggests that later life is not as traumatic as is popularly believed, despite limitations of the studies and despite the fact that declines and losses have constituted the dominant paradigm for studies of older age. Although older persons often have poorer physical health and greater functional limitations than younger age groups (e.g., Kaplan 1992; Verbrugge 1989), older age cannot simply be equated with health problems (Rowe and Kahn, 1997; Stahl and Feller 1990). Interestingly, some studies have found that older persons tend to be more optimistic about their health than middle-age persons (e.g., Cockerham, Sharp, and Wilcox 1983; Rakowski and Cryan 1990; but see Roberts 1999). Other studies have reported that older adults are no more likely than members of younger age groups to feel lonely (e.g., Creecy et al. 1985) or to evidence symptoms of psychological distress (see Hendricks and Turner 1995). However, this chapter has not focused upon adaptation to *specific* life events which may occasion distress, but rather upon "adaptation to aging" writ large. In the next chapter, I

---

[11]Although the magnitude of these associations tend to be rather modest for all age groups (Baltes and Baltes 1990), larger correlations have been found among older samples (e.g., Rozzini et al. 1988).

[12]Research in the area of developmental psychology has done far more in this regard, but is beyond the scope of this book. For an excellent treatment of psychological perspectives on older women, see Barbara Turner and Lillian Troll's edited collection *Women Growing Older* (1994), especially the chapter by Margaret Hellie Huyck on the relevance of psychodynamic theories for understanding gender in later life.

focus specifically on adaptation to the death of a spouse, a life event perceived as stressful by most who experience it, and for which older persons are at greater risk than younger ones.

Conclusions About Gender Differences

This review has shown that conclusions to be reached about gender differences in adaptation to aging depend upon the measure under consideration. As a group, women seem to fare better than men on some dimensions, but worse on others. It is difficult to ascertain clear patterns of gender differences for some of these dimensions due to measurement variation and the diverse samples that are often used. However, some general conclusions can be drawn.

In the ultimate sense of "adaptation," women quite simply live longer on average than men. This fact is well-known, but is worth repeating here since mortality has been used as an indicator of adaptation to aging. In addition, most of the empirical evidence shows that women are more likely than men to have one or more confidants outside of marriage. Women also may be more likely than men to have maintained long-term intimate friendships over their lives. However, what women and men say about their friendships in general may not characterize their specific relationships (Walker 1994). The evidence is mixed concerning gender differences in frequency of interaction with others or amount of organizational involvement. However, qualitative dimensions of social interaction are better predictors of well-being than quantitative ones. Both older women and older men tend to report generally high levels of happiness and satisfaction with their lives.

On the other hand, men can expect to live out their lives with fewer chronic illnesses. At all ages, men also are less likely to suffer from depression, but this gender difference narrows in later life. And gender differences in depression are "balanced out" by the fact that men are more susceptible than women to other forms of psychological distress, specifically personality disorders.

An undisputed gender difference concerns men's greater economic resources (Hardy and Hazelrigg 1993). (I will reiterate that at this point, aggregate categories of men and women are being compared. Later in the chapter, I address how a sole focus on gender obscures the importance of race-ethnicity in understanding economic disparities.) Economic resources, in turn, are predictive of better mental and physical health and better coping skills. These patterns are supportive of structural arguments that focus on men's and women's differential access to resources. To the degree that men's material resources exceed women's, we should expect more adaptive outcomes on the part of men. Although resources are clearly implicated in health outcomes, hypotheses concerning gender, health, and socioeconomic resources have not been tested systematically. The need to consider socioeconomic and political factors in health status and behaviors is increasingly recognized, however, and more researchers are turning their attention in this direction (e.g., Bound et al. 1996; House et al. 1992; James, Keenan, and

Browning 1992; Reynolds and Ross 1998; Schoenbaum and Waidmann 1997; Williams 1992).

Explanations based on traditional gender roles are even further from empirical verification. Gender roles have been inferred rather than tested in most studies of adaptation to aging, and competing explanations can account for results that seem to reflect the effects of gender roles. For example, Pearlin and Schooler's report (1978) of greater coping skills among men may be attributable to men's greater material resources, rather than to qualities associated with a masculine role. Given consistent findings of greater intimacy and confiding among women, this dimension of social functioning seems most amenable to a gender role explanation. Yet, research also suggests that expressions of intimacy among men as well as women are contingent upon particular interaction settings, challenging the assumption of a fixed gender role (see Winstead et al. 1997). More generally, women's and men's adaptation cannot be evaluated adequately in terms of a simple dichotomy, pitting all women against all men, whether adaptation is conceptualized in terms of physical or mental health, subjective well-being, social functioning, or some other dimension.

Gender Differences in Life Events and Adaptation to Aging

Earlier I reviewed gender-difference arguments concerning whether women or men experience more life changes in older age, and how adaptation to aging is impacted by role changes and life events—one's own life events as well as involvement in the life events of others. Some evidence does suggest that older women experience more major life events than older men—or that they are more likely to report such events. One study found that women age fifty-five to seventy-five reported more life events during the prior decade than men in this age group (Szinovacz and Washo 1992). Maximiliane Szinovacz and Christine Washo raise the possibility that women may report more life events than men due to gender-specific recall bias. That is, women simply may *report* more events than men, as opposed to actually experiencing more of them. If this is so, the authors believe that by recalling more of these events, women would seem to attach greater salience to the events. Women are thought to report (or to actually experience) more life events than men because they are more involved in crises involving their family members and friends (see also Kessler and McLeod 1984). The authors use gender role socialization to explain women's greater involvement in the life crises of family and friends. However, these studies did not measure attitudinal or behavioral adherence to traditional gender roles, nor did they assess potential differences in women's and men's involvements in their social networks. Thus, it is not possible to assess the empirical merits of this argument compared to other possible explanations. For example, because spousal bereavement is a more probable experience for women than men, we might *expect* that older women would score higher on a life events inventory for this reason alone.

A further component of these arguments stresses women's involvement in the life events of their family and friends. In particular, women's provision of care to those who are ill or otherwise require care may be detrimental to their own health and well-being. Much research has documented that women perform the bulk of family caregiving, which "directly affects both their economic status and their health in old age" (Arendell and Estes 1991:220) (see also Hooyman 1992; Marshall et al. 1990; Seccombe 1992). Although gender role theory often is used to explain these patterns, it is not sufficient to explain why women do most of the caregiving (Finley 1989). This explanation ignores power differentials between women and men in society and in interpersonal relationships, reflected in the low value placed on the work that women do and the general lack of concern for the costs of caregiving to women (Walker 1992).[13]

SOME ATTEMPTS TO MOVE BEYOND GENDER DICHOTOMIES

In this section, I examine three controversies in the gerontological literature which bear on gender and adaptation to aging: whether involvement in multiple roles is helpful or harmful to women's health; whether gender role androgyny promotes successful adaptation to aging; and whether a homosexual orientation facilitates adaptation to aging. These debates move beyond dichotomous comparisons between women and men, but they continue to revolve around traditional gender roles. Parsonsian assumptions continue to serve as the bedrock for these arguments, describing and circumscribing the nature and functioning of women's and men's roles.

Multiple Roles: Bane or Blessing?

Some scholars have moved beyond gender dichotomies by making comparisons among women (and less often, among men) with differing family and work experiences. For example, lifelong homemakers have been compared with women who have participated in the labor force (e.g., Depner and Ingersoll 1982; Freudiger 1983; Keith 1982). Recent years have witnessed more sophisticated assessments of family and work experiences, using multivariate analyses and controlling for potentially confounding factors (e.g., Adelmann 1994; Barnett, Marshall, and Pleck 1992; Moen, Dempster-McClain, and Williams 1992; Penning 1998).

---

[13]Although the health and economic costs of intensive caregiving have long been established in the research literature, policymakers have attempted to contain the costs of health care to older adults by maintaining or increasing caregiving responsibilities in the family (Arendell and Estes 1991).

The question underlying much of this research is whether women fare better or worse when they occupy traditional gender roles, and, more broadly, whether multiple roles in the realms of family and work are helpful or harmful for women's health and well-being. Men often have been excluded from these studies, with the rationale that they do not have to juggle or trade off work and family roles as women do, or that men are better able than women to sustain identities in both of these spheres (e.g., Bielby and Bielby 1989; Regan and Roland 1985; but see Penning 1998). Not surprisingly, the answers to these questions are more complicated than simply whether multiple roles are good or bad for women's well-being, or whether men are better able than women to sustain multiple roles.

The belief that multiple roles are inherently stressful has long been assumed. The reasoning was that individuals who take on more roles are likely to experience role conflict (incompatible expectations associated with different roles) and role strain or overload (having too many role demands and too little time to perform them). Role conflict and strain, in turn, were thought to produce stress and exhaustion, eventuating in psychological and/or physical impairments (Thoits 1987a). This reasoning is consistent with Parsonsian theory, which assumes not only that societal members share comparable expectations for particular roles, but also that individuals are motivated to internalize and conform to these expectations. Thus, "incompatible or burdensome expectations create serious personal dilemmas" (Thoits 1987a:12). From this perspective, married women who are employed would be at risk for serious health problems. Women's roles of wives and mothers have been considered incompatible with labor force participation, producing both role conflict and role strain.

Empirical research has not borne out this line of reasoning. It is clear that homemakers do not enjoy health advantages over married women who are employed (Lewin-Epstein 1986; McKinlay et al. 1990). In fact, a number of studies have shown the converse, with employed women reporting less illness, fewer days of disability, and less anxiety than homemakers (e.g., Kessler and McRae 1982; Lewin-Epstein 1986).

To explain such findings, Jessie Bernard and others (e.g., Gove 1972; Gove and Tudor 1973; see also Coombs 1991) have argued that women's traditional roles are detrimental to their health. Exemplifying the blended gender role/ resource approach reviewed in the previous chapter, these authors stress that gender roles are stratified rather than complementary and equal, producing differences in women's and men's access to valued resources. Bernard speaks of women "dwindling" into their roles as housewives, losing self-esteem and a sense of identity ([1972] 1978:42). Her argument that marriage is more beneficial to men than it is to women is supported by studies showing that married men are mentally healthier than married women (Gove 1972; Gove and Tudor 1973; Keith 1980; Rosenfield 1989; see also Coombs 1991; Thoits 1987b). Employment can benefit women by providing them with avenues for self-fulfillment beyond the family, along with economic and social resources (Gore and Mangione 1983). Other writers have argued more generally that role accumulation provides individuals with greater access to resources and alternative sources of gratification (Gerson 1985; Rosenfield 1989).

Although research is largely supportive of the thesis that multiple roles are beneficial (Adelmann 1994; Barnett et al. 1992; Coleman, Antonucci, and Adelmann 1987; but see Penning 1998), the gains are not limitless. Evidence suggests a threshold effect for multiple roles (Stoller and Pugliesi 1989; Thoits 1986), beyond which role demands take a toll on health and well-being. Sarah Rosenfield (1989) argues convincingly that personal control is key to understanding this threshold effect. According to Rosenfield, married women have greater symptoms of psychological distress because they "are more often in positions of low power as housewives and in positions of high demands when employed" (1989:87). Increased power or gratification provided by employment can be offset by losses in personal control, due to the overload of responsibilities from both jobs and family life. Thus, the effect of women's employment "is not consistently positive because it often trades one source of low control for another" (p. 77).

A further key to understanding the effects of multiple roles concerns how individuals themselves evaluate their situations. Peggy Thoits asserts that role expectations "are not as clear, consensual, rigid, and monolithic" as the traditional view of multiple role occupancy has assumed (1987a:12). The importance of considering individuals' perceptions of their situations is demonstrated by Coverman (1989), who found that role overload was not nearly as important in predicting psychological symptoms among women, compared to the women's *perceptions* of role conflict. If women perceive their roles as conflicting with one another, they are likely to suffer psychological distress (see also Franks and Stephens 1992).

Mid-life women have been the primary focus in these studies (Barnett et al. 1992), with the assumption that they are most likely to face conflicts and demands from multiple roles (e.g., Brody 1985; Brody and Schoonover 1986). However, some researchers have extended these investigations to men and to older women (e.g., Barnett et al. 1992 ; Moen et al. 1992; Penning 1998). For example, Phyllis Moen and colleagues have contended that multiple role occupancy is especially important for older women, since they are more likely than men to spend their later years alone "without the presence (and support) of a spouse" (1992:1613), and hence in greater need of additional roles. Other researchers have been interested in long-term effects of multiple role occupancy, asking whether lifelong homemakers fare better or worse in older age compared to married women who have been employed (e.g., Keith 1982).

Although we can conclude broadly that multiple role occupancy is beneficial—to a point—for adults of all ages (Gerson 1985; Rosenfield 1989; Rushing, Ritter, and Burton 1992; Stoller and Pugliesi 1989), it is very difficult to understand more about this issue without considering particular contexts in which individuals interact and attach meaning to their experiences. This point is underlined by one of the few longitudinal studies of multiple role occupancy and aging, the study by Phyllis Moen and colleagues (1992) referenced above. This study found that women who occupied multiple roles in 1956 were likely to do so thirty years later, a finding consistent with the continuity theory of aging. All of these women were wives and mothers at mid-life, but some had also taken on volunteer or paid work activities, while others had not. Doing volunteer work earlier in their lives (measured as of 1956) predicted better health for the women when they were older (measured as of 1986). However, women who had worked for pay at mid-life had *poorer* health in older age, compared to women who had not been employed (and controlling for the women's previous health levels).

This finding contrasts with other studies that have found beneficial effects of employment on women's mental health, reviewed above. To understand this finding, information is needed about the types of jobs the respondents held and, even more importantly, how they evaluated their paid work and family commitments. Did the women perceive the demands in these realms as in conflict with one another, or as excessively demanding of their time and energy? As the authors conclude, further research on the linkages between role attachments and health must consider individuals' preferences and choices, as well as their levels of autonomy.

Androgyny and Adaptation to Aging

Research on multiple roles moves beyond gender dichotomies by examining the influence of marital, parental, and employment roles and experiences. These researchers have not simply assumed that women share the same roles, but have considered variations in the type and number of their roles (and, less often, have considered role variations among men). Although some who pursue this line of study have argued that women and men who occupy similar roles will show equivalence in their psychological health and well-being (a structural approach), they have conceded that it is virtually impossible to locate groups of women and men to study who occupy equivalent social roles (e.g., Thoits 1986). Others have argued that differences in women's and men's personalities and behaviors grow smaller in later life, reflecting a process of gender role androgyny. Furthermore, androgyny has been thought to facilitate adaptation to aging (e.g., Gutmann and Huyck 1994; Livson 1983; Sinnott 1977, 1982; Turner 1982).

From this line of reasoning, aging frees women and men from restrictive social expectations attached to their own gender, bringing improved health and well-being. There is also an implicit suggestion that older men and women will enjoy more egalitarian relationships with one another because they come to share similar traits. Women are thought to develop presumed male characteristics of independence and assertiveness as they grow older, while retaining female traits of nurturing and emotional expression. Older men are thought to take on female traits (or to allow the female sides of themselves to surface), while retaining masculine ones. Because many of the stereotypically male traits are socially valued, while presumed female traits generally are not (e.g., Lubinski, Tellegen, and Butcher 1983; Morgan, Affleck, and Riggs 1986; Taylor and Hall 1982; Whitley 1984), writers taking this point of view have predicted that women's self-concepts should improve in later life (e.g., Turner 1979). Although the converse would seem to apply to men (suffering lower self-esteem when they take on socially devalued female characteristics), proponents of androgyny have portrayed men as also benefitting from androgynous roles because they are freed from the emotionally restrictive and stressful expectations associated with masculinity (Guttman and Huyck 1994; Livson 1983; Maracek 1979).

Probably because many people (including myself) have found this argument appealing, the androgyny and aging thesis has been generally accepted in the gerontology literature (e.g., Aiken 1995; Cunningham and Brookbank 1988; Hooyman and Kiyak 1995; Markson 1995; Pratt and Norris 1994; Rybash, Roodin, and Santrock 1991; Turner 1982). Indeed, references are made to the "normal androgeny (sic) of later life" (e.g., Jerrome 1990:199). However, empirical evidence for this thesis is limited, insofar as androgyny is conceptualized as a role or set of psychological traits.

An article often cited as support for androgyny and aging, written by Jan Sinnott (1977), illustrates both conceptual and methodological shortcomings of this argument. Sinnott claimed that androgynous individuals show flexibility in their gender roles over their lifetimes, modifying their roles when needed. Androgyny was conceptualized in this study, as it is in most, as a blending or merging of culturally-defined feminine and masculine characteristics. According to Sinnott, androgynous individuals age more successfully, displaying greater autonomy and life satisfaction in older age than those who cling to rigidly defined gender roles—and in the ultimate sense of "successful aging," that they also live longer! (See also Kline 1975.)

For support, Sinnott cited a variety of studies believed to have "some flaws," but which were "generally accepted as valid by students of aging" (1977:461). From the vantage point of more than twenty years later, it is clear that many of the studies were badly flawed methodologically, and others simply were not designed to test what Sinnott wished to demonstrate. For example, to support the thesis that androgynous individuals live longer, Sinnott cited a study of long-lived elderly (Jewett 1973), whose personalities were characterized as androgynous—combining "independence, interest in work, activity, and strength with adaptability, nurturance, family concerns, and acceptance of emotions" (Sinnott 1977:461). However, since there was no control group, we have no clue how this sample differed from persons who did not live long enough to be included in the study, who may have exhibited equally "androgynous" personalities. Nor do we know much about how androgyny was assessed.

Subsequent studies of androgyny addressed this issue by using standardized sex role inventories. Sandra Bem's Sex Role Inventory, or BSRI, has been the most popular. The BSRI contains a battery of items reflecting stereotypic masculine and feminine characteristics. ("Forceful," "self-reliant," and "analytical" are examples of the masculine items, while "affectionate," "gentle," and "gullible" are included in the feminine list.) The instrument treats masculinity and femininity as independent dimensions, such that individuals can score high (androgynous) or low (undifferentiated) on both dimensions, or high on one and low on the other. In the latter case, respondents would be categorized as predominantly feminine or masculine, and their sex role category can be at variance with their biological sex (i.e., men can be categorized as feminine, and women as masculine (see Bem 1977).

A review of the literature shows that androgyny, as it has been assessed by these instruments, is not an effective predictor of health or well-being at any age (see Deaux and Kite 1987). If anything, it is simply the presence of high instrumental (or "masculine") traits that are associated with better mental health and well-being—traits that are socially valued (Frank, Towell, and Huyck 1985; Lubinski et al. 1983; Morgan et al. 1986; Taylor and Hall 1982; Whitley 1984). Other studies have found that sex-role classification, whether "masculine," "feminine," or "androgynous," does a poor job of predicting any health outcome (Lubinski et al. 1983; Windle 1986).

In addition to empirical challenges, androgyny has been critiqued on conceptual grounds. Despite its emancipatory promise, Bem's (and most others') concept of androgyny is built upon stereotypes of masculinity and femininity, which are considered integral components of personality. An androgynous individual is not free of these stereotypes, but must incorporate *both sets*. Equally paradoxical is the fact that instruments measuring androgyny treat presumed masculine and feminine qualities as universal constants (Morawski 1990).

David Gutmann's work on androgyny and aging also is frequently cited (e.g., Arber and Ginn 1995; Markson 1995; Szinovacz 1989b; Thomas 1994). His approach differs from those discussed thus far, both in how androgyny is conceptualized and how it is measured. He agrees, however, that masculine and feminine qualities are universal, or nearly so.

Citing ethnographic data published in 1957 (Barry, Bacon, and Child), Gutmann states that "the central themes in female socialization across cultures are nurturance, responsibility, and to a lesser degree, obedience" (1997:86). Males, in contrast, are "almost universally socialized toward achievement and self-reliance" (p. 86). According to Gutmann, the driving force behind these patterns of socialization is preparation for parenthood, which is required to ensure survival of the society. Human potential encompasses both masculine and feminine qualities, for both men and women. However, the "parental imperative" dictates that each sex cultivate the qualities which will ensure effective parenting and relinquish those which would interfere with it. Men are required to suppress passive, nurturing tendencies so that they can provide effective protection to the young. Women are required to suppress aggressive tendencies in order to be "a provider of emotional security to children and of emotional comfort to the providing husband" (p. 87). For each sex, this adaptive restriction "closes out psychological tendencies that could interfere with adequate parenting, and it leads individuals to seek their completion, their lost omnipotentiality, not within themselves but through procreant alliances with the heterosexual other" (pp. 87-88).

In older age, when parental duties have been completed, men and women are able to reclaim the qualities they gave up in the service of parenthood. In fact, the renounced traits are those which come to be emphasized in older age. In this sense, Gutmann's thesis is a theory of role reversal rather than androgyny (see McGee and Wells 1982). "Older women reclaim the aggression that can no longer hurt their young" (Gutmann 1997:113). For older men, "the current sets in the opposite direction," toward pacifism, sensitivity, and dependency (p. 122).

Gutmann has examined these ideas cross-culturally using the Thematic Apperception Test (TAT), a projective assessment tool. Subjects are shown a series of cards which depict ambiguous scenes and are asked to tell stories about them. The themes that emerge in these stories are then analyzed by the researcher. Based upon his studies of the Navajo, Maya, the Druze of Galilee and the Golan Heights, and residents of Kansas City, as well as findings of additional studies conducted by his colleagues and students, Gutmann reports that TAT results provide cross-cultural support for the parental imperative thesis (Gutmann 1994, 1997).

It is difficult to reconcile Gutmann's reports with a growing anthropological literature stressing the diversity and complexity of gender across cultures. Since the mid-1970s, feminist anthropologists have challenged the view that women universally are associated with the domestic or private sphere of life and that men universally are associated with the public sphere (see Lamphere 1997). The thesis that women are universally subordinated also has been challenged. Although male dominance is widespread, women "typically have power and influence in political and economic life" (Rosaldo 1980:394). Furthermore, men take an active and important role in child care in some societies. To cite just one example, Barry Hewlett (1997) reports that among the Aka, a hunter-gatherer group located in the tropic forest of Central Africa, both fathers and mothers "embrace the parenting role," but fathers are more likely than mothers to show affection while holding their infants. Fathers "are characterized by their affectionate and intimate relations with their infants. Aka infants bond with their fathers because they provide sensitive and regular care" (p. 51).

Reflecting specifically on Gutmann's work, Jeanne McGee and Kathleen Wells (1982) observe that the parental imperative thesis assumes a "traditional" conjugal relationship (a protecting father paired with a nurturing mother), ignoring the diversity of family patterns found both within and outside the United

States. Nor has a pattern of gender convergences found much empirical support (see Thompson 1994).

The validity of the TAT methodology also has been widely questioned (e.g., Belsky 1999; McCrae and Costa 1984; McGee and Wells 1982). Robert McCrae and Paul Costa cite research showing that "TAT stories change from one time to another, and so do the scores derived from them" (1984:84). The authors state that subjects' performance on these tests is subject to "verbal skill, motivation, and perceptual problems" (p. 84). Even more to the point, "careful research studies using projective tests to measure traits or predict outcomes have had uniformly disappointing results" (p. 85). Indeed, among the Middle-Eastern Druze—a group cited by Gutmann as an exemplar of androgyny in older age—"the old men are respected as leaders and decision makers; they are anything but passive" (McCrae and Costa 1984:87).

Critiques of androgyny are not new. In fact, Sandra Bem, one of the architects of the concept, was also one of the first to draw attention to its limitations (1978). However, the androgyny and aging thesis has shown great lasting power in gerontology.

To understand this issue, we must distinguish between androgyny as assessed by the BSRI and other trait measures or as imputed by researchers via the TAT, and behaviors that individuals themselves may define as masculine and feminine. With regard to the former, supporting evidence is sparse. Beyond the conceptual problems associated with androgyny, described above, trait-based measures have not yielded much empirical support for the androgyny thesis (see Deaux and Kite 1987). And as noted above, the TAT approach to assessing androgyny has generated more controversy than consensus.

On the other hand, evidence shows that people define particular behaviors as "male" or "female," and that they *expect* gender-linked differences in human behavior (Bastida 1987; Sinnott 1984; Thompson 1992). Furthermore, evidence suggests that current cohorts of older persons *believe* that they are expected to become "androgynous." In Jan Sinnott's 1984 study, a sample of persons age sixty and older was asked to describe themselves *as others expect them to be*. Many of the respondents indicated that others expected them to exhibit high levels of masculine as well as feminine characteristics. A woman who had been recently widowed elaborated on this issue, saying that since her husband had died, others expected her to handle "both roles"—her own, and her husband's—whereas previously they had expected her to be "feminine" only.

This statement is revealing. To the degree that individuals themselves characterize some behaviors as "feminine" and others as "masculine," it is likely that many women and men *do* become more "androgynous" in later life (see McGee and Wells 1982). A social constructionist approach which emphasizes individuals' own definitions differs from trait-based measures of masculine and feminine personality, and also differs from the assumption that role changes will bring more or less stable transformations in individuals' personalities. Life changes that are associated with older age, such as the death of a partner, can bring greater similarities in the kinds of things that women and men do, which in turn will shape their interactions with others and consequently their definitions of themselves and others. These definitions may change depending upon new (or renewed) contexts and interactions.

To illustrate, numerous studies have documented that the division of labor among married couples tends to be heavily gendered. Women perform most of the household work even when wives are employed and husbands are unemployed or retired (Blair and Johnson 1992; Keith and Wacker 1990; Vinick and Ekerdt 1992). A woman who considers paying the bills her husband's job and defines this as a "masculine" task may well consider herself more masculine when she takes on that task after she is widowed. If she subsequently forms a new household with someone else and renegotiates the division of labor with her new partner, she may relinquish the tasks she considers "masculine" and come to redefine herself as more "feminine."

Similarly, men who are widowered, or whose wives are in poor health and require care, are likely to take on behaviors they consider "women's work," and their self-definitions may change accordingly. This conclusion was reached by Lenard Kaye and Jeffrey Applegate (1994), regarding men who were performing intensive caregiving to their wives or other family members. Kaye and Applegate found that the men's self-definitions "did not vary significantly in relation to their marital status, employment status, age, physical health, or whether they were caring for a spouse or another relative" (p. 223). The study suggests that the context shared in common by the men—their "common experience of heavy engagement in family caregiving" (p. 223)—shaped the men's views of themselves as nurturant and caring.[14] Although these findings are suggestive of how the experience of caregiving can shape men's gendered identities, the researchers relied upon a modified version of Bem's checklist of "masculine" and "feminine" characteristics. We do not know how the men themselves defined and evaluated these characteristics, or whether the men identified with these characteristics prior to engaging in family caregiving.

A focus on individuals' own definitions and interpretations, and how these emerge within particular contexts of social interaction, emphasizes the potential fluidity of gendered identities. The BSRI and other trait measures are premised on "situation-free self-attributions of relatively enduring qualities," (McGee and Wells 1982:124) and cannot possibly capture these dynamics. Jan Sinnott's statements (1977, 1984) on androgyny and aging stress that individuals show flexibility in their gender roles over their lifetimes. However, this conceptualization

---

[14]These men viewed themselves as possessing more "feminine" qualities (gentle, compassionate, warm, loving) than "masculine" qualities (analytical, competitive, aggressive, forceful). However, self-sufficiency was most commonly named as a quality they saw themselves possessing.

relies upon the researcher's determination of which respondents fit a situation-free "androgynous" personality profile (a feature shared with Gutmann's methodological approach) and which do not, in addition to making dubious claims concerning the health and longevity benefits of androgyny.

In sum, a definition of androgyny based upon presumed personality traits moves beyond the dichotomy of masculinity versus femininity, but simply adds a further pre-defined category. Evidence to date does not convince that this category is useful or valid.

Sexual Orientation and Adaptation to Aging

While it is manifestly true that the study of aging has been the study of heterosexuals (Cruikshank 1990), there has been some speculation that a homosexual orientation facilitates adaptation to aging (Berger 1982; Friend 1990; Kimmel 1995; Quam and Whitford 1992; Teitelman 1987). The reasoning parallels the arguments for androgyny: a homosexual orientation is thought to encourage flexible gender roles throughout life, which in turn provide greater adaptability to change and more positive self-identities. Richard Friend (1990), for example, argues that older lesbians and gay men have had greater freedom than their heterosexual peers to learn skills that are non-traditional for their gender. Because they are not bound to traditional roles, Friend says, older homosexuals may be better prepared for changes and losses associated with aging.

These arguments have remained in the realm of speculation, however. There is no evidence that homosexuals age more successfully than heterosexuals, but also no evidence that they age less successfully, either. Findings of life satisfaction and self-acceptance among older gay men and lesbian women are based on samples who feel comfortable about identifying themselves as homosexual—a unique group indeed among today's older cohorts (see Adelman 1991; Quam and Whitford 1992). Those who have agreed to participate in studies have reported many of the same concerns voiced by older heterosexuals, revolving primarily around health, income, and social support (Lee 1987; Quam and Whitford 1992). Some concerns, however, are unique to lesbians and gays in a homophobic society: Fears of rejection when they come out to family members and friends; concerns about discrimination in housing, employment, health care, and long-term care (Quam and Whitford 1992). In fact, for every benefit that has been proposed for growing old as a homosexual, another, equally potent cost has been enumerated (e.g., Adelman 1991; Berger 1982; Quam and Whitford 1992).

Richard Friend notes that the two elements common to today's older gay and lesbian people are a homosexual identity and the fact that they came of age during a particular socio-historical period (1990:99). Beyond these elements, the population of older homosexuals is characterized by great diversity (Kimmel 1995), just as is true for older heterosexuals and doubtless is true for older bisexuals. Although research in this area is still meager, references to sexual orientation are becoming somewhat more common in gerontological works (e.g., Aiken 1995; Gradman 1994; Thomas 1994). The years to come should witness a larger accumulated body of knowledge on sexual orientation and the life course.

I turn now to examining adaptation from a life course perspective, which is premised on the importance of considering sources of diversity across individuals, historical time, and social space. Gender and sexual orientation are two important sources, but neither is sufficient to understand how people adapt to aging, or to life changes at any age.

BEYOND GENDER DIFFERENCES: ADAPTATION TO AGING IN LIFE COURSE PERSPECTIVE

Greater attention has been paid to differences between women and men— whether expected or observed—than to sources of similarity between them, or to sources of differentiation within groups of women and within groups of men. Given the diverse samples used in the reviewed studies, often varying not only in the region sampled, but also the respondents' age, race, education, income, etc., it is not at all surprising that so many conflicting findings regarding gender differences have been reported.

In addition, although some authors of the reviewed studies have cautioned that findings of gender difference may be less applicable to future cohorts (e.g., Barer 1994), the context for aging seldom is given much attention. Not only are individuals' personal histories often overlooked, but also the broader socio-historical context in which they grow old. Even those studies based on a social constructionist approach, in which gender is viewed as an emergent property of social interaction, seldom explicitly consider the historical context—personal or societal—in which those interactions take place (e.g., West and Zimmerman 1987).

My purpose in this section is to outline the features of a life course perspective which bear on adaptation to aging and to discuss relevant research findings. The discussion is organized using the model advanced in Chapter 2, which highlights the multiple levels of analysis encompassed by a life course approach. These are personal histories of experience; social location and membership in social groups; birth cohorts; and the broader societal context.

While relatively few studies of adaptation to aging have been based fully on a life course perspective, findings from many studies help to explicate and support different facets of this approach. These findings are helpful for this discussion because they help to fill in the broad outlines of a life course perspective. However, they cannot provide a satisfactory illustration of the perspective or the unique insights that it can provide. Further, the multi-level model utilized here helps to disentangle and clarify the levels of experience encompassed by a life course perspective, but it does not highlight the crucial linkages and intersections between these levels. For this reason, I conclude this section by discussing several exemplars of a life course perspective, each of which focuses rather narrowly on a selected cohort and population, and a selected dimension of adaptation to aging.

Employing the Multi-Level Life Course Model

Personal Histories

From a life course perspective, the ways in which we adapt to change in later life are likely to reflect earlier patterns of adaptation. Individuals develop preferred methods of coping with changes in their lives, which in turn impact their health and well-being (see Costa et al. 1991). This is not to say that we maintain the same patterns over our lifetimes, with little potential for personal growth or change (e.g., Lieberman 1992), or that different situations do not call forth different responses (Folkman and Lazarus 1980). Rather, proponents of a life course perspective recognize that although older age presents some unique challenges and opportunities, it is not disconnected from earlier phases of life.

The importance of previously established patterns has been shown for social relations and health outcomes in later life. Toni Antonucci has conducted extensive research on what she terms "convoys of social support," in which social relations are seen as "often, but not always, having stable and enduring qualities, and as having an important and cumulative influence on the individual" (Antonucci 1991:261; also Antonucci and Akyama 1987b). Her research has confirmed that social relationships tend to be relatively stable over time, and that early social relations affect well-being in older age. Other studies show that friendship patterns established early in life lay the foundation for later friendships (Matthews 1986; Roberto and Kimboko 1989).

Health also has long-term, cumulative effects. Phyllis Moen and her colleagues (1992) found that women who had health problems during their childhood or early adulthood had poorer health and less functional ability in older age than women without early health problems. Other researchers have shown that prior history of illness helps to predict future health problems, for both physical and mental health (Fischer et al. 1979; Tausig 1986). While these findings would seem rather obvious—indeed, health practitioners include a medical history as a standard preliminary diagnostic—researchers have paid greater attention to the impact of recent life events on health, than they have to respondents' long-term histories of health and illness (Tausig 1986). From the evidence available thus far, it is clear that we must consider what has come before in peoples' lives to understand their current health status, social relationships, and other resources, and to anticipate the levels and types of resources which are likely to be available in the future.

Social Location and Social Groups

Personal histories—past, present, and future—are configured by individuals' positions in social hierarchies and by their membership in social groups, including families and households. Studies focusing primarily or solely upon gender differences neglect other sources of diversity and inequality. The importance of considering linkages between gender and other dimensions that help to define the life chances available to individuals is highlighted by studies of poverty in older age.

Research on adaptation to aging has documented the importance of economic resources for health and well-being (e.g., Crimmins et al. 1996; Harel, Sollod, and Bognar 1982; Longino, Warheit, and Green 1989; Markides 1989a). Furthermore, it is well-known that as a group older women's incomes and assets fall far short of men's (Burkhauser 1994; Holden 1989). However, a singular emphasis on gender can lead to misleading conclusions about who is likely to "suffer more" from the effects of poverty in their older age.

When gender is used as the sole lens through which statistics on poverty are examined, conclusions can easily be drawn that older women are worse off than older men: unmarried older women are more likely to fall below the poverty line than unmarried older men, and they have significantly lower median incomes (Dressel 1988). These patterns hold within racial-ethnic groups. Based on population data for 1982, Meredith Minkler and Robyn Stone (1985) reported that among older unmarried elderly whites, nearly half of the women but only about a third of the men fell below 125 percent of the poverty line. Similar patterns were found for older unmarried elderly blacks: 80 percent of the women fell below this line, compared to 64 percent of the men. Minkler and Stone concluded that "elderly women represent . . . the single poorest segment of American society" (1985:109) (see also Burkhauser 1994). In response, Paula Dressel (1988) noted that unmarried black men are more likely (64%) than unmarried white women (49%) to fall below 125 percent of the poverty line, and that their median incomes from Social Security are significantly lower. Among married couples, whites received a median benefit of $7,670 from Social Security in 1982, compared to $5,920 for black couples.[15]

As Dressel puts it, "the point is not to debate which oppression is worse, gender or race. Rather, it is to argue that the history of the U.S. political economy mandates that analysts take race into account, along with gender, age, and other

---

[15]More recent census data show the same patterns. Data published for 1992 show, for example, that 10.3 percent of all men age seventy-five and older were classified as poor, compared to 19.8 percent of women in this age group (U.S. Bureau of the Census, 1996a, Table 4-4). Within racial-ethnic groups, poverty rates for persons age seventy-five and older were, for whites: 8.1 percent for men and 17.8 percent for women; for blacks: 34.8 percent for men and 42.8 percent for women; and for persons of Hispanic origin: 18.8 percent for men and 32 percent for women (U.S. Bureau of the Census, 1996a, Figure 4-9).

relevant factors" (1988:179; see also Dressel, Minkler, and Yen 1999). Taking an additional relevant factor into consideration—that of household composition—shows that within the older population, older women of color who live alone are at greatest risks for severe poverty (Hardy and Hazelrigg 1993).

Living arrangements—As noted in the previous chapter, living arrangements are linked with a range of outcomes in older age, including poverty. Those who live with others are less likely to be poor than those who live by themselves (Hardy and Hazelrigg 1993). Risks for poverty help to explain why older persons of color—both women and men—are more likely than whites to live in extended family households (Ford et al. 1990; Himes, Hogan, and Eggebeen 1996; Mutchler 1990). These living arrangement patterns extend across age groups and marital statuses—married as well as unmarried persons of color are more likely to live in extended family settings compared to non-Hispanic whites.

Economic need clearly plays a role in these patterns, as well as cultural preferences (Ford et al. 1990; Himes et al. 1996). The availability of family members also is important. Namkee Choi (1991) found that among widows of color, those who had raised more children were less likely to live alone. In a further study which considered the national origins of older unmarried Hispanics in the United States, Barbara Zsembik (1993) showed that the availability of kin helped to determine the living arrangements of Mexican Americans and Puerto Ricans, but not Cubans.

The importance of distinguishing within the broad category of racial ethnic "minorities" also is shown by Jeffrey Burr (1992), who examined the influence of cultural factors on living arrangements. Burr found that among unmarried women age fifty-five and older in the United States, Asian Indian women are *more* likely to live alone than white women. Burr reports that the Asian Indian women who are most acculturated (those who speak English well, use public transportation with ease, or were born in the United States) are most likely to live alone, mirroring "the preference of the dominant group" (p. 221). On the other hand, older Chinese and Japanese Americans are more likely than non-Hispanic whites to live in extended family households, regardless of their country of birth, the use of English in the home, or their level of education (Kamo and Zhou 1994). These results held for both women and men in these racial-ethnic groups.

Thus, although non-Hispanic whites are more likely to live alone than most other racial-ethnic groups, differing patterns and predictors of household structure have been found for differing groups. Studies which consider the intersections of gender and race-ethnicity can provide fuller understanding of how women and men in diverse groups adapt to aging. However, within racial-ethnic groups, it is important to note that older women are more likely to live alone than men, and they are more likely to live in poverty (Hardy and Hazelrigg 1993; Zsembik 1993).

Birth Cohort

The increasing numbers of older adults in society has been identified as a potent force for change. In particular, the larger size of today's older cohorts has been thought to increase their political power and produce improvements in their position in society (see Uhlenberg 1988; Wallace et al. 1991). Following this argument, the next fifty years should bode well for older persons. Americans age sixty-five and older are expected to grow from 33.5 million in 1995 (about 13% of the total population) to 79 million by the year 2050 (20% of the total population) (U.S. Bureau of the Census 1996b, Table J). If this line of reasoning is correct, racial minorities should also gain in political power because they are the fastest-growing segment of the older population. In 1990, racial minorities made up about 10 percent of the population over sixty-five. Their representation within the older population may increase to 20 percent by the year 2050 (U.S. Bureau of the Census, 1996a, p. 2-14).[16]

Although this optimistic argument is appealing, the link between cohort size and cohort advantage is not so simple (Uhlenberg 1988). It is true that the economic position of today's older cohorts has improved over previous cohorts. In 1960, one-third of Americans age sixty-five and older were classified as poor (U.S. Senate Special Committee on Aging 1992:56). This proportion fell to 12 percent in 1993 (U.S. Senate Special Committee on Aging 1997:93). Economic gains have not been enjoyed equally within the older population, however. Despite increases in Social Security benefit levels during the past several decades, economic inequality is greater within the older population than it is within the non-elderly population (Crystal and Shea 1990).[17] Stephen Crystal and Dennis Shea report that the elderly who are best-off economically "mask the presence of economic disadvantage among a substantial proportion of the elderly popula-tion" (p. 441). For example, nearly 35 percent of African American women age

---

[16]For the groups categorized as racial minorities by the U.S. Bureau of the Census, the following trends are projected from 1990 to the year 2050: The proportion of African Americans is expected to grow from 8 percent of the total population age sixty-five and older to 10 percent. Those of Asian, Pacific Islander, American Indian, Eskimos, or Aleut heritage will grow from less than 2 percent of the older population as of 1990, to 8 percent by 2050. If Hispanic origin also is considered, the proportion of older "minority" Americans could exceed 20 percent by the year 2050. Americans of Hispanic heritage can be of any race. In 1990, 4 percent of all older Americans claimed Hispanic origin. This proportion is expected to grow to 16 percent of the total older population by the year 2050 (U.S. Bureau of the Census, 1996a, pp. 2-14–2-16).

[17]Furthermore, the poverty criterion is more stringent for older adults than it is for younger persons. In 1992, the federal poverty threshold for single households was $7,295 for the fifteen to sixty-four group, but was even lower—$6,729—for persons sixty-five and older. Thus, a sixty-four year old with an annual income of $6,730 would be classified as poor, but a sixty-five year old with the same income would not. For two-person households, the poverty thresholds in 1992 were $9,443 for the fifteen to sixty-four age group, compared to $8,487 for the 65+ age group (U.S. Bureau of the Census, 1996a, p. 4-16). For a discussion of the development and history of the official poverty thresholds, see Fisher (1992).

sixty-five through seventy-four were classified as poor in 1992. The poverty rate for African American women age seventy-five and older is even higher, at 43 percent (U.S. Census, 1996a, Figure 4-9).

What of future older cohorts? We know that African Americans, Mexican Americans, and other racial-ethnic minorities will have higher levels of education relative to today's older cohorts, a pattern also true for older non-Hispanic whites (Bould, Sanborn, and Reif 1989; Somers 1985). Education is inversely related to functional disabilities and chronic diseases and conditions—higher education levels are associated with lower risks for these health problems (Longino et al. 1989). On the other hand, the effects of educational gains among future cohorts may be overridden by economic disadvantages faced by segments of the population (e.g., Crystal and Shea 1990; Higginbotham 1997; Lynch and Minkler 1999; Reskin and Padavic 1994; Rubin 1996). For this reason, Sherman James and colleagues suggest the strong possibility that "current racial disparities in health will remain constant, if they do not actually increase, in the years ahead" (1992:39). Along similar lines, Beth Hess (1986) argues that, despite women's increased educational attainment and labor force participation, economic disparities in the workplace—in particular, continuing sex segregation in occupations—are likely to continue, bringing continued economic disparities. Considering this feature along with women's greater life expectancies relative to men, Hess argues that "all women run the risk of outliving their resources" (p. 132)—now, and for the foreseeable future (see also Burkhauser, Duncan, and Hauser 1994).

Societal Context

Changes in the societal context help to shed light on why a substantial proportion of unmarried white women and many women and men of color are unlikely to gain significant economic ground in the future. In recent decades, the economic restructuring of U.S. society has become an increasingly important facet of this context (DiPrete and Nonnemaker 1997). While it is true that job opportunities have increased in such fields as medical services, financial services, and information processing (Schulz 1995), it is also true that industrial jobs in the United States have lost ground relative to the expansion of jobs in the service sector (Rubin 1996). Compared to jobs located in the industrial sector, those in the service sector typically offer lower levels of pay and fewer benefits, if any are offered at all (Reskin and Padavic 1994; Rubin 1996).

Hispanic and African American working-class men are disproportionately likely to experience economic dislocations brought about by industrial job loss and declining manufacturing employment (Eitzen and Zinn 1989). On the other hand, employment opportunities have expanded for working-class women of color, affording them dubious "benefits" of these structural changes. Stanley Eitzen and Maxine Baca Zinn point out that "the 'typical' job is a non-union, service sector, low-paying job occupied by a woman" (1989:133; see also Hayward and Liu 1992; Reskin and Padavic 1994). Together, these features mean that significant proportions of older women and men are likely to retire from jobs in which pension benefits are small or nonexistent. As of 1990, nearly fifty-two million workers lacked pension coverage on their current job. Among full-time workers in 1988, only 26 percent of those working in non-professional service industries enjoyed pension coverage. In comparison, more than 60 percent of the full-time workers in manufacturing industries were covered by employer-sponsored pensions (Schulz 1995:Table 7-1).

Furthermore, given the current political climate in which the "social security" of public pensions has become an ever-larger question, economic sufficiency may be further jeopardized for vulnerable older adults (see Hendricks, Hatch, and Cutler 1999). Ninety percent of Americans age sixty-five and older receive Social Security benefits, making it the most common source of income for this age group. Among poor older adults, whose incomes lie at the bottom one-fifth of the older population, Social Security represents nearly 80 percent of total family income. In contrast, Social Security accounts for only 18 percent of family income among the richest quintile. (For a further comparison point, Social Security provides about 60% of total family income for older persons who fall in the middle of the income distribution (Reno 1993).) Although Social Security payments are unequally distributed within the older population—reflecting their higher earnings, the richest quintile receives $1.72 in Social Security income for every $1 received by the poorest quintile—economic disparities among older adults would be even greater without this public pension program (Crystal and Shea 1990). These data underscore the fact that some groups of older adults are more dependent upon state policies than others, and that policy changes consequently will have greater impact on their lives (Hendricks and Hatch 1993).

Exemplars of Life Course Research

The preceding section illustrates key facets of a life course perspective on adaptation to aging—the importance of personal histories, social location, birth cohort, and the larger societal context. While this approach provides information about differing levels of experience, and how each of these impacts adaptation to aging, it does not highlight their interdependence. What are the unique insights that can be gained from studies based on a life course perspective?

I have selected three sets of studies which address this question, focusing here on depth rather than breadth of study. Consistent with a life course perspective, these researchers identify particular birth cohorts for study, spell out the characteristics of their informants in some detail, and consider the personal histories of their informants as well as the social-historical contexts in which they have lived. While their conclusions cannot be extended to other groups without further study, they provide hypotheses that can be taken up in studies of different populations and subsequent cohorts.

The research foci for the exemplars I have chosen correspond to the three central dimensions of adaptation investigated in this chapter. The first bears on social relationships and intimacy in older age; the second on mental health; and the third examines an issue relevant to physical health in later life. By using a life course perspective, each study provides insights about adaptation in later life that challenge conclusions yielded by conventional approaches, which neglect or ignore altogether essential life course dimensions.

Exemplar #1. Veterans' Reunions and Emotional Intimacy among Older Men

Earlier in this chapter, I reviewed studies of interpersonal relationships and emotional intimacy, focusing on reported gender differences. Although most researchers have concluded that women are far more likely than men to develop and maintain intimate relationships with others, Scott Swain (1989) argues persuasively that men may simply express intimacy somewhat differently than women. Swain also hypothesizes that men may have fewer opportunities for same-sex intimate relationships as they grow older. His own research focused on college-age men, however, and Swain did not focus on life course dimensions (i.e., respondents' histories of experience, potential cohort effects, and so forth).

A challenge to Swain's hypothesis is found in Glen Elder and Elizabeth Colerick Clipp's (1988) life course study of men's wartime experience and social ties. Data from this longitudinal study, which began in the 1930s and continued through the 1980s, emphasize the "extraordinary bonding of men who fought and survived together" (p. 323). The study population consisted of men born in the 1920s, who were veterans of World War II or the Korean War.

Elder and Clipp show that reunions provide opportunities for these men to share painful memories, and in the process to reaffirm and strengthen their bonds with one another. The reunions "mark the interaction of individual and historical time and they bring together veterans who once shared an intense and affectively significant experience. The group reassembles to honor lost members and to reaffirm surviving ties" (p. 321). Furthermore, data from the study indicate that sharing wartime experiences in a supportive environment helps to alleviate veterans' emotional problems and feelings of guilt.

Many American men who are now in their seventies have served in the Armed Forces. Only 14 percent of the veterans in Elder and Clipp's study had attended reunions of their unit, but this figure would represent a considerable number of older men in the larger population who have maintained long-term ties with their comrades. This study clearly challenges assumptions that emotional intimacy with other men is unimportant or nonexistent among (heterosexual) men (e.g., Weiss 1983).[18]

---

[18]Such assumptions have focused implicitly upon heterosexual rather than gay men. Most of the veterans in Elder and Clipp's study were married, suggesting that most of them were heterosexual.

On the other hand, the study focuses on rather extreme conditions which lay the groundwork for overt expressions of intimacy among this sample of wartime veterans. Those who attended reunions were more likely to have experienced the loss of friends or comrades during combat, compared to veterans who never attended reunions. Other, less extreme contexts may also favor expressions of intimacy by and among older men, and provide benefits for their mental health and well-being. For example, Lenard Kaye and Jeffrey Applegate report that "a long-standing sense of deep affection and intimacy surfaced regularly" in their interviews with men who were providing care to ill or disabled family members (1994:223).

Exemplar #2. Economic Hardships and Older Women's Mental Health

Glen Elder's work is also represented in this second set of studies, which examine the impact of economic hardships experienced earlier in women's life course.

The resource explanation reviewed previously in this book contends that greater access to socioeconomic resources will produce better adaptation to aging. While this is doubtless true in general (e.g., Crimmins et al. 1996; House et al. 1992), studies using a life course perspective show that this formula cannot be applied in a deterministic way. The context for aging must be considered.

Glen Elder and Jeffrey Liker's longitudinal study of Depression-era women (1982) provides an excellent case in point. Born near the turn of the century, the women in this study bore children during the economically prosperous 1920s, and experienced the "bust and boom" of the 1930s and 1940s as mothers, wives, and often as labor-force participants as well. Elder and Liker found that economic loss experienced during the Depression helped to prepare these women to cope with losses and life changes as they grew older.

However, the adaptive features of early hardships were highly contingent upon the women's social class positions. Elder and Liker argue that the educational, economic, and status resources of middle-class women provided them with greater problem-solving skills and a stronger sense of self-worth. On the other hand, working-class women had fewer of these resources on which to draw when they experienced economic losses and family hardships during the Depression. According to Elder and Liker, these women were more vulnerable to long-term psychological problems, including feelings of inadequacy and dissatisfaction with life.

Elder and Liker's sample was composed primarily of non-Hispanic white women. The in-depth interviews of older African American women conducted by Katherine Allen and Victoria Chin-Sang (1990) show that the cultural context of resource scarcity must also be considered. Although the economic status of this sample was not described, one-third of the women interviewed had no formal schooling beyond sixth grade, and an additional 40 percent of the sample had not completed high school. Rather than displaying insecurity and low self-esteem, as would be inferred from the results of Elder and Liker's study, themes of self-reliance and pride in their accomplishments emerged consistently from these women.

The women in Allen and Chin-Sang's sample were born between 1896 and 1923, representing a much broader birth cohort than the Elder and Liker sample. From a life course perspective, long-term effects from an historical event such as the Depression would differ if that event was experienced by a child, or by a young adult with family and/or labor force responsibilities.

Nonetheless, results from both of these studies suggest that individuals who experience "smooth sailing" throughout their lives may have greater difficulties adjusting to changes and losses in older age. The strength and resilience of groups with long-term histories of confronting discrimination and inequitable opportunities should not be overestimated, thus overlooking the real difficulties these groups face (see Sokolovsky 1990). However, these groups can and often do provide important sources of psychological and social support for their members (e.g., Peterson 1990).

Exemplar #3. Multiple Role Involvement and Older Men's Physical Health

I noted previously that research on multiple role involvement has tended to focus on mid-life women, with the assumption that they are under the most pressure to juggle work and family roles (e.g., Barnett and Baruch 1985; Baruch 1984; Brody and Schoonover 1986; Brody et al. 1987; Long and Porter 1984; Moen et al. 1992). Results from these studies indicate that participation in multiple roles provides health benefits, but only to a point. A threshhold effect has been suggested, beyond which role demands exact health tolls rather than benefits (Rosenfield 1989; Stoller and Pugliesi 1989; Thoits 1986). However, the *nature* of these role involvements and how individuals assess them are likely to be far more important than their sheer numbers. In other words, the context for social roles must be considered.

Some studies have examined these questions with groups other than mid-life, predominantly Caucasian women. I have selected research conducted by Beth Rushing, Christian Ritter, and Russell Burton (1992) to discuss here. Using longitudinal data from a cohort of men who were born between 1907 and 1921, Rushing and colleagues examine the effects of multiple role involvement on older men's physical health. The most valuable feature of this study is its exploration of how race serves as a context for the men's roles.

This line of reasoning emphasizes that "specific role combinations, as well as the quality or characteristics of those roles, are the factors that make roles healthy or not" (Rushing et al. 1992:127). Furthermore, the authors argue that race differences in the acquisition and content of social roles will impact how those roles affect individuals' health. "In a society in which race is one of an individual's most important statuses, being of one race or another clearly places a person in a social context within which roles take differential meaning and carry differential consequences" (p. 136).

Rushing and colleagues focus especially on employment, which they believe will be a more salient role for those who are less certain of acquiring it. Because African Americans face greater obstacles in the acquisition of this role relative to Caucasians (reflected in large race differences in unemployment rates), being employed is hypothesized to exert a stronger effect on African Americans' health, in the direction of greater health benefits. The authors argue that this relationship may be especially strong for the cohort of African American men included in this study. Born in the early part of the century, these men have led their lives in a societal context of pervasive racial discrimination in education, employment, and other opportunities.

The men in this study were surveyed in 1976 and again in 1981. These longitudinal data enabled the researchers to control for the men's prior health status (measured in 1976), and thus to examine changes in their health over a five-year span. In general, those who occupied more social roles showed a smaller increase in their health limitations, from time 1 to time 2. The social roles assessed in the study were employment, marriage, and being a supporter (the latter was measured by whether the respondent had one or more dependents, other than his wife). Of these roles, employment had the most consistent effect on health, and, as hypothesized, this relationship was stronger for the African American men.

In addition, particular role configurations were important for the men's health. The authors note that the simple presence or absence of a social role may not impact a person's health, but may have an effect in combination with other roles. For example, being married showed a health-protective effect only when it was considered in combination with other roles (being employed or being a supporter). Consideration of these more complex relationships (rather than considering only the presence or absence of particular roles) was helpful in explaining the health of men of both races, but more so for the African American men.

Summary

The life course studies described here address several controversies bearing on gender and adaptation to aging. The study by Elder and Clipp (1988) challenges the notion that older men lack avenues for expressing emotional intimacy with other men—and also refutes assumptions that heterosexual men do not value emotional intimacy with other men, or that they are incapable of forming such relationships.

In another study reviewed here, Elder and Liker (1982) examine the impact of economic hardships on older women's mental health. This study is notable because it focuses attention on the life course impact of socioeconomic resources to explain older women's well-being, rather than relying on the more usual explanation focusing upon traditional gender roles or the long-term effects of socialization into those roles. At the same time, the study challenges the simple assumption that greater access to socioeconomic resources produces better adaptation to aging. Both this study and the research of Allen and Chin-Sang (1990) demonstrate that the context for aging must be considered, including women's and men's social locations (e.g., their social class and race) and the historical times in which they have lived.

Finally, the research reported by Rushing and her colleagues shows that multiple role involvement is generally beneficial to older men's physical health, a topic more often studied with mid-life women. This study also hypothesized and found that employment provides greater health benefits to African American than to Caucasian men. The reasoning underlying this hypothesis is that African Americans face greater uncertainty in acquiring employment in a racist society, and thus this role should have greater salience for them.

The studies described here did not include samples of both women and men, and hence did not make gender comparisons. Such comparisons are not incompatible with a life course approach, although life course researchers often have confined their attention to one gender—as well as to a specified birth cohort, racial-ethnic group, and/or a particular social class. In this way, some important sources of variation are controlled, allowing for a more intensive and effective study of other sources of variation. This approach has been used effectively in both quantitative (e.g., Rushing et al. 1992) and qualitative studies (e.g., Allen and Chin-Sang 1990) of the life course, as well as in studies that combine these methodologies (e.g., Elder and Liker 1982).

For example, by limiting their attention to a cohort of older African American and Caucasian men, Beth Rushing and her colleagues were able to focus attention on how race may serve as a context for these men's social roles. An alternative approach would be to compare a cohort of African American women and men (or a cohort of women and men of another racial-ethnic and/or social class group), and to focus attention on how gender may serve as a context for employment, family, and other social roles. Taking a life course perspective, hypotheses and findings based on gender would be grounded within a particular historical period, and would consider respondents' personal histories and social locations. In this way, potential similarities as well as differences between women and men could be identified, and understanding could be gained about the life course factors underlying these patterns. Glen Elder's life course study of children of the Great Depression (Elder 1974; Elder and Rockwell 1979), discussed in the previous chapter, fits these criteria.

Considering the study by Rushing and colleagues in particular, a further and necessary next step is to examine how individuals assess the meaning and content of their involvements in employment, family, and other realms of experience over their lifetimes. These researchers use a life course framework for their hypotheses and findings, but they do not examine how race shapes social experience from the point of view of the participants themselves. The content and meaning of social roles may be what is most important to individuals' health, rather than the presence or absence of particular roles, combinations of these roles, or numbers of roles.

CONCLUSION

In this chapter, I hope to have accomplished two central goals. The first objective has been to document the limitations of theoretical and empirical efforts that have focused on gender differences in adaptation to aging, to the neglect of other life dimensions that also impact adaptation. Traditional gender role theory has constituted the central framework for these efforts. Passed on from the earliest gerontological theories, gender role explanations remain popular in contemporary research efforts, despite a lack of empirical support. Indeed, precious little empirical investigation has actually been conducted to assess the impact of gender roles on adaptation in older age. Rather, it has simply been assumed that one gender or the other will fare better or suffer more in aging, due to the presumed characteristics of women's and men's traditional roles, or the long-term effects of socialization into these roles. Equally paradoxical is the fact that traditional gender roles have been used to explain *both* why women should fare better than men in adapting to aging and also why they should fare worse.

A review of the empirical literature shows mixed evidence for gender differences in adaptation. Little if any support can be found for gender role explanations, primarily because they have almost never been tested directly, but also because findings of gender difference are so inconclusive. On some dimensions of adaptation, such as social relationships—and, in particular, confiding and intimacy with others—women appear to fare better. Even here, the findings are not without controversy. Karen Walker (1994) suggests that people report friendship behaviors which correspond to their cultural notions of what men and women are like, and that their own friendship interactions may be inconsistent with these notions. To the degree that longevity can be used as an indicator of adaptation, this dimension provides incontrovertible evidence that women, as a group, fare better than men. On the other hand, men tend to have fewer long-term chronic illnesses than women (but their higher rates of mortality may mask men's health problems). Men are less likely than women to suffer from depression, but this gender difference narrows among older age groups. Furthermore, at all ages men apparently are more susceptible than women to personality disorders.

As is obvious from this review, there is no clear pattern of gender differences in adaptation to aging. Even when attention is focused on a specific dimension of adaptation, the gender differences that have emerged tend to be rather small in magnitude, and (with the exception of mortality) conflicting findings have been reported. These conclusions are in line with other reviews of gender difference research. Previous reviews have not focused on gender differences in later life, however, and there has been some recent discussion that gender differences in aging require more research attention (e.g., Barer 1994; Reitzes et al. 1995). I hope to have shown that a focus on gender differences in adaptation to aging is not particularly fruitful, and in fact often leads to misleading conclusions.

Thus, the second central goal of this chapter has been to demonstrate how adaptation to aging can be understood from a life course perspective, moving beyond a focus on gender differences. Using the multi-level framework described in Chapter 2, I have illustrated key facets of this perspective as these bear on selected aspects of adaptation to aging. Gender is crucial to consider, but must be considered in conjunction with race-ethnicity, social class, sexuality, and age, and grounded in social-historical context.

This discussion was not intended as a comprehensive treatment of all life course dimensions, but rather to illustrate differing levels of experience encompassed by a life course perspective. In order to illustrate intersections between these levels and how they can be fruitfully studied, I concluded by examining three sets of exemplary life course studies. In their use of a life course approach, these studies provide a richer understanding of adaptation to aging. Although the studies were not designed to do so, they also challenge some conclusions concerning gender and aging that have been reached in previous research.

This chapter has demonstrated that many challenges, if not pitfalls, are inherent in the study of adaptation to aging. Foremost among these is the fact that adaptation remains a fuzzy concept, despite its wide usage. Linda George has noted that "adaptation is a very broad concept that encompasses almost all human behavior" (1987:5-6). When does adaptation to aging begin? What is the point of demarcation from earlier points in the life course to older age? In the literature reviewed here, the *processes* by which individuals adapt to aging have seldom been addressed. Rather, most of these studies have assessed what are considered to be outcomes of adaptation processes: social relationships; mental health and subjective well-being; physical health and longevity.

This chapter has examined adaptation to aging writ large. The chapters that follow are focused more narrowly on the two life events that have been thought to have the greatest impact on adaptation in older age: the death of a spouse and retirement from paid labor. Each of these experiences has been framed primarily in terms of role losses, and each has generated great debate concerning whether men or women are likely to suffer more from the experience. Importantly, as life "events," these experiences also lend themselves more readily to a focus on *process:* individuals' responses will vary depending upon the length of time that has elapsed following that experience. As I will show, this is more true for spousal bereavement than it is for retirement.

In the succeeding chapter, I examine the explanations and empirical evidence for gender differences in adaptation to the death of a spouse, followed by an analysis of how a life course perspective helps us to understand this experience. Chapter 5 follows a similar plan, focusing on retirement from paid labor. The goals of these chapters are, in general, the same as those I have pursued here: to investigate the theoretical explanations and empirical research bearing on gender differences; to document the limitations of these approaches; and to illustrate insights that can be gained from using a life course approach. Along the way, we will encounter a series of long-standing controversies concerning spousal bereavement and retirement, and how women and men respond to these life experiences.

CHAPTER
4

Adaptation to the Death of a Spouse

When people have been asked to name the life events they believe are the most undesirable or which require the most readjustment, the death of a family member has headed the list (Arbuckle and de Vries 1995; Tausig 1986). In a study that has come to serve as the benchmark for research on life events (Holmes and Rahe 1967), independent raters assigned the maximum score of 100 points to spouse's death, reflecting raters' views that this event requires tremendous readjustment. In contrast, only 47 points was assigned to retirement from paid labor. The following chapters will show that spousal bereavement is in fact more consequential for most people's health and well-being than retirement.

Nonetheless, both retirement and spousal bereavement have figured prominently in the gerontological literature as the central life events of older age. Both have been assumed to require extensive adaptive efforts on the part of individuals. The focus on these experiences as role losses reflects functionalist concerns, as does the assumption that individuals must adapt to these changes in order to regain equilibrium. Functionalism also is implicated in the assumption that equilibrium or a steady state characterized the individual's life prior to retirement or bereavement.

Furthermore, following from functionalist assumptions of role differentiation, these experiences have been linked closely to gender roles. Elaine Cumming and William Henry (1961) provide the quintessential functionalist statement on women's and men's presumed primary roles in relation to these later-life experiences. In their view, "widowhood is to women what retirement is to men, the conclusion of the central task of adult life" (1961:154). Consistent with this assumption, women have constituted the central focus for research on spousal bereavement, with female-only samples commonly used (Umberson et al. 1992). Until fairly recently, retirement research has shown a parallel focus, examining issues and problems assumed to hold primarily for men, and frequently using male-only samples (Hatch 1987).

It might be argued that these research patterns simply reflect social reality. Women are more likely than men to experience the death of a spouse and to remain unmarried following bereavement. Nearly half of American women who are age sixty-five or older are widowed, compared to the 14 percent of men in this age group who are widowered. Among the oldest-old—those who are eighty-five years of age and older—these figures rise to 79 percent for women and 39 percent for men (U.S. Bureau of the Census 1996a, Table 6-2). And, as a group, men have been more likely than women to have lifetime histories of paid employment from which to retire (Clark 1988). However, the gendered dimensions of these research traditions reach beyond the relative risks that women and men face for experiencing these life changes.

One need only look to the language used to describe spousal bereavement and retirement from paid labor. It is commonly accepted that women who lose a spouse through death are called widows, and that men who undergo this experience are called widowers (e.g., Aiken 1995:212; Cox 1996:196; McPherson 1990:323). Yet "widowhood" is the term used most frequently to describe both women's and men's bereavement, rather than a term that encompasses both genders[1] (e.g., Aiken 1995:212; Cox 1996:196; McPherson 1990:323). (For this reason, the term "widow/erhood" is used here.) And although "worker" and "retiree" are gender-neutral terms, equally applicable to both women and men, closer inspection of some works reveals that at times they have been used to refer only to men, conveying the implicit assumption that only men work and retire (e.g., Anderson, Burkhauser, and Quinn 1983; Atchley 1976b; Bradford 1979).

In light of the historical focus—both theoretical and methodological—on women as widows and men as retirees, it is fascinating to find that more often than not, men have been assumed to suffer more than women from the effects of *both* of these experiences. Not only has retirement been traditionally considered a more important and difficult experience for men than for women, but most theoretical discussions also have cast men as experiencing greater problems than women when a spouse dies.

To some extent, empirical studies that have made gender comparisons support the conjecture that spousal bereavement is more difficult for men. (As I will show in the following chapter, a similar claim cannot be made for retirement from paid labor.) This observation must be accompanied with the caveat that findings of gender differences are typically small in size, and contradictory results are frequently reported. In this way (and not surprisingly), research on widow/erhood suffers from the same limitations as other literatures surveyed in this book. To the degree that gender differences in risks for these problems exist, studies do suggest that men are more vulnerable than women to losses in their social resources following the death of a spouse, and that bereaved men may also be in somewhat greater jeopardy than bereaved women for declines in their health. On the other hand, if the definition of adaptation is expanded to include economic well-being, most reports show that widows, as a group, face greater challenges than widowers on this dimension.

[1] This pattern contrasts with the more usual practice of employing generic male terms.

This chapter examines the theoretical and empirical literature on gender and adaptation to the death of a spouse. I also examine a number of controversies surrounding this experience in addition to those bearing on gender differences. Bereavement has been thought to produce a range of negative outcomes for surviving spouses, including decrements in their social and economic resources and declines in their mental and physical health—sometimes to the point of causing premature death. It has also been assumed that spousal bereavement is more stressful when it occurs at younger rather than older ages. To what degree are these beliefs about adaptation to the death of a spouse warranted? More generally, what dimensions are important to consider in order to understand how surviving spouses respond to bereavement? This chapter addresses these questions and also examines how spousal bereavement can be placed in life course perspective, moving beyond a focus on gender differences.

EXPLANATIONS FOR GENDER DIFFERENCES IN ADAPTATION TO THE DEATH OF A SPOUSE

In the main, the theoretical perspectives applied to gender differences in adaptation to the death of a spouse are parallel (and often derived directly from) those used in the broader literature on adaptation to aging (see Chapters 2 and 3). Traditional gender roles have been the dominant explanatory framework used in prior decades, and this remains true today. From this perspective, widows are vulnerable to the loss of instrumental-economic support provided by their husbands, including the status and identity provided to women by their husbands, while widowers lose the socio-emotional and housekeeping support provided by their wives. Writers taking a gender role approach often consider how women's and men's health, economic, and social resources are impacted following bereavement, providing a "blended" gender role and resource approach to gender differences in adaptation. Also present in the literature are structural explanations focusing on the effects of skewed sex ratios in older age. One version of this latter argument proposes that widows' numerical dominance gives them important advantages over widowers in adapting to bereavement. An opposing argument has also been made, however—that widowed women's numerical dominance is problematic because it intensifies women's rivalry over the available men.

Both gender role and resource/structural perspectives have been used to explain why men should suffer more than women from the effects of spousal bereavement. However, both types of perspectives have also been used to explain why this experience should be more difficult for women than for men. Beyond the fact that very few efforts have been made to test these theoretical arguments, they do not provide a clear direction for positing the relationships that might be tested, if one were inclined to do so. Nonetheless, questions concerning which gender suffers more when a spouse dies, and why, continue to be raised in gerontology textbooks (Aiken 1995:213; Atchley 1994:355; Cox 1996:195-197; Kimmel

1990:471-472; Thorson 1995:234-238, to name a few), and research efforts (e.g., Barer 1994; Cohler 1991; Lee, Willetts, and Seccombe 1998; Stroebe and Stroebe 1993a). Some of these authors contend that in general, problems of adjusting to the loss of a spouse are worse for a woman than for a man (e.g., Aiken 1995), while others (more frequently) assert the reverse (e.g., Barer 1994; Cohler 1991; Lee et al. 1998; Stroebe and Stroebe 1993a; Thorson 1995). Sometimes statements are made that resolving the question of "which gender suffers the more" awaits further empirical evidence (Stuart-Hamilton 1994:121). I believe that it is useful to review these debates and their conceptual and empirical limitations, to pave the way for moving beyond them.

I first examine explanations that depict men as suffering more than women from the effects of spousal bereavement, and then turn to explanations that posit the reverse.

Gender Role and "Blended" Explanations

Men Suffer More

Since traditional gender role theory assumes that family roles are central to women's status and identity, it would seem reasonable that a parallel assumption would be made concerning the loss of those roles; the death of a spouse should bring more serious consequences for women than for men. Interestingly, this is not usually the case. In Cumming and Henry's classic work (1961), the argument is made that the death of a spouse is "a desolating experience for men" (p. 154) but not for women. This is so, they say, because widowerhood is an unexpected experience for men, but also, and more importantly from the authors' perspective, because it deprives men of their "mediator into the world of kinship and culture" (pp. 154-155) upon whom they have relied.

Cumming and Henry believe that widows face special problems of redefining their identities because "a woman is usually given her social identity through her husband's occupation" (p. 156). However, they do not consider the task of identity reformulation to be especially problematic for widowed women. In Cumming and Henry's view, society provides consideration to widows and, in fact, widowhood is characterized as an "honored state" (p. 157). The authors believe that widows also are advantaged because women can retain the prestige associated with their husbands' accomplishments. Widows with children can identify with them as well, and with the children's successes and careers (presumably when children are male). Also, due to women's presumed specialization in emotional tasks, Cumming and Henry assert that they are able to quickly revive connections with their kin. And finally, "widows have a ready-made peer group in other widows, and there is reason to believe that they join this very happily" (p. 157). From Cumming and Henry's perspective, widows may lose financial status, but that is about all that they lose.

Subsequent works have echoed the same gender role assumptions articulated by these early functionalists, especially those concerning women's presumed social-emotional specialization. Like Cumming and Henry, these writers have emphasized that traditional gender roles facilitate women's adaptation to bereavement, but hinder men's adaptation. In particular, bereavement is thought to increase men's risks for social isolation, which in turn is linked with increased risks for health problems. In this way, a "blended" explanation for adaptation to bereavement also is proposed, which incorporates the influence of gender roles and individuals' access to resources.

Social-emotional losses—Many writers have agreed that women have stronger support networks than men, that they often depend upon other women for intimacy and affection, and thus that women undergo far less social disruption following bereavement than men are likely to experience (Barer 1994; Blau 1973; Booth 1972; Ferraro 1989b; Rawlins 1992; Rowe and Kahn 1987; Thorson 1995). Many also agree that gender role socialization is the mechanism by which this is accomplished (e.g., Barer 1994; Elwell and Maltbie-Crannell 1981; Ferraro, 1989b). For example, Kenneth Ferraro (1989b) suggests that gender role socialization allows widows to express their feelings more openly than widowers, and to make greater use of their social support networks. Active engagement in this grief-work is seen as helping to reduce stresses associated with the death of a spouse. Other writers proposing gender differences in bereavement refer more simply to men's dependence on their wives' social and emotional skills, and do not necessarily ground this in socialization, although this is implied (e.g., Berardo 1970; Rawlins 1992).

Loss of homemaking services—From a traditional gender role perspective, men are the instrumental specialists, bringing home the bacon, while women are considered the emotional specialists in the family (Parsons 1955). However, this perspective implicitly casts women as "instrumental specialists" as well, because they are assumed to have primary responsibility for homemaking and housekeeping activities. Consequently, women are assumed to specialize in emotional as well as instrumental tasks (though the latter are very different from men's), while men are excluded entirely from expertise in the emotional realm.

Thus, in addition to losing their source of emotional support and intimacy and the person who has mediated their contacts with kin and community, men are thought to suffer when they are widowered because they lose the "homemaker-housekeeper" on whom they have relied (Hyman 1983; Umberson et al. 1992). Herbert Hyman argues that widowers often cannot manage household tasks by themselves, while widows are "capable of managing domestic matters quite well" (1983:92).

Indeed, widows are portrayed in many of these writings as capable and independent, while widowers are cast as dispirited and lonely, leading "sad lives" (Hyman 1983:92), and unable to care for themselves. Knud Helsing and colleagues are especially illustrative in their claim that "added emphasis is needed on studies involving the weaker sex—the widowed males" (Helsing, Szklo, and Comstock 1981:808). Such assertions are quite interesting given traditional gender role assumptions which stress men's instrumental, dominant roles relative to women. The implicit conclusion is that men are strong only to the degree that women are available to support and nurture them.

Effects on men's health—From a traditional gender role perspective, men suffer when their spouse dies because they lose the social, emotional, and house-keeping support their wives provided. Even more significantly, writers have argued that losses in these realms impact men's mental and physical health, sometimes to the point of causing premature death.

In addition to affecting well-being directly (greater social resources translate into greater well-being) (e.g., Baldassare, et al. 1984/85), social resources are thought to exert indirect or "buffering" effects by helping individuals cope with stressful experiences such as the death of a spouse (e.g., Wan 1982). Following this reasoning, if men are more vulnerable to social losses following bereavement, they will also be more vulnerable to decrements in their mental and physical health (Arens 1982/83; Umberson et al. 1992; Wortman et al. 1993). Conversely, women's greater access to supportive relationships may provide important health benefits to them following widowhood (Umberson et al. 1992).

Men's vulnerability to health problems following the death of a spouse has been linked not only with the loss of social and emotional support previously provided by their wives, but also with the loss of their wives' skills in home-making and housekeeping. This argument has been elaborated in various ways, but each variation hinges on the assumption that women and men perform different tasks within marriage. For example, Rowe and Kahn (1987) argue that men are more susceptible than women to health problems and early death fol-lowing bereavement because they rely on their wives for emotional support as well as for meal preparation and nutritional needs (see also Young, Benjamin, and Walls 1963).

Other writers also have argued that taking over household tasks is stressful for men (Arens 1982/83; Berardo 1970; Kohen 1983; Umberson et al. 1992). They contend that taking on these unfamiliar tasks may reduce the time men might otherwise spend developing new relationships, which could provide the social support benefits lost to them through widowerhood. (The converse is never considered: the time that women devote to household tasks reduces *their* opportunities for pursuing new relationships or other activities.) More convinc-ing, perhaps, is the suggestion that widowers' performance of household tasks produces strains associated with the work itself, or simply because these tasks are associated with women's work (Umberson et al. 1992). Housework is "deviant" for men to perform, but, in addition, such tasks are social liabilities because they have low status (Arens 1982/83).

From a traditional gender role stance, women who become widowed take on responsibilities associated with the other gender, such as financial and household management. However, these new activities usually are viewed as advantageous to women: they require women to become more independent, provide linkages with the larger society, and carry greater prestige than "women's work." Thus, according to this line of reasoning, although changes in women's roles may be stressful, they are also potentially very rewarding (Arens 1982/83). Umberson, Wortman, and Kessler (1992) go further, by suggesting that women's health may actually be enhanced when they are widowed because they are relieved from the burdens of performing household tasks and providing emotional support to their spouses. The work by Umberson et al. is relatively unique in this body of literature in that the researchers tested these theoretical arguments empirically. I will review this effort shortly, along with other empirical studies of bereavement.

Women Suffer More

Gender roles have taken center stage in positing women's greater problems in widowhood, just as they have dominated explanations for why bereaved men should face greater hardships. Both sets of arguments are based on the same central assumptions (i.e., specialization of roles by gender, especially the assignment of nurturing qualities to women and instrumental ones to men), but differ in how these assumptions are elaborated.

Loss of identity and status—From a traditional gender role perspective, women lose their primary identity when they are widowed. Although Cumming and Henry (1961) believe this loss pales in comparison with widowers' problems, other writers take widows' (presumed) loss of identity as their central concern. Dorothy Heyman and Daniel Gianturco argue that the "loss of the homemaking role central to the self-esteem and gratification" (1973:362) of married women is responsible for greater declines in women's well-being following widowhood relative to that of men's. Raymond Carey (1979) also believes that women suffer more than men when a spouse dies because women have been encouraged to build their identities around their husbands.

Furthermore, some writers have assumed that women lose status upon widowhood (e.g., see Barrow 1989:94; Kimmel 1990:471; Stevens-Long 1988: 346). The male role is more prestigious, they argue, and a woman's status often reflects her husband's social position. Thus, widowhood is thought to remove the source of women's status. Note that this argument is directly contrary to the gender role argument of Cumming and Henry, reviewed earlier, who contend that widowed women are able to retain their husbands' prestige—and that, in any event, widowhood is an "honored state" for women.

Social-emotional losses—Women's presumed specialization in the social and emotional realm has been viewed as an important advantage for their adaptation to widowhood (Barer 1994; Blau 1973; Booth 1972; Ferraro 1989b; Rawlins 1992; Rowe and Kahn 1987). This is the central reason why many writers taking a gender role perspective have argued that men suffer more from bereavement than do women. However, other writers who focus on gender roles have contended that women's social-emotional specialization is actually a liability. If affective features of the marital relationship are of greater importance to women than to men, then women will miss those features more when marriage ends (Carey 1979; Keith and Schafer 1985). A logical outcome of these assumptions is that men's instrumental orientation may lead them to *prefer* less social support than that desired by women. Consequently, some scholars have argued that men are not harmed if their social networks are reduced following widowerhood (Longino and Lipman 1982; Spitze and Logan 1989). In a statement sure to draw ire from men who have suffered the death of a beloved wife, Raymond Carey suggests that women may have "deeper emotional attachments toward their husbands than men do toward their wives" (1979:168).

Thus, in contrast to the thesis that widowers are vulnerable because they depended upon their wives' social-emotional expertise, Glenna Spitze and John Logan state that "women have been socialized to be more dependent than men" (1989:108; see also Arbuckle and de Vries 1995; Stroebe and Stroebe 1983). As a consequence, widows may be seen by others as requiring greater social support, and may also view themselves in this light. In a related vein, Vira Kivett (1978) has argued that women have been socialized to be passive, inhibiting them from taking an active role in reaching out to friends. Kivett also suggests that socialization-induced passivity hinders women from adapting to a new social role after they are widowed. These arguments, focusing on women's presumed passivity and dependence (and men's strength and independence), seem to be more consistent with the assumptions of traditional gender-role theories, which stress men's relative independence and women's dependence (e.g., Turner 1970), than arguments which posit bereaved men's dependence on women. However, both forms of this gender role argument remain primarily in the realm of speculation, as I will show shortly.

Economic resources—Clearly, arguments concerning whether women or men experience greater problems following the death of a spouse have depended upon the specific dimensions of adaptation under consideration. Compared to issues of social functioning and health, gender differences in economic resources have figured less prominently in theoretical treatments of "who suffers more" from bereavement. Writers who consider this issue have argued that women's economic dependence on their husbands brings higher risks for poverty following bereavement (e.g., Morgan 1986; Umberson et al 1992). Economic strictures, in turn, are linked with widows' physical and mental health problems (Longino et al. 1989; Wilkinson, Darby, and Mant 1987). Leslie Morgan (1976), for example, attributes much of women's mental distress in widowhood to the effects of economic strain. In addition, Robert Atchley (1975) argues that low income can restrict the transportation available to widows, reducing their opportunities for social participation (see also Ferraro and Barresi 1982).

Women's greater likelihood for experiencing the death of a spouse also has been considered, along with a lower standard of living they may expect in widowhood. Greater longevity and a lower chance for remarriage (Babchuk and Anderson 1989) mean that many older women can expect to live out their lives in a widowed status, and risk exhausting their economic resources prior to their own death (Hess 1986). Together, these dimensions have been seen as decreasing older women's quality of life, reflecting greater problems on the part of widows relative to widowers (e.g., Carey 1979; Rawlins 1992).

Effects of Skewed Sex Ratios

Gender role theories have dominated discussions of which gender suffers more in bereavement, along with explanations which consider the combined effects of gender roles and widow/ers' access to resources. Structural explanations have also been proposed, which focus on the effects of sex ratios. In later life, most women are widowed, while most men are married. This gender difference is due to several factors, including women's greater longevity, the convention of women marrying men several years older than themselves, and women's lower likelihood of remarriage (Stroebe and Stroebe 1983; Sweet and Bumpass 1987). However, like the gender role explanations reviewed above, arguments based on sex ratios do not provide a clear direction for positing gender differences in adaptation to the death of a spouse. Furthermore, as I show below, some sex ratio arguments also incorporate elements of gender role theory.

Men Suffer More

Karen Altergott (1985) proposes that numerical dominance gives widows important advantages over widowers. According to Altergott, individuals whose gender-marital status combination is a numerical majority will have more peers available to them, and they will enjoy greater social acceptability. Those whose gender-marital status is a numerical minority "may be less readily recruited into community involvement" (Altergott 1985:70).

Zena Smith Blau also has argued that bereavement adversely affects men because it places them "in a position different from that of most of [their] age and sex peers" (1961:431). Thus, the death of a spouse reduces men's opportunities for social contacts with their peers, and relegates them to a socially "deviant" status (see also Gallagher, Thompson, and Peterson 1982). A related argument is that since widows are more numerous than widowers, less attention is given to widowers' needs, such as in community support programs for bereaved spouses (Stroebe and Stroebe 1983).

Women Suffer More

Of course, unequal sex ratios can also be seen as placing heterosexual *women* in a disadvantaged position, since there are fewer available men for them to partner (Atchley 1975; Babchuk and Anderson 1989). (This argument also hinges upon the convention that women are far less likely than men to date and marry younger partners.) Some writers have linked this structural argument with a traditional gender role argument. Drawing from the traditional gender role thesis that marital and family roles are those most highly valued by women, some scholars have argued that widowhood places strains on women's relationships with their married friends. Nicholas Babchuk and Trudy Anderson (1989) believe that widowhood will reduce women's same-sex friendships due to rivalry and jealousy over married women's husbands. This argument also derives in part from presumed structural effects, since rivalry would be less of a problem if more men were available. Zena Smith Blau (1973), for example, argues that rivalry over married women's husbands is heightened in older age groups where women greatly outnumber men. However, women's rivalry with one another over men is thought to be *exacerbated*, not produced, by unfavorable sex ratios; such rivalry is assumed also at younger ages, when sex ratios are more equal.[2]

Summary

Explanations for "who suffers more" when a spouse dies have come primarily from traditional gender role theory and "blended" gender role/resource explanations, but arguments focusing on the effects of unequal sex ratios have also been proposed. Gender role and structural/resource explanations have been used to explain why men should suffer more from bereavement, and have also been used to explain why women should suffer more. Although the former argument has been proposed more frequently (widowers at greater risk than widows), the converse argument seems equally tenable—or equally untenable. For gender role explanations in particular, the same central assumptions are used to posit gender differences in both directions. Given the critique of gender role theory offered in Chapter 2, these arguments are not particularly compelling on conceptual grounds. However, it is difficult to discard them decisively as an explanation for gender differences in spousal bereavement, to the degree that such differences exist, since they have almost never been tested empirically.

Drawing from both gender role and resource explanations, direct as well as indirect effects of bereavement have been proposed. The direct effects most

---

[2] In contrast, gender role theorists have portrayed men's competition with other men as healthy and productive, revolving around sports (thereby fostering "team spirit" and bonding with other men) and economic competition (e.g., Chafetz 1974; Turner 1970).

commonly proposed for men have focused on losses in the social, emotional, and housekeeping support provided by their wives. These losses, in turn, are thought to reduce men's health and well-being. For women, direct effects of widowhood have been seen as primarily economic. Gender role theory is implicated here in women's economic dependence upon their husbands (e.g., Umberson et al. 1992). Economic strictures, in turn, are thought to impact women's health and social resources.

In the following section, I review empirical studies of spousal bereavement, focusing especially on those that have compared women and men. With rare exceptions, these works have not attempted to test either gender role or structural explanations for gender differences in spousal bereavement. Rather, when gender differences are found, one or the other of these explanations typically has been proposed to account for the findings. A study that I will review (Umberson et al. 1992) is notable because these researchers hypothesized *a priori* that depression among widows and widowers would be predicted by different sources of strain, and their findings appear to support a gender role explanation. Even in this research, however, respondents' attitudinal or behavioral adherence to gender roles was not assessed. Furthermore, a structural argument, which does not rely directly upon the effects of gender roles, can also be made to explain some of the findings. For this study and others, little direct support exists for theories of gender difference in adaptation to the death of a spouse.

ADAPTATION TO BEREAVEMENT AND THE EMPIRICAL RECORD ON GENDER DIFFERENCES

How do men and women respond to the death of a spouse? Do widowers experience greater problems than widows on some dimensions of adaptation? Conversely, are women at greater risk than men for some types of problems following bereavement? To what degree can empirical support for theories of gender differences be inferred from the available evidence?

In this section, I evaluate empirical research which pertains to these questions, including the dimensions of adaptation discussed in the previous chapter: social relationships, mental health and coping, physical health and mortality. I also consider research on economic changes following the death of a spouse. Economic well-being is not considered a specific "dimension of adaptation"—middle- and upper-class people would, by definition, be viewed as adapting more effectively than working-class and poor people. However, economic resources clearly are implicated in adaptation processes and outcomes, and there has been some controversy in the literature concerning gender differences in economic losses following bereavement.

As a first step in evaluating this body of research, I review some methodological issues that are unique to studies of bereavement.

Methodological Issues

Samples and Research Designs

Most studies of bereavement have been based on samples of women (e.g., Arling 1976; Holden, Burkhauser, and Myers 1986; Hong and Duff 1994; Hyman 1983; Lopata 1973, 1993; Morgan 1981; O'Bryant 1988, 1991; O'Bryant and Morgan 1990). Those that include both genders often have had small, geographically limited samples (e.g., Dimond, Lund, and Caserta 1987; Gallagher et al. 1983; Gass 1989; Heyman and Gianturco 1973; Lee et al. 1998; Parkes and Brown 1972). Although there has been much speculation about gender differences in bereavement, relatively few studies have made systematic comparisons between women and men, using representative samples.

In addition to a greater focus on women in studies of bereavement, many of the samples also have been limited to white, predominantly middle-class respondents (Umberson et al. 1992). Until recently, studies of bereavement also have focused mainly on mid-life or younger widows (Wortman and Silver 1990). According to Lund, Caserta, and Dimond (1993), no systematic investigation of older adults and bereavement existed until 1979, when the National Institute on Aging established a funding priority for this topic. This historical pattern is rather surprising in light of the importance accorded to spousal bereavement by early gerontologists.

Methods of sampling also vary across studies of bereavement; each presents different methodological concerns. Many of the early studies of bereavement drew respondents from patient populations, including those seeking psychiatric treatment. Control groups were seldom included, consisting of non-bereaved patients, or bereaved individuals who had neither sought or been referred for treatment (see Hyman 1983). Although non-clinical and national samples have become more prevalent in the literature, a number of bereavement researchers have continued to utilize clinical populations or other selected groups (for example, self-help groups) for their samples (see Arbuckle and de Vries 1995).

Some researchers have used death records to obtain the names of surviving spouses (e.g., Gallagher et al. 1983; Gass 1989; O'Bryant 1988, 1991; O'Bryant and Morgan 1990). This approach provides a less biased sample than those based on patient populations, but representation typically is compromised by high refusal rates. Those who are recently bereaved often are understandably reluctant to participate in a study. For example, Dolores Gallagher and colleagues (1989) used death certificates to identify spouses of persons who had died in the preceding two to four weeks, yielding a 30 percent response rate.

Other studies have used more conventional sampling techniques. Many of these have been confined to local areas, which vary in geographic locale and in the composition and density of the older population (Kohen 1983). National surveys provide greater representation, but few have been designed for the specific purpose of studying spousal bereavement. As a consequence, information often is not available on important factors such as length of time since bereavement. Margaret Stroebe and colleagues point out the tradeoffs between studies based upon large probability samples (which provide generalizable data, but may offer superficial information about bereavement) and smaller, non-representative studies (which may provide fuller data on bereavement, but with limited generalizability) (Stroebe, Hansson, and Stroebe 1993).

Additional tradeoffs are offered by studies which are undertaken for purposes other than studying bereavement. Because the study was not designed with bereavement specifically in mind, the respondents were not treated as "special characters" by the researchers (Hyman 1983:14) (i.e., researchers may treat bereaved respondents differently than other respondents, potentially biasing the results). Nor would specific connections between bereavement and other information asked in the study be suggested (directly or indirectly) by the researchers to the respondents (Hyman 1983). Thus, such studies can provide a "double-blind" advantage.

As is true for other areas of social research, cross-sectional studies of bereavement have been more prevalent than longitudinal approaches (e.g., Amato and Partridge 1987; Arbuckle and de Vries 1995; Arens 1982/83; Arling 1976; Lee et al. 1998; Umberson et al. 1992). A common procedure has been to compare bereaved and married persons, with the assumption that data from married respondents can be used to represent the attitudes, behaviors, and situations of widows and widowers prior to their bereavement (Ferraro and Barresi 1982). Such comparisons can misrepresent pre-bereavement characteristics. In particular, characteristics attributed to bereavement, such as depression, may derive from the fact that healthier persons are more likely to remarry (Umberson et al. 1992).[3] Since men are more likely than women to remarry, this selection factor also will bias results concerning gender differences.[4]

A cross-sectional alternative to comparing bereaved and married persons has been to rely on retrospective data supplied by respondents about their lives prior to bereavement (e.g., Lopata 1973). However, this approach introduces other potential biases. Kenneth Ferraro argues that retrospective data are especially questionable for studies of stressful life events because respondents "may have difficulty in recalling accurately what life was like before confronting bereavement" (1984:455).

Longitudinal studies of bereavement can help to address these problems, by tracing respondents prior to and following changes in their marital status or by studying the course of bereavement. More of these studies have become

---

[3] Umberson, Wortman, and Kessler (1992) present a cross-sectional alternative to this dilemma, which is discussed later in the chapter.

[4] Lee and colleagues (1998) contend that this selection factor would not seriously bias study results because remarriage following the death of a spouse is relatively uncommon.

available in the past decade (e.g., Dimond et al. 1987; Gallagher-Thompson et al. 1993; Lund et al. 1993; Stroebe and Stroebe 1993b; Wortman et al. 1993). Although longitudinal studies are superior to cross-sectional approaches when studying the effects of life changes, there are methodological drawbacks to these designs as well, including selective attrition and testing effects (Stroebe et al. 1993).

The Need for Controls

Until relatively recently, few studies of spousal bereavement controlled for potentially spurious relationships (Homan et al. 1986). In addition to gender and length of time since spouse's death (Arbuckle and de Vries 1995; Lee et al. 1998; Umberson et al. 1992), other relevant factors include number of years married (Dimond et al. 1987), age and birth cohort (Thompson et al. 1984), racial-ethnic heritage (Markides 1989a), living arrangements (Homan et al. 1986), employment history (Smith and Zick 1986), education, income, and social class (Arbuckle and de Vries 1995; Longino et al. 1989; Morgan 1986).

The need for adequate control groups is arguably the most serious methodological issue in studies of gender differences in adaptation to the death of a spouse. For example, because women are more likely than men to suffer from depression (or are more likely to be diagnosed as depressed),[5] this main effect of gender must be taken into consideration before conclusions can be drawn about the effects of bereavement. In fact, because women's rates of depression are about twice that for men in the general population (Aneshensel et al. 1991), cross-sectional studies showing equivalent or only slightly higher depression rates for widows compared to widowers suggest a greater impact of bereavement on men's mental health (Stroebe and Stroebe 1983). Similarly, it cannot be concluded that spousal bereavement has more devastating effects on men simply because widowers have higher mortality rates than widows: Mortality rates for men of *all* marital statuses are higher than those for women. Prospective studies can avoid this problem by examining changes in individuals' health and well-being prior to and following bereavement. In the absence of such studies, adequate control groups must be used (i.e., comparing widows with women in other marital statuses and widowers with men in other marital statuses) to assess gender differences in life satisfaction, depression, mortality, or other outcomes following bereavement (Stroebe and Stroebe 1983). An investigation of these various outcomes follows. I begin this empirical review by examining economic changes following bereavement.

[5] Women's greater likelihood of being diagnosed with depression can be traced in part to clinicians' biases (e.g., Broverman et al. 1970), but self-reported data also reveal more symptoms of depression among women (Holzer, Leaf, and Weissman 1985; Radloff 1975; Weissman and Myers 1978).

Economic Well-Being

It is well-documented that bereaved spouses have fewer economic resources on average than continuously married couples (Hyman 1983; McCrae and Costa 1993; Morgan 1981; Zick and Smith 1986, 1991). However, the death of a spouse is not solely responsible for this pattern. Due to their lower life expectancies, members of poorer socioeconomic groups are likely to be over-represented in the category of bereaved spouses (see Morgan 1981). Other couples may experience economic declines in the period prior to the spouse's death. Health problems can affect a spouse's employment opportunities, which in turn will impact the couple's income, pension benefits, and investment opportunities (Zick and Smith 1991).

Although widows and widowers tend to have lower incomes than continuously married couples *prior* to their spouse's death, economic declines also can be linked directly to the death (due to loss of the spouse's income, for example, or the loss of pension benefits that do not extend to survivors) (Morgan, 1991; Zick and Smith, 1991). However, longitudinal studies show somewhat smaller economic changes following spousal bereavement than would be concluded from cross-sectional data (Morgan 1981; Zick and Smith 1986).

Gender Differences in Economic Well-Being

It seems self-evident that widows would be in greater economic jeopardy than widowers (Burkhauser, Holden, and Feaster 1988; Fengler and Danigelis 1982; Holden, 1989; Morgan 1984b, 1986). As a group, women have lower earnings power than men, and displaced homemakers confront serious difficulties in finding adequate employment (Morgan 1984b, 1991). Older women face reduced Social Security benefits when their spouse dies, and frequently the reduction or withdrawal of private pension benefits (Arendell and Estes 1991; Older Women's League 1999). It is thus interesting to find that there has been some controversy over gender differences in economic vulnerabilities following bereavement.

According to Ken Smith and Cathleen Zick, "Counter to the conventional wisdom, widowers appear to be just as likely to experience economic hardships as are widows, other things being equal" (1986:629). This conclusion was based on results from a longitudinal study of widows and widowers and from comparisons of bereaved spouses and continuously married couples.

Smith and Zick's contention that widowers and widows are equally likely to experience poverty illustrates the different ways in which gender has been assessed and assigned meaning by social scientists. In this study (and in other quantitative works), a variable for gender was included in the analyses, along with a number of control variables. One of these control variables was work experience. Smith and Zick's central finding was that "the sex of the widowed individual never matters" in predicting poverty after a spouse's death, but that "years of work experience always matter" (p. 629). Greater work experience was found to minimize the chances of falling into poverty, for both men and women.

What Smith and Zick do not address is that work experience is itself a gendered phenomenon. As a group, men have been more likely than women to have lengthy and continuous labor force histories (Hayward and Liu 1992; Reskin and Padavic 1994), especially among whites (Anderson 1988; Jones 1985). That gender *is* important in understanding economic changes following bereavement has been demonstrated in a number of other studies, including several authored by Zick and Smith. In a related study based on the same data set, these researchers reported that both men and women were likely to experience dramatic declines in their economic well-being after widowhood, but that widows were more likely than widowers "to experience changes that lead them to extreme poverty" (Zick and Smith 1986:673). A further study published in 1988 showed that "the death of a spouse translates into a substantial economic loss, particularly for widows" (Zick and Smith 1988:233). In addition, a longitudinal study focusing specifically on older persons found that retired men, as a group, were *not* at greater risk for poverty when their spouse died (Burkhauser, Butler, and Holden 1991). Both women and men who experienced bereavement had fewer economic resources than continuously married couples, but only women showed an increased risk for poverty at the time of their spouses' death. Together, these research findings support the commonly-held view that the death of a spouse places women, as a group, in greater economic jeopardy relative to men.

Considering paid work experience, race-ethnicity, and other important elements in addition to gender provides a fuller understanding of economic risks associated with spousal bereavement. (I take up this issue in the latter part of this chapter, in considering a life course approach to spousal bereavement.) Economic resources also are implicated in widows' and widowers' adaptation, as reflected in their social functioning, health, and coping.

Social Relationships

Empirical studies challenge the popular belief that bereavement brings loneliness and social isolation (Babchuk and Anderson 1989; Cleiren 1993; Ferraro and Barresi 1982). In fact, several studies have found higher rates of contact with friends, family, and neighbors among widows and widowers than among married persons (Kohen 1983; Powers and Bultena 1976), though network size apparently declines following spousal bereavement (Morgan 1984a). Widows and widowers "may have fewer relationships, but rely on them more fully" (Kohen 1983:57).

Gender Differences in Social Relationships

Some studies indicate that women's social contacts are intensified following widowhood, relative to those of bereaved men. In this regard, Herbert Hyman (1983) found that widowed women had higher levels of interaction with non-kin than married women, but he found no differences between widowers and married men. In an analysis of data from the longitudinal Retirement History Study, which I conducted with Kris Bulcroft (Hatch and Bulcroft 1992), widows reported more frequent contact with their friends than did other unmarried respondents, including widowers. In contrast, widowers and divorced men showed the greatest declines over time in the frequency of their friendship contacts. Other studies also have found that spousal bereavement affects men's social relationships more adversely than women's (Berardo 1970; Pihlblad and Adams 1972; see also Dimond et al. 1987).

Conflicting findings have been reported by Robert Atchley (1975) and by Kenneth Ferraro and Charles Barresi (1982), who concluded that bereavement produced greater increases in *men's* social participation relative to that of women. From the results of his study, Atchley (1975) proposed that men's higher income provided them with greater access to transportation, which in turn facilitated their social participation. Although Ferraro and Barresi's (1982) sample was drawn from a low-income population, it is probable that the men's average income was higher than the women's. Following Atchley's reasoning, gender differences in income (apparently not controlled in Ferraro and Barresi's analyses) might help to explain why widowers reported higher rates of interactions with friends than did the widows. However, this reasoning would not apply to the comparable finding that Ferraro and Barresi reported for interaction with neighbors, as transportation would not be an issue.

It is not surprising that conflicting findings should emerge in these studies of widow/erhood, since the larger literature on gender differences in social resources also is contradictory (see Chapter 2). I have noted that this is especially true for quantitative measures of network size and frequency of contacts. Fewer studies have examined qualitative changes in social relationships following bereavement, and whether these changes differ for women and men.

Janet Kohen's study (1983) is helpful in this regard. Based on a sample fifty-five years and older, Kohen found gender differences in interaction among both married and bereaved respondents. For both marital groups, women were more likely than men to say that they shared their concerns with persons close to them. In addition, married respondents were more likely than bereaved respondents to turn to family members when they were worried, while bereaved respondents were more likely than the married to rely upon friends. Of all respondents, widowers were least likely to turn to family members for support, a finding Kohen believes is due to men's relatively weaker ties with their children. Her results suggest that widows are more likely to have close relationships with their children, while widowers must choose from a narrower set of alternatives to replace the intimacy their wives had provided.

Thus, Kohen concludes that following bereavement women have "more anchorage points available to them for expanding their social roles" (1983:63) than do men. These conclusions can only be suggestive, as this is a cross-sectional study. However, parallel findings have been reported by Umberson, Wortman, and Kessler (1992), who found that men but not women experienced strained relationships with their children following bereavement. As discussed in the previous chapter, studies also show that married men are more likely than women to rely upon their spouse as their primary source of intimacy, and that widowers are less likely than widows to name a confidant. Together, these research results suggest that men are more likely than women to experience strains or losses in their social relationships following bereavement. However, such vulnerability apparently declines over time. Research reported by Dale Lund and colleagues (1990) found that widowers were less likely than widows to have a confidant immediately after their spouse's death, but that this difference disappeared within two years.

Mental Health and Coping

Early studies of bereavement were based on patients in psychiatric institutions, providing a model of pathological bereavement that was adopted in subsequent research (see Sanders 1989). Although bereavement continues to be seen as "a stressor of immense proportions" (Sanders 1989:180), and is thought to produce overwhelming, debilitating effects on the health and well-being of survivors (Parkes 1993), researchers have emphasized that such effects typically are concentrated in the period immediately following bereavement (Faletti et al. 1989; Gallagher et al. 1983; Shuchter and Zisook 1987, 1993; Thompson et al. 1989). Furthermore, making the point that "normal" and "pathological" bereavement must be distinguished, Phillip Bornstein and colleagues concluded that for most persons experiencing bereavement, "grief is grief and is not a model for psychotic depression" (1973:566) (see also Hansson, Remondet, and Galusha 1993). I will return to questions concerning the course of bereavement later in the chapter.

Few writers have gone as far as Edgar Borgatta and Rhonda Montgomery (1986) in suggesting that the death of a spouse can produce beneficial effects on survivors' health and well-being, but some of the widows in Helena Lopata's (1973) study reported "compensations" following the death of their husbands. This was especially true when the marriage was antagonistic or when lengthy caregiving of an ill spouse had affected the respondent's health. Recognition of multiple, sometimes conflicting, responses to bereavement is reflected in some researchers' efforts to evaluate "positive" (well-being, life satisfaction) as well as "negative" (grief, depression) dimensions of mental health (Arens 1982/83; Lund, Caserta, and Dimond 1986a; O'Bryant 1991).

Due to the complexity of responses to bereavement and the difficulty of unraveling cause-and-effect relationships, research to date provides few conclusions about coping styles or strategies that are productive of "good" versus "poor" adaptation to bereavement (Stroebe et al. 1993). Is it better to repress one's memories about the loved one (see Cleiren 1993:28), for example, or is it better to confront "emotion-laden memories and associations . . . until tolerance for the memory is developed" (Weiss 1993:280)? As I will discuss in greater detail, great diversity has been found in how individuals respond to bereavement. Based on extant research, no one set of responses is clearly associated with better coping.

Gender Differences in Mental Health

Although the evidence is far from conclusive with regard to whether women or men "suffer more" on mental health dimensions following the death of a spouse, research suggests that men are in somewhat greater jeopardy (see Lee et al. 1998; Stroebe and Stroebe 1983, 1987; Umberson et al. 1992). Because women have higher rates of depression and self-reported distress than men, within-gender control groups are needed to evaluate potential effects of bereavement on mental health dimensions when longitudinal data are not available (Stroebe and Stroebe 1983). (The antisocial personality disorders for which men are more prone are seldom investigated in studies of bereavement.) However, because healthier persons are more likely to remarry, comparison of bereaved spouses with currently married spouses may overestimate the effects of bereavement (Umberson et al. 1992).

To address this problem, Debra Umberson and her collaborators combined *all* persons who had ever been widow/ered, and compared women and men in this group with those who had ever been married but who had not experienced the death of a spouse. The researchers emphasize that this is the most conservative approach to estimate effects of bereavement, but they conducted additional analyses to evaluate separately those respondents who had remarried following their spouse's death, and also compared bereaved spouses to those who were currently married. The results showed that men were more vulnerable than women to depression following the death of a spouse. These gender differences were explained in part by considering the length of time since bereavement (but see Lee et al. 1998 for a different conclusion). This variable is important to consider since depression and distress are greater in early stages of bereavement, and men typically have been bereaved for shorter periods (women live longer, and thus have been widowed for a longer period).

This study is noteworthy not only in its attention to control groups and its inclusion of important control variables such as length of time since bereavement.

It is also one of the very few studies to test specific hypotheses concerning gender differences in widow/erhood, rather than to offer explanations *ex post facto* for observed differences (see also Lee et al. 1998). Debra Umberson and her colleagues hypothesized that depression among widowers would be connected with sources of strain that were different from the strains confronting widows. For widowers, dependence upon their wives for emotional and social support and for household management was expected to help explain their vulnerability to depression. A different source of strain—that of vulnerability to economic problems—was hypothesized as an important predictor of depression among widows.

The three sets of strain variables were assessed differently, depending upon the source of strain under consideration. Strains in social relationships were measured by asking respondents whether others make too many demands upon them and whether others are critical of them. Respondents were also asked about supportive aspects of their relationships with others, including whether they had confidants with whom they can share their most private thoughts and feelings. Financial strain was measured by respondents' satisfaction with their current finances, the extent of their difficulty with making monthly payments on bills, and the extent to which end-of-month finances were sufficient to make ends meet. Finally, strains in the area of household management were assessed by counting the number of tasks respondents performed in the past week, the number of home maintenance tasks performed in the past year, the number of hours spent doing housework in the past week, and also by asking respondents whether anyone helps them with the housework. Although these latter sets of variables are termed "household management strains," the items assessed the number of tasks and the amount of time respondents spend performing them, and do not ask respondents directly about dissatisfactions or difficulties they may be experiencing in this area (as do the social and economic strain variables).

Consistent with their hypotheses, the researchers found that widowers' depression was predicted by strains associated with household management, while widows' depression was predicted by financial strains. The hypothesis that widowers' depression would be linked with strains arising from social relationships was not supported. On the other hand, although widowers were less likely than widows to report having a confidant, widowers who reported having a confidant seemed to derive greater mental health benefits from this social support than did the widows. This latter finding is supportive of gender role arguments which stress men's reliance on the social and emotional support provided by their wives, and their consequent health problems when that support is no longer available.

Although this study concluded that widowers are more vulnerable to depression than widows, longitudinal research conducted by Dale Lund and his colleagues found more similarities than differences in widows' and widowers' levels of depression and life satisfaction (Lund et al. 1986a; Lund et al. 1993). However, these researchers did not examine potential gender differences (or potential similarities) in the sources (or predictors) of depression and life satisfaction, as did Umberson et al. Outcomes that appear equivalent for women and men (or any comparison groups) can be predicted by different sources.

Gender Differences in Coping

If men are more vulnerable than women to depression following bereavement, it would seem that widowers also would evidence poorer coping strategies compared to widows. Based on the few studies that have examined this question, processes of adapting to bereavement seem to be more similar than different for widows and widowers (Gallagher et al. 1989; Gass 1989). Furthermore, although Kathleen Gass (1989) found that older widows and widowers utilized similar coping strategies, a number of the strategies used by *women*, not men, were linked with poorer mental health. The use of a greater number of coping strategies was also linked with poorer mental health among women. In contrast, only one coping strategy, "self-blame," was related to poorer mental health for men, and the number of coping strategies that the men used was unrelated to their mental health.

Gass believes that the women in her sample may have faced more bereavement-related problems than the men, particularly financial problems, and thus that they needed to marshall more coping behaviors. Since the widowers had higher economic and occupational status than the widows, these resources may have reduced their need to employ more ways of coping (Gass 1989:91).

Dolores Gallagher and her colleagues (1989) also found more similarities than differences in the coping strategies used by older widows and widowers. However, men more consistently used the "action-oriented" coping strategy of keeping busy, which the authors believe is consistent with traditional gender role patterns. It should be noted that gender differences in the "keeping busy" strategy were extremely small, and that the study apparently did not control for economic resources.

Morbidity and Mortality

Not surprisingly, bereavement has been considered detrimental for physical as well as mental health—sometimes to the point of causing premature death (Bowling 1987; Ferraro 1985/86, 1989b; Gallagher et al. 1982; Parkes and Weiss 1983; Rowland 1977; Stroebe and Stroebe 1983). Consistent with these assumptions, many studies have shown elevated health problems (Ferraro 1985/86; Parkes and Brown 1972; Thompson et al. 1984; Wan 1984) and mortality (Cox and Ford 1964; Helsing et al. 1981; Helsing and Szklo 1981; Kraus and Lilienfeld 1959; Parkes, Benjamin, and Fitzgerald 1969; Rees and Lutkins 1967; Wolinsky and Johnson 1992) among bereaved spouses. However, these effects typically have been documented with "simple relationships between marital status and either morbidity or mortality" (Ferraro 1985/86:9).

Studies using longitudinal data and/or matched control groups have produced some conflicting findings. A number of these studies concur with the bulk of the literature cited above: declines in physical health following bereavement have been reported (Ferraro 1985/86; Parkes and Brown 1972), as well as increased mortality (Helsing et al. 1981; Helsing and Szklo 1981; Parkes et al. 1969; Rees and Lutkins 1967), especially within the first few weeks or months of a spouse's death. However, other studies have found negligible or no effects of bereavement on physical health (Heyman and Gianturco 1973; Murrell, Himmelfarb, and Phifer 1995; Wan 1984; Wolinsky and Johnson 1992) or mortality (Clayton 1974; Murrell et al. 1995; Ward 1976). Margaret Stroebe and Wolfgang Stroebe offer what seems to be the most reasonable conclusion that can be reached at this time—that "the loss of a loved one is associated with extreme mental and physical suffering, not for everyone, and not always lastingly, but for a significant minority" (1993a:175).

If we accept that physical health and mortality risks *are* associated with bereavement for a "significant minority" of spouses, we must ask what these associations actually mean. Other factors may help to explain observed relationships involving morbidity and mortality, beyond the romantic notion of survivors "pining away and dying of grief" (Helsing et al. 1981:802). The length and severity of illness experienced by the deceased spouse (which may produce health strains on the caregiving spouse), pre-existing illness in the survivor, or "common process" (whereby husbands and wives are exposed to similar conditions, including similar diets, household cigarette smoking, and so forth, which can cause deleterious effects in both spouses) can help to explain increased morbidity and mortality among survivors (Borgatta and Montgomery 1986; Smith and Zick 1994; Young et al. 1963).

Gender Differences in Morbidity and Mortality

Studies showing increased morbidity and mortality among bereaved spouses often have also found that men are at greater risk than women (Helsing et al. 1981; Helsing and Szklo 1981; Parkes and Brown 1972). This finding has been reported in studies based on younger samples as well as older ones (Rees and Lutkins 1967; Wan 1984). This apparent gender difference must be viewed with some caution, however, given the methodological limitations associated with studies of bereavement and mortality.

An interesting finding in this regard was reported by Edgar Borgatta and Rhonda Montgomery (1986). They re-analyzed the data used in research conducted by Knud Helsing and his colleagues (Helsing et al. 1981; Helsing and Szklo 1981), which had found increased mortality for widowers but not for widows following bereavement. Noting that respondents who became widow/ered had been included twice in this prospective study (counted once as a married subject, and again as a bereaved subject), Borgatta and Montgomery eliminated the duplicated cases and found a positive relationship between widowhood and *survival* for the female sample. Though this finding differs radically from the originally published reports (bereavement associated with enhanced survival rather than with mortality), it is noteworthy that both sets of findings suggest a health disadvantage for widowers relative to widows.

Borgatta and Montgomery point out that spousal bereavement typically occurs in later life, and that lengthy illness often precedes death in older populations. Because women typically outlive their husbands, they are likely to take on a spousal caretaking role. The writers hypothesize that the spouse's death releases the survivor from the burdens and stresses of caregiving, eventuating in better health. Although these researchers are unique in asserting that widowhood can enhance longevity, a longitudinal study found that respondents' health improved over the long term following bereavement (Murrell et al. 1995).

Evaluating the Empirical Record

Clearly, the death of a spouse is consequential for individuals' lives. Not all of the potential changes occasioned by bereavement are negative, nor are their effects typically uniform. For example, it is to be expected that a spouse's death would generate changes in the social and familial relationships of surviving spouses, and in their self-concepts and identities (Lopata 1996; Shuchter and Zisook 1987). However, bereavement does not inevitably (or even typically) bring loneliness and social isolation to widows and widowers (Babchuk and Anderson 1989; Ferraro and Barresi 1982; Kohen 1983). Furthermore, although some surviving spouses experience long-term dislocations in their social identities, others are able to identify and pursue new opportunities for growth and development (Lopata 1996; Lund et al. 1986b).

It is true that declines in mental health are commonly found among widows and widowers in the period immediately following bereavement. Depending upon the study under consideration, this period ranges from a few months (Lund et al. 1989) to the first year or two following the spouse's death (Faletti et al. 1989; Gallagher et al. 1983; Thompson et al. 1989). Even within this initial period of bereavement, surviving spouses often evidence multiple, conflicting responses to their loss (Arens 1982/83; Lund et al. 1986a; O'Bryant 1991).

For a minority of surviving spouses, bereavement may also bring increased risks for physical health problems and possibly increased risks for mortality (Stroebe and Stroebe 1993a). In view of the methodological limitations of most of the studies which report such findings (see McCrae and Costa 1993), this conclusion is offered only tentatively. In particular, few of these studies utilize baseline data on respondents' health measured prior to bereavement. Furthermore, alternative explanations for increased risks for morbidity and mortality among bereaved respondents can be advanced. It is possible that some surviving spouses literally become ill and die of grief, but other factors (or more probably, a combination of various factors) also can account for these patterns (see Stroebe and Stroebe 1993a).

Conclusions about Gender Differences

Conflicting images have been suggested for women as widows and men as widowers. Helena Lopata (1996) argues that widowed women have been portrayed in dismal terms as "ever-limited, ever-suffering, ever-dependent" (1996:xiv). While it is doubtless true that negative images of widows and widowhood have long held sway, bereaved men also have been portrayed in negative terms. In fact, as I have shown, writers more typically have argued that men's difficulties following the death of a spouse outweigh those faced by women. Herbert Hyman, for example, argues that older men who are alone lead "a sad life" and often cannot manage by themselves, an image that contrasts sharply with his description of widowed women as capable and independent (1983:92) (see also Berardo 1970; Helsing et al. 1981).

Beyond the methodological limitations of many of these studies, which I have reviewed in some detail, conclusions about which gender suffers more following the death of a spouse depend upon the outcomes that are emphasized. In general, empirical studies lend support to the view that widowers are at greater risk than widows on the dimensions of social support and mental health. Given the methodological limitations of extant research on physical health and mortality following bereavement, I do not place great confidence in findings of gender differences on these dimensions, but I will note that most of these studies have found greater risks among men relative to women. On the other side of the dichotomous gender coin (considering only gender, and ignoring race-ethnicity and other sources of diversity), widows face greater risks for economic hardships than widowers (Burkhauser et al. 1991; Zick and Smith 1986, 1988).

What do findings of gender differences in widow/erhood reflect? Gender role explanations have been the dominant paradigm to explain gender differences in spousal bereavement, but they have almost never been tested. One of these rare exceptions, the study conducted by Debra Umberson and colleagues (1992), hypothesized that different sources of strain would predict depression among widows and widowers. These researchers argued that differences in the benefits afforded by traditional gender roles in marriage would produce different sources of vulnerability for bereaved men and women. Consistent with the researchers' hypothesis, depression among widowers was predicted by performing household tasks, which presumably their wives had performed previously. Furthermore, fewer widowers than widows reported having a confidant, but among those who did, the emotional benefits afforded by a confidant apparently were greater for the men than for the women. Although the magnitude of this gender difference was small, the finding is potentially important. The lack of social support—and especially the lack of a confidant—has been the most frequently preferred explanation for why men would "suffer more" than women from bereavement. For women, on the other hand, "a primary benefit of marriage . . . is financial security" (p. 19), and as the researchers had hypothesized, depression among widows was predicted by financial strains.

This cross-sectional study does not provide baseline information about the respondents prior to their bereavement, including their household division of labor, social support patterns, economic dependency, and so forth. Rather, the researchers assume that respondents and their spouses held traditional gender roles prior to the spouse's death. Support for this conjecture is provided by another study (Lund et al. 1993), in which bereaved respondents were asked about the tasks they had performed prior to spouse's death. The majority of older widows and widowers (73%) said that performing the tasks previously taken care of by their spouses had made their coping in bereavement more difficult. The skills which respondents reported that they lacked fell along "predictable" lines (1993:246). Women reported that they lacked skills in home repair work and in managing financial records and legal affairs, while men said that they had difficulty doing the cooking, shopping, and housecleaning which their wives had performed.

These findings are suggestive of a gender role interpretation, but neither of these studies tests the theory. To support a gender role explanation, respondents who score higher on traditional gender roles (whether assessed by behavioral or attitudinal measures) should be at greater risk for strains and poorer adaptation outcomes than respondents who score lower on gender role measures.

What of resource explanations? Although economic well-being generally is not considered a dimension of "adaptation"—and hence conclusions regarding gender differences in adaptation are weighted toward other outcomes—many studies have found that economic resources are important to bereavement outcomes, including mental health and coping, physical health, and mortality. More simply, widows are more likely than widowers to be poor (e.g., Burkhauser et al. 1991).

Not surprisingly, employment history, with its linkages to income, savings, and pensions, goes a long way toward explaining women's risks for poverty in widowhood (Smith and Zick 1986). In the study by Umberson and colleagues (1992) economic strain predicted depression among widows. In another study, differences between married and widowed women's morale disappeared when their income and employment status were controlled (Morgan 1976). These findings can be interpreted from a gender role perspective, which emphasizes married women's dependence upon their husbands for economic support (and hence a gendered division of family functions) (e.g., Umberson et al. 1992). However, the findings can also be interpreted from a structural perspective which emphasizes women's and men's access to socioeconomic resources, rather than their presumed gender-linked personality traits, attitudes, or behaviors (e.g., Hatch and Bulcroft 1992; Moore 1990).

In order to test a resource explanation, both women and men who occupy marginal socio-economic positions should fare more poorly from the effects of spousal bereavement than those who occupy more advantaged positions—regardless of their attitudinal or behavioral adherence to traditional gender roles. Some partial support for this perspective is found in a study by Colin Parkes and Robert Weiss (1983), who reported that respondents of less advantaged social class standing showed poorer outcomes following bereavement, assessed by changes in emotional and physical health, socializing, and economics. This study did not examine potential gender differences in these outcomes, however.

Other structural arguments have focused on the effects of skewed sex ratios in society. Widows may fare better (e.g., Altergott 1985) or worse (e.g., Babchuk and Anderson 1989) than widowers when they are more numerous. A study by Carolyn Balkwell (1985) found that younger age at widowhood was associated with poorer morale among Mexican American and Anglo widows, but not among African American widows. Balkwell conjectures that because African American women have higher risks for experiencing widowhood at younger ages, they will have a stronger support system of widowed friends within their own ethnic group. This argument is similar to that made by Zena Smith Blau (1973), reviewed earlier in this chapter to explain fewer problems of adjustment among widows compared to widowers.

Lawrence Hong and Robert Duff (1994) take up this question in their study of widows residing in retirement communities. They found that widows were more socially active and expressed greater satisfaction with their lives in communities with higher ratios of widowed to married women. Hong and Duff suggest that such environments offer greater opportunities for single and same-sex activities, which in turn may promote feelings of well-being among widows. In contrast, communities with higher ratios of married to widowed women may promote "a heterosexual dyadic life style favoring the married couples" (p. 351) from which widows may feel excluded, diminishing their feelings of life satisfaction. (The social activities and life satisfaction of widowers and married men were not examined in this study.)

Other studies, which have not focused specifically on widowhood, provide modest support for the thesis that women have greater economic and political power in low sex ratio societies (low numbers of men relative to women) than in high sex ratio societies (see South and Trent 1988). From these findings, it might be inferred that more programs and support services would be available to women in societies where women predominate, such as the United States, than in societies with higher sex ratios. Stroebe and Stroebe (1983) have suggested that numerical dominance provides widowed women with more community services and programs oriented to their needs. However, the level of socioeconomic development present in a society is probably a better predictor of the existence of such programs than the sex ratio (see South and Trent 1988). Furthermore, even where women predominate, they do not have *greater* power in a society relative to men. The availability of community services such as "widow-to-widow" support groups is one thing; the availability of an adequate income on which to live is quite another. As I will discuss in the following section, no consistent social program has been developed to meet the economic needs of homemakers who become displaced through widowhood, despite the social labeling of widows as one of the few categories of the so-called "worthy poor" (Lopata and Brehm 1986).

BEYOND GENDER DIFFERENCES: ADAPTATION TO BEREAVEMENT IN LIFE COURSE PERSPECTIVE

Although questions concerning gender differences continue to be raised in the literature, the need for a more complex investigation of women's and men's adaptation to the death of a spouse is evident. Relatively few empirical studies have made systematic comparisons between widows and widowers. Of those that have, some studies have found few or no gender differences (e.g., Lund et al. 1986a, 1990, 1993), while others suggest modest differences between widows' and widowers' adaptation (e.g., Gallagher et al. 1989; Gass 1989; Lee et al. 1998; Stroebe and Stroebe 1983, 1987).

Increasingly, writers are calling attention to additional life course dimensions that may influence women's and men's responses to bereavement. Race, social class, birth cohort, and the circumstances surrounding the spouse's death have been cited as potentially important (e.g., Arbuckle and de Vries 1995; Stroebe and Stroebe 1993a, 1993b; Stroebe et al. 1993; Wortman and Silver 1990). The impetus for this broader investigation of bereavement has come primarily from empirical studies that have found great diversity in how individuals—both women and men—respond to the loss of a spouse.

Limitations of Extant Models of Bereavement

Empirical evidence has highlighted the shortcomings of approaches that homogenize responses to bereavement—not simply those that focus on dichotomized gender differences, but more fundamentally the models that have been proposed to describe the course of bereavement, which have been assumed to hold for both women and men (e.g., Bowlby 1960; Kavanaugh 1972; Kübler-Ross 1969). Among the many models that attempt to explain grieving, most share in common the following three stages (several models propose four or more stages): 1) disbelief, shock, and denial; 2) acute symptoms of grief and social withdrawal; and 3) resolution. Commonly, resolution implies a return to "normal functioning" or pre-bereavement equilibrium (Zisook 1987; see also Wortman and Silver 1990).

Writers proposing these models have cautioned that the stages may not be experienced in a fixed order, and that some individuals may not go through all of them (e.g., Kavanaugh 1972; Kübler-Ross 1969; Zisook 1987). The potential for overlap between the stages also has been recognized (e.g., Bugen 1977). These cautions are necessary, since the results from empirical studies have challenged central assumptions about bereavement embodied in the models.

For example, Dale Lund (1989b) examined several longitudinal studies of bereaved spouses to conclude that some aspects of bereavement may continue for many years, or may never end (see also Zisook, Shuchter, and Lyons 1987; Shuchter and Zisook 1993). Feelings of stress due to spouse's death were commonly reported after five years. Some respondents stated explicitly that they "do not feel they will ever 'get over' their loss but that they have learned to live with it" (Lund 1989b:221). These findings call into question the assumption that resolution is an inevitable end point to the grieving process, or at the least suggest that resolution can mean quite different things to different persons.

Furthermore, intense grief does not inevitably accompany bereavement. Camille Wortman and Roxane Cohen Silver (1990) analyzed data from five longitudinal surveys of bereavement, four focusing on the loss of a spouse (the fifth focused on the loss of a child). Across the surveys, they found that attenuated or "absent grief" was quite common, with substantial numbers of individuals showing only low or moderate distress across all of the measurement points. Nor was there evidence that lower initial levels of grief predicted poorer subsequent mental or physical health, refuting the common assumption that experiencing intense initial distress (or "working through the loss") is required for healthy adjustment.

There is no doubt that bereavement is a process. Longitudinal studies using frequent, closely-spaced measurement points show significant changes over time in respondents' reports of grief, depression, anxiety, anger, and stress, as well as their life satisfaction, morale, self-esteem, and so forth (Lund et al. 1989; Zisook et al. 1987). Many bereaved persons do share some similar general patterns in their responses, often experiencing intense grief and depression in the first few months, followed by gradual, but uneven, improvements after this initial period (Lund 1989b). Lund, Caserta, and Dimond describe the course of bereavement as "a roller coaster of many ups and downs with gradual improvement over time" (1993:247). There is little empirical support for specific stages of bereavement, however (Aiken 1991).

Rather, great diversity has been observed among individuals in the intensity, duration, and course of bereavement (see Shuchter and Zisook 1993). A life course perspective helps to identify elements which contribute to this diversity, and places them in sociohistorical context. In the following sections, I examine how the experience of spousal bereavement is shaped by personal histories of experience; social location and membership in social groups; birth cohort; and the broader societal context.

Employing the Multi-Level Life Course Model

Personal Histories

A variety of life pathways lead to spousal bereavement, which in turn influence the direction of widows' and widowers' subsequent experiences. This section examines some features of personal history as they bear on individuals' responses to bereavement, and how these patterns are conditioned by life course dimensions that include but are not limited to gender.

Age at bereavement—The death of a spouse becomes more likely with advancing age, but can occur at any point in the adult life course. I discussed in Chapter 2 how life course researchers have characterized life events as "on-time" or "off-time," depending on whether those events occur at normatively prescribed ages (McLanahan and Sørensen 1985; Wortman and Silver 1990). Spousal bereavement and other major life events which take place "off time" have been thought to hinder individuals' coping and disrupt the subsequent flow of events in their lives (e.g., Brim 1980; Wortman and Silver 1990). Following from this thesis, bereavement should be bring more severe consequences when it is experienced at younger rather than older ages.

Supportive evidence for the "off-time" thesis comes primarily from earlier, less methodologically rigorous studies (Ball 1977; Carey 1979; Morgan 1976). These studies found poorer mental health among younger bereaved respondents compared to older ones. However, researchers who have utilized comparison groups and controlled for the length of time since widow/erhood have not found a relationship between age at bereavement and mental health outcomes (e.g., Umberson et al. 1992), or, more precisely, have not found a direct relationship.

Age at bereavement can exert *indirect effects* on individuals' well-being. A clear ramification of age at bereavement concerns **remarriage**, which becomes less likely with increasing age. Remarried (and continuously married) persons have greater economic resources and they report better mental health and well-being than those who are widow/ered, a conclusion that has been reached for both women and men (Umberson et al. 1992; see also Gentry and Shulman 1988).[6,7] However, the probabilities for remarriage are unevenly distributed across gender and racial-ethnic groups. At all ages, remarriage rates are higher for men than for

---

[6] However, most studies show that the health benefits men derive from marriage and remarriage are greater than those derived by women (see Coombs 1991). This issue is examined more fully in Chapter 6.

[7] According to Umberson et al. (1992), it is not known whether remarriage offers mental health benefits, or whether mentally healthy persons are more likely to remarry. However, the latter thesis would not account for the disparate chances for marriage and re-marriage found for women compared to men, or across racial-ethnic groups.

women and higher for non-Hispanic whites than other racial-ethnic groups (Glick and Lin 1986; Morgan 1991; Sweet and Bumpass 1987).

Age at bereavement also is associated with the risk of **falling into poverty**. Economic problems are commonly experienced by widows and widowers of all ages, but apparently are less severe when bereavement occurs prior to age fifty (Morgan 1991; Smith and Zick 1986). On the other hand, longer marriages can help to "insulate" surviving spouses from dire poverty (Smith and Zick 1986:629; see also Holden and Kuo 1996).

Due to the significance of employment for financial well-being, as well as for social interaction and support, **entry (or re-entry) into the labor force** has been advocated as an important adaptive mechanism for widows (Morgan 1980, 1984b). In her study of mid-life widows age thirty to forty-four, Leslie Morgan (1980) found that most of these women were already employed. A subsequent study (Morgan 1984b) of widows age fifty-eight to sixty-three showed that fewer of these older women (about one-third) were already employed when their husbands died. Among those who were not already employed, approximately 18 percent entered the labor force. Many of these women had not previously been employed and a number of them reported problems in finding jobs. However, most of the widows over sixty who were not already employed said that they had not considered looking for work. Morgan cautions that women entering widowhood who are not already in the labor force face job competition and discrimination, and that these obstacles increase with women's age. Both men and women face increasing job instability and declining earnings as they grow older, as well as discriminatory hiring practices (Eglit 1989; Mueller, Mutran, and Boyle 1989; Rodeheaver 1990; U.S. Senate Special Committee on Aging 1997); these problems are exacerbated for women and minorities (Couch 1988; Gibson and Burns 1992; Morgan 1984b; Rodeheaver 1990).

Circumstances surrounding the death—The circumstances surrounding the spouse's death also have been linked with the survivor's adaptation. One of these—having some forewarning of the spouse's death—has received a good deal of research attention, but has yielded mixed findings concerning survivors' adaptation. Theoretically, it would seem that having some forewarning of the death would be beneficial, as this would help spouses to prepare emotionally for their impending loss. Forewarning may aid preparations in other realms as well, allowing couples time to make wills and engage in financial planning if they had not already done so.

Forewarning is one of the factors underlying the "timing thesis" discussed above, since younger spouses are less likely than older ones to anticipate and hence to prepare emotionally for widow/erhood. Thus, in light of the relative lack of support for the timing thesis, it is perhaps not surprising that the research evidence is mixed concerning whether forewarning is helpful or harmful for surviving spouses' mental health and well-being (cf. Ball 1977; Gallagher et al.

1982; Hill, Thompson, and Gallagher 1988; Stroebe and Stroebe 1993b; Umberson et al. 1992). In part, these mixed results might be understood by recognizing that the anticipation of bereavement is often associated with lengthy illness of the spouse, and that caring for a chronically ill spouse can be taxing (Wortman and Silver 1990). Indeed, much research attests to the emotional and physical costs of long-term intensive caregiving by spouses (Fitting et al. 1986; George and Gwyther 1986; Johnson and Catalano 1983; McFall and Miller 1992). For this reason, forewarning may not have a beneficial impact on the mental health and well-being of surviving spouses.

It is how people *reflect upon and attach meaning* to their impending loss during the forewarning period that is important. In a retrospective study, Jacqueline Remondet and colleagues (1987) examined how adaptation to a spouse's death was impacted by the surviving spouse's rehearsal of the event. Those who engaged in "cognitive rehearsal" prior to their spouse's death— dwelling on the impending death and its implications—reported greater problems in adapting to the loss. In contrast, "behavioral rehearsal," in which the soon-to-be surviving spouse made social comparisons between themselves and other bereaved spouses or otherwise made plans for the future, was associated with higher well-being after the loss.

Survivors' distress is heightened when additional crises are experienced at or near the time of bereavement (Vachon et al. 1982; see also Wortman and Silver 1990). Some of these crises may reflect problems that were already present when the spouse died, such as chronic health problems on the part of the survivor (which may have been produced or exacerbated by caregiving efforts). Other crises may arise from the loss itself. For example, due to financial difficulties following a spouse's death, some widows and widowers may have to move from their homes (Wortman and Silver 1990).

Continuities over the life course—Bereavement occasions multiple, often profound changes in the lives of surviving spouses. At the same time, it is important to recognize patterns that are likely to continue over the long term. For example, although kin networks apparently shrink somewhat following spousal bereavement, the level of family interaction established prior to the spouse's death is a strong predictor of subsequent interaction (Morgan 1984a; see also Lund et al. 1990). Economic and health resources show similar patterns. John Bound and colleagues (1991) found that women's living standards declined 18 percent on average following widowhood, but the women's economic status prior to widowhood was the best predictor of their subsequent economic status. Other investigations have shown that individuals' health prior to bereavement is the strongest predictor of their health afterward (e.g., Fenwick and Barresi 1981).

In addition, many of the consequences that have been linked with spousal bereavement have shown only short-term effects. In Kenneth Ferarro's study (1985/86), respondents reported health declines immediately after bereavement, but only minimal effects persisted over the long-term (see also Fenwick and Barresi 1981; Ferraro, Mutran, and Barresi 1984). Similarly, Dimond, Lund, and Caserta (1987) found that buffering effects of social relationships on mental and physical health were limited to the first three weeks of bereavement. Other studies have found few if any long-term effects of bereavement for bereaved spouses' morale, perceived well-being, or depression (Balkwell 1985; McCrae and Costa 1993). As Robert McCrae and Paul Costa point out, this does not mean that "the loved one has been forgotten or the sense of loss does not remain" (1993:206). Rather, "individuals learn to accept their loss, and it appears widowhood ultimately ceases to have much effect on day-to-day mood and functioning" (p. 206).

Relationship with the deceased and survivor's personality—Learning to live with the loss may depend upon the nature of the marital relationship prior to the spouse's death and the personality of the surviving partner. Evidence suggests that bereaved spouses experience greater difficulties when their relationships with the deceased were characterized by ambivalence or high levels of psychological dependency (Parkes and Weiss 1983). Parkes and Weiss argue that if ambivalence and dependency are reflective of particular relationships, "they also reflect the personalities of the individuals who form those relationships" (p. 20). Such individuals may have had difficulties throughout their lives in forming satisfactory relationships. They may have greater difficulties in terminating the relationships they do form, as these relationships may be perceived as "more nearly irreplaceable" (p. 20).

Social Location and Social Groups

Some features of personal histories that have been described thus far—age at bereavement, chances for remarriage and (re)employment, and circumstances surrounding the spouse's death—are shared, at least in part, by others who share similar positions in the social structure. Membership in families and households also impact the experience of bereavement and its outcomes.

Social class—As noted earlier in this chapter, spousal bereavement increases the risks for economic problems (e.g., Smith and Zick 1986), but those in poorer groups have lower life expectancies and thus are more likely to become bereaved in the first place (Morgan 1981). Very little is known about how spousal bereavement is experienced by women and men in different social classes. In one of the few studies to do so, Colin Parkes and Robert Weiss found that respondents of poor and working-class standing "had grieved in much the same way as those of higher status" (1983:50). That is, grieving processes were not distinctive across social class groups. On the other hand, less advantaged social class standing was associated with poorer outcomes following bereavement, assessed by changes in emotional and physical health, socializing, and economics. Race was not a significant predictor of bereavement outcomes when social class was controlled.

Race and ethnicity—Most of the empirical evidence concerning spousal bereavement has come from samples of middle-class white women (Wortman and Silver 1990). Although few in number, studies of bereavement based on other racial-ethnic groups have challenged some commonly-held assumptions. For example, studies that have focused explicitly on respondents' racial-ethnic heritage challenge the assumption that bereaved spouses lack rituals to help them mourn and which help guide others' reactions to the mourning (e.g., Perry 1993; Younoszai 1993).

It is true that many societal prescriptions for mourning have disappeared over time in the United States, at least within the majority population. Earlier in the century, wakes and other postmortem rituals were common, allowing public expressions of grief (Aries 1974). Lewis Aiken argues that by the 1990s American funerals became "a rather cut-and-dried affair," characterized more by efficiency than by ritualism and the expression of grief (1991:2). However, Barbara Younoszai observes that openly emotional responses to death are expected among Mexican Americans, and that "no one is ashamed to cry and to freely express their grief" (1993:76). Hosea Perry (1993) also contends that mourning among African Americans of both genders is less formal and more emotional than among the white majority. Note that emotional responses are expected among both women and men, contrasting with traditional gender role assumptions that men are not allowed to express their emotions in public, or that men are unable or unwilling to cry openly (e.g., Glick, Weiss, and Parkes 1974).

Traditional rituals and customs to help guide mourning continue among many groups in the United States. Mexican Americans, African Americans, and Native Americans have retained distinctive funeral and mourning rituals, as have Buddhists, Muslims, Jews, and other groups (Brokenleg and Middleton 1993; Cytron 1993; Gilanshah 1993; Irish 1993; Perry 1993; Truitner and Truitner 1993; Younoszai 1993).

Responses to bereavement thus may be shaped by cultural meanings attached to death, such as whether relationships with the deceased are expected to continue in an after-life. Beecher, Madsen, and Anderson (1988) assert that the grieving process was facilitated among Mormon widows who believed in the church's teachings of eternal family relationships for the faithful. Particular religious or philosophical orientations "might lead individuals to incorporate the loss into their view of the world, and hence be protected from distress" (Wortman and Silver 1990:245; but see Stroebe and Stroebe 1993b).

Households and families—African Americans and Hispanic Americans are more likely than non-Hispanic whites to live in extended family households (Ford et al. 1990; Manuel and Reid 1982; Mutchler 1990; Wolf 1984). These patterns extend across age groups and marital statuses (i.e., married as well as unmarried persons of color are more likely to live in extended family settings compared to non-Hispanic whites). Widows and widowers of color also have more children and siblings than non-Hispanic whites (Morgan 1991; Sweet and Bumpass 1987) and, according to some studies, have greater contact with family members (Ford et al. 1990; Manuel and Reid 1982; Morgan 1984a). These patterns should not be taken to imply that minority elders "are automatically and overwhelmingly surrounded by kin" (Manuel and Reid 1982:41).

Whether due to cultural factors, economic need, or, more likely, a combination of these (see Mutran 1985), family support among African Americans seems to be less contingent on an individual's marital status compared to the informal support patterns observed among non-Hispanic whites. Elizabeth Mutran (1985) found that widow/erhood was an important predictor of family support among older whites (greater support was provided to widows and widowers than to those with living spouses), but not among older African Americans. This finding is consistent with other studies showing that older African Americans are more likely than whites to seek and receive aid from a large and varied pool of informal helpers, including not only extended family members, but also friends and neighbors (Chatters, Taylor, and Jackson 1985; Gibson 1982, 1986; Hatch 1991).

Birth Cohort

Potential cohort effects are almost never mentioned in studies of adaptation to bereavement, despite the fact that most of these works are cross-sectional and their results may well reflect such effects. An obvious cohort-related issue concerns changes in workforce experiences among married women and the impact that these changes can have on widows' economic well-being and autonomy in the future. Future cohorts of older widows will have greater labor force experience, job skills, and education, which in turn will influence their ability to retain incomes above the poverty level after their husband dies (Morgan 1991). (I explore this issue more fully in the next section, including racial-ethnic differences in widows' workforce experience and economic independence.)

Other potential cohort effects concerning bereavement processes or outcomes are less manifest. It has been suggested that today's cohorts of young men and boys are more emotionally open and expressive with other males, compared to older cohorts (see Kimmel and Messner 1989). If this is so, future cohorts of married men may be less dependent upon their wives as their primary source of emotional intimacy, eliminating the linchpin that many writers have proposed to account for widowers' risks for depression and health problems.

Risks for bereavement and birth cohorts—The likelihood of bereavement has changed for successive cohorts. Historically, the death of a spouse has been a more common experience for women than for men in the United States, but lengthening life expectancies have further increased women's risks for spousal bereavement. In 1890, the wife was the surviving spouse in 56 percent of all marriages (Mineau 1988). Today, most older women can expect to outlive their spouses, if the marriage is not terminated earlier through divorce. As of 1998, nearly one-third of American women age sixty-five to seventy-four were widowed. Slightly over one-half of women age seventy-five to eighty-four were widowed, compared to three-quarters of women age eighty-five and older (Lugaila 1998, Table 1).

For both women and men, increased life expectancies have produced a higher average age of bereavement. During the eighteenth and early nineteenth centuries, young widows and widowers were relatively common (Blom 1991). New demographic trends emerged at the beginning of the nineteenth century. Especially among the white majority, women and men began to live longer, with greater increases among women. Spousal bereavement increasingly became associated with older age, and with older women in particular (Blom 1991; Markides 1989b).

The feminization of old age has been a more recent phenomenon among racial-ethnic minorities because these groups have had higher fertility and mortality rates. For Hispanic groups, continuing immigration also has been important. These populations remain relatively "young" in comparison to the non-Hispanic white population. However, the proportion of older adults is growing in these groups, along with widening sex imbalances in favor of women (Angel and Hogan 1992; Markides 1989b).

In fact, the population of racial-ethnic minority elderly is expected to increase at a faster rate than elderly in the non-Hispanic white population (see Chapter 3). Sex ratios are expected to decline as these populations age. By the year 2000, the sex ratio is expected to drop to 56.1 for African Americans age sixty-five and older, compared to 65.3 for whites of this age group (Markides 1989b).[8] These demographic trends "will almost certainly mean more widowhood among black and Hispanic women in the near future" (Markides 1989b:99).[9]

Societal Context

The societal context for spousal bereavement has changed dramatically over the century. Demographic trends have increased the likelihood that bereavement will occur at older rather than younger ages, and have also increased the likelihood that women will undergo this experience. Economic dimensions of widowhood also have changed greatly over this period, with a general increase in widowed women's abilities to maintain independent households. In the following sections, I examine these and other factors that bear on the larger context for spousal

---

[8] Sex ratios reflect the number of men per 100 women.

[9] Racial-ethnic minorities are more likely than whites to be widow/ered. The Bureau of the Census (1996a, Table 6-2) reports that for the year 1993, rates of widowhood among "young old" women (age 65 to 74) were 34 percent for whites, 44 percent for African Americans, and 36 percent for Hispanics. Among men of this "young old" age group, rates of widowerhood were 9 percent for whites, 16 percent for African Americans, and 14 percent for Hispanics.

bereavement, focusing especially on widows' economic autonomy and well-being. I have selected this focus because economic resources are implicated in all of the dimensions of adaptation examined here.

Widows' economic autonomy—Changes in the economy and in social policies governing the family have impacted the autonomy of widowed women. These patterns have been dependent upon women's racial and social class origins. For the most part, African American women historically have been compelled to seek employment outside the home. Greater proportions of black wives have been employed compared to white wives, and also compared to immigrant women of similar socioeconomic background to themselves. An important reason for African American women's employment lies in the fact that black men earned less than other groups of men, including those who were foreign-born (Jones 1985). Consequently, black women more often have been family wage earners than other women, and less often economically dependent upon their husbands. However, women and men of all racial-ethnic groups face greater risks for poverty when they are single than when they are married; these risks are greater for women and racial-ethnic minorities (Chapter 3).

Sarah Nelson argues that Native American women also have had greater autonomy than women in "mainstream American culture" (1988:39), and that widows in Native American groups historically have suffered fewer social and economic penalties. Among these groups, matrilineal societies[10] such as the Navajo, Western Apache, and Zuni apparently have treated widowed women the most favorably. Nelson observes that despite mainstream American contact, Native American women continue to have importance, and are unlikely to be penalized economically or otherwise within their cultures when they are widowed.

The economic dependence of women in all social classes has been fostered by the legal system (e.g., protective legislation and laws designating husbands as the head of the family) and by a stratified labor market (Lopata and Brehm 1986; Smith 1987). Most women have had limited possibilities for maintaining their standard of living outside of marriage (Blom 1991). Reflecting the importance of economic factors in women's marriage patterns, widows have been less likely to remarry when they were able to maintain a satisfactory standard of living on their own (Blom 1991).

Although women continue to earn significantly less than men on average, their participation in paid labor has risen dramatically over the century. This trend is especially pronounced for white women, but is applicable to women of other racial and ethnic groups as well (Reskin and Padavic 1994). In 1900, less than 4 percent of married women were employed; that figure rose to 62 percent by 1997 (U.S. Bureau of the Census 1998, Table No. 654). Dorothy Smith (1987)

---

[10]Lineage is traced through the mother in matrilineal societies.

maintains that corporate capitalism's demand for women's labor (e.g., as clerical, sales, and service workers) has weakened the ideological and political "compact" restricting the employment of married women, hence weakening wives' dependence on husbands. In addition, the income generated by women's wage labor increasingly is required to maintain the family's standard of living (May 1987). Thus, "the relation of dependency is no longer fully viable" (Smith 1987:50).

Social policies and widowhood—The state plays a central role in defining and regulating relations of dependency. In the United States, Social Security programs (including the Old-Age, Survivors, and Disability Insurance program and the Supplemental Security Income program) and Aid to Families with Dependent Children have provided some assistance to older American widows and to mothers of minor children, who otherwise would be dependent upon family members for support. On the other hand, historical documents attest to the fact that family members with the means to provide support do not always do so. Over the years, community agencies have attempted to sue adult children for their parents' support. Some older parents themselves have filed suits against their children (see Lopata and Brehm 1986). More importantly, "poor persons usually have poor relatives" (Coll 1969:21) who are unable to support another family member.

The trend toward state and federal responsibility for the poor, along with the enactment of Social Security, has enabled more older adults to maintain autonomous households (Markides 1989b) and has helped to ease intergenerational conflicts over financial matters (Kingson, Hirshorn, and Cornman 1986). These changes have been especially consequential for widowed and other unmarried women due to their risks for poverty.

This is not to say that social policies meet the economic needs of poor widows. State and federal programs for the poor are hardly generous, reflecting a continuing American preoccupation that adequate public support will encourage indolence among the poor and increase their numbers (Katz 1989). Furthermore, although older women and widows with children have been considered "the quintessential worthy poor" (Katz 1989:67), no consistent social program has been developed to meet the needs of women who have depended upon a male breadwinner and who experience economic distress in his absence (Lopata and Brehm 1986).

Helena Lopata and Henry Brehm note that U.S. social policy has viewed widows "only as mothers and carers of surviving children or as older women deprived of the husband's earnings or social security benefits" (1986:75). For example, Aid to Families with Dependent Children was implemented to assist the mothers of young children and Social Security benefits are contingent upon the surviving spouse's age and retirement status. Younger widows are eligible for Social Security only if they have dependent children of the deceased beneficiary in their care. Social insurance programs (specifically the Supplemental Security Income program and the Old-Age, Survivors, and Disability Insurance program) are welfare programs for elderly indigent, for disabled persons of all ages, and for minor children. The needs of women who had depended upon their husbands for economic support, but who were neither elderly nor the caretakers of dependent children are not addressed. Over the years, policymakers have considered offering temporary aid to women who fell between these categories, but have failed to do so (Lopata and Brehm 1986).

It is commonly assumed that Social Security was enacted to assist older wives and widows who had not been employed, as well as labor force retirees. However, as Lopata and Brehm show, the major thrust of this legislation was to provide financial aid to older workers who retired, and in the process to create job openings for younger persons. Social Security was implemented in 1935, a time of widespread unemployment. "The welfare of older wives and older widows was not the purpose of the act, even tangentially" (Lopata and Brehm 1986:49). It was only after the Social Security program met with sustained public criticism that it was amended, in 1939, to include dependents of the beneficiary. The program subsequently has undergone numerous additional modifications, including the extension of benefits to those who divorce or remarry. (As of 1978, benefits are not reduced for women or men over the age of 60 who remarry (Lopata and Brehm 1986).) Even so, spousal benefits are not provided when marriages last less than ten years. If the primary beneficiary retires early and draws Social Security payments prior to age sixty-five, his (or her) benefits are permanently reduced, as are any spousal benefits, no matter how long a widow may outlive her husband. Furthermore, although the average age of women's widowhood in the United States is fifty-five, Social Security spousal benefits do not become available until the age of sixty. This "widow's gap" creates a period of great economic insecurity for many women (Older Women's League 1999), buttressing the contention that U.S. social policy has never been oriented to meet the needs of women who have depended upon a husband's wages, and who have been "encouraged" to do so by economic and political forces in society.

Thus, it may be misleading to claim that federal policies provide economic independence to poor widows in their later years, or to poor elders more generally. Beyond the frequently low levels of benefits which necessitate assistance from family members, family-related dependencies are reinforced by the provisions of extant programs (for example, by permanently reducing survivors' benefits if the primary beneficiary retires early, as noted above) (see Hendricks and Hatch 1993).

An Exemplar of Life Course Research

Thus far, I have reviewed research findings that illustrate differing levels of a life course perspective on spousal bereavement—widows' and widowers' personal histories, their social locations and birth cohorts, and some features of the larger social structure. Most of these findings come from studies that were not based explicitly on a life course perspective, but which offer insights that fit one or more dimensions of this perspective (for example, studies that consider aspects of bereaved spouses' personal histories, but neglect their social locations, birth cohorts, or the larger societal context for spousal bereavement).

Katherine Allen's (1989) study of older unmarried women takes into consideration key dimensions of a life course perspective. Findings concerning the women's life histories and current situations were grounded in their social location, their birth cohort, and the broader societal context. The study is of particular interest here because it examines the women's own interpretations of their experiences and accomplishments in life and their autonomy and adaptation to aging.

This qualitative study was based on American women who were born in the year 1910, and was limited to white, native-born, working-class women. These selections allowed Allen to focus on women of comparable racial-ethnic heritage and socioeconomic status, and who represent a single birth cohort. In this way, Allen was able to make systematic comparisons between women who are similar in their social location and their place in historical time, but who differed on the basis of their marital histories—those who had married and subsequently became widowed and those who had remained single throughout their lives.

From in-depth interviews with fifteen widowed and fifteen never-married women, Allen found that all of the women had maintained strong connections to their families throughout their lives. The widowed women's family careers in adulthood had focused primarily on their roles as wives and mothers. The women who never married had "fulfilled a related set of expectations for some members of their cohort and class" (p. 127), focused on providing care to a parent. According to Allen, this cohort of never-married women from working-class backgrounds "followed a life course pathway that was consistent with older familistic norms of keeping a daughter at home to care for a widowed mother or aging parent" (p. 127).

Both groups of women characterized their current situation as a time of being alone, but most valued their independence and their freedom from former responsibilities. Most of the women, both widowed and never-married, also felt that they had adjusted well to older age.

However, the widowed and never-married women differed in how they evaluated their accomplishments in life, revealing their perceptions of an "acceptable lifestyle" for women of this cohort, class, and race-ethnicity. While the widows believed that "they had experienced all that life offered," many of the never-married women felt that their lives had been "uneventful or dull," or otherwise were regretful about their lives (p. 126). Both the widows and the never-married women evaluated the roles of wife and mother as more valuable than alternative roles associated with remaining single. Furthermore, both groups of women expressed stereotypical views of women who never marry as socially "deviant," although the never-married women did not apply this label to themselves. An implication of this study is that the widows' perception of having led fulfilling and valuable lives provided them with a source of well-being in older age that was not available to women who had not married—despite the fact that the never-married women had also provided considerable caregiving to family members over their lifetimes.

Allen argues that "the findings in this study were linked to the historically essential role of spinster found in the past" (p. 133). Women of this cohort and class had few economic resources to enable them to remain single voluntarily. Rather, their life course decisions concerning whether to marry or to remain single and provide parent care were shaped by family pressures and needs.[11] Allen points out that the small size of her sample and the selection criteria she utilized necessarily limit the generalizability of her study. However, the selection criteria are also a strength of the study because the results are grounded in social and historical context. Future works can determine whether findings from Allen's study may apply to women in other social classes, racial-ethnic groups, or birth cohorts.

In this regard, it is important to point out that the rising trend toward singlehood observed among younger and mid-life women is linked more closely with their abilities to maintain themselves economically than with family pressures on women's marital decisions (Allen 1989; Sweet and Bumpass 1987). Future cohorts of older women will have had greater personal choice in whether to marry or to remain single, along with greater opportunities (and greater pressures) to participate in paid labor throughout their adult lives. To the degree that Allen's findings may extend to women of other birth cohorts and social locations, it seems reasonable to predict that fewer older women in future cohorts will evaluate their accomplishments in life primarily or exclusively on the basis of whether they fulfilled gendered expectations for marriage and motherhood.

CONCLUSION

Debates over how people adapt to the death of a spouse have often included debates over gender differences. The direction of these differences has been a subject of controversy—do men experience greater difficulties when a spouse dies, or do women fare more poorly? Debates have also arisen concerning gender differences on specific dimensions of adaptation—do widowers experience greater difficulties than widows on some dimensions, but fewer problems on others? Or are observed gender differences in adaptation to spousal bereavement

[11]Allen did not ask the never-married women about their sexual orientation. This important omission could alter her conclusions regarding the women's lack of personal choice in remaining single. It is possible that for some of these women, family pressures to remain single and provide parental care was matched with a personal preference to remain unmarried. See a subsequent article (Allen 1995) for the author's reflections on heterosexism and her own experiences.

simply an artifact of sampling, measurement, or some other methodological feature of the studies?

Although the evidence is far from conclusive, research findings for gender differences in adaptation to spousal bereavement are somewhat more convincing than those that have been reported for the broader, more nebulous area of adaptation to aging (Chapter 3). Some evidence suggests that the death of a spouse brings greater mental health problems to men than women, possibly due to men's greater reliance on their wives for social support and confiding. Many writers have proposed such patterns and interpreted them from a gender role perspective.

On the other hand, women as a group are in greater economic jeopardy than men when their spouse dies. Economic outcomes generally are not considered a specific "dimension of adaptation." However, many studies have found that income adequacy predicts health and well-being following bereavement. Explanations for women's higher risks for poverty following bereavement have drawn on gender role theory (focusing upon women's and men's differing roles in marriage), as well as elements of a structural perspective (focusing upon gender differences in earnings, work histories, and so forth).

Neither explanatory framework has been tested systematically in the large body of studies I have reviewed. The study by Debra Umberson and her colleagues (1992) represents an exception: different sources of strain, related to women's and men's "marital roles," were hypothesized to predict depression among widows and widowers (see also Lee et al. 1998). However, even in this study, respondents' gender roles were not measured, only inferred on the basis of their marital status. A partial test of the sex ratio argument also has been conducted. Robert Hong and Lawrence Duff (1994) hypothesized and found that widows were more socially active and reported greater life satisfaction when they lived in retirement communities with higher ratios of widowed to married women.

Although gender role and structural explanations for gender differences have not yet been tested systematically, the gender difference focus of both of these explanatory frameworks holds limited promise. Findings of gender differences in bereavement processes or outcomes tend to be rather modest (e.g., Gallagher et al. 1989; Gass 1989; Lund et al.1990; van Zandt, Mou, and Abbott 1989), and some studies of bereavement have not found any gender differences (e.g., Lund et al. 1986a, 1993; Stroebe and Stroebe 1993b; Thompson et al., 1989). Economic well-being following bereavement represents an exception in this regard, since most studies show substantially greater risks for poverty among widows compared to widowers. However, not all widows face equal risks for poverty, nor do all (or even most) widowers enjoy economic well-being. These features are emphasized by a life course perspective.

In this chapter and in the preceding one, I have discussed research findings which illustrate different facets of a multi-level life course model. Use of this model helps to disentangle the multiple layers of phenomena encompassed by a life course perspective; each of these facets are important in helping to understand adaptation to aging and later-life events. At the same time, such an approach oversimplifies the complexities of the perspective. For this reason, I have discussed some research exemplars of a life course approach.

In this chapter, I selected Katherine Allen's (1989) study of widowed and never-married women from the 1910 birth cohort, who share a similar social location in their social class background, race, and nationality. In her use of a life course perspective, Allen shows that normative expectations are indeed important: the women's perceptions of societal expectations for their gender impact their evaluations of their own lives. In contrast to most gender-role theorists, Allen shows that these gendered expectations, and their impact on the women's lives, must be grounded in social and historical context.

Spousal Bereavement and Aging

Spousal bereavement has been considered a major event of later life, but this experience can occur at any point in the adult life course. In fact, given the theoretical emphasis on spousal bereavement in the gerontological literature, surprisingly little empirical research has been devoted specifically to the study of bereavement in older age (see Lund et al. 1993). This pattern is changing somewhat, with an increasing number of works devoted to older widows and widowers (e.g., Burkhauser et al. 1991; Choi 1991; Heinemann and Evans 1990; Lee et al. 1998; Luborsky and Rubinstein 1990; Lund 1989a; O'Bryant 1991; Sable 1991).

Relatively few studies have made systematic comparisons among widows and widowers of varying ages. Among the better-designed works that have done so, little support is found for the assumption that bereavement is more detrimental for individuals' mental and emotional well-being when it occurs "off-time"—i.e., when it occurs at younger ages—than when it occurs "on-time" in older age (Umberson et al. 1992). I argued in Chapter 2 that the timing thesis assumes that individuals in diverse groups are subject to the same social norms. Thus, this thesis runs counter to the central insight provided by a life course approach, which stresses the importance of considering sources of diversity across space and time.

Evidence does show that the timing or age of bereavement can have critical repercussions on individuals' risks for poverty and their chances for remarriage, employment, or re-employment. For these outcomes as well, issues of timing do not operate in a social and historical vacuum. Other life course dimensions of individuals' lives also must be considered in order to understand the impact of bereavement, or any life event, beyond the age at which that event was experienced—including gender, race-ethnicity, and social class, and the intersections between these.

Parallels Between Divorce and Spousal Bereavement

Many of the problems faced by widows and widowers also are relevant for women and men who divorce (Lund 1989b). In fact, divorce has been thought to bring greater disruption and more disadvantages to individuals' lives than the termination of marriage through widowhood (e.g., Hyman 1983; Riessman and Gerstel 1985; Wan 1982). Thomas Wan (1982) contends that as a result of social stigma, less interpersonal support is offered to divorced persons than to those whose spouse dies. Naomi Gerstel (1989) agrees, pointing out that although divorced persons are no longer "statistically deviant," greater numbers do not ensure an absence of stigmatization. Beyond issues of inter-personal support, the state provides greater economic support to women whose marriage ends in the death of spouse than to those who divorce (Older Women's League 1999).

State policies and programs "make important distinctions between women in terms of whether the marriage ended by divorce or death of the spouse" (Morgan 1991:13). Although economic supports afforded to widows have "many flaws and loopholes" (Morgan 1991:13), widows have been perceived as justifiably needy since their marriages were terminated through no fault of their own. Divorce has been assumed to represent a voluntary ending to marriage, and fewer economic supports have been made available through the state to divorced women (Lopata and Brehm 1986). Policy changes such as no-fault divorce have not improved the economic position of divorced women (Arendell 1987).[12]

Similar patterns of gender differences have been posited for both divorce and spousal bereavement. That is, while divorced women are at greater risk for economic deprivation (e.g., Morgan 1991), divorced men are thought to face greater problems in the areas of health and social relationships (e.g., Goldscheider 1990; Hyman 1983; Spanier and Thompson 1984). Kris Bulcroft and Richard Bulcroft (1991) found that although divorce had negative effects on older parents' contacts with their adult children, these effects were stronger for men than for women. The timing of divorce was also important: men who divorced when their children were younger had the lowest rates of parent-child interaction when their children were grown.

It is possible that the long-term effects of divorce reported by Bulcroft and Bulcroft may be even more pronounced among future cohorts. Although joint custody has become more common (about ten percent of divorcing couples share custody) (Teachman 1991), women continue to be far more likely than men to have custody of children. Older cohorts in the future will be more likely to have experienced divorce during their lifetimes, whether in their younger years, at mid-life, or in older age.

---

[12]Terry Arendell points out that "the legal implementation of divorce favors men in both community-property and common-law states" (1987:131).

To date, divorce among older adults has been uncommon, a pattern which is expected to change in the near future. Cohorts who will reach retirement age in the twenty-first century have been on the forefront of massive social changes, taking part "in the rapid growth of labor force participation among women, the tremendous rise in divorce and in childbearing out of marriage, and the overall decline in marriage and remarriage" (Goldscheider 1990:531). Divorce rates consequently are expected to rise *within* the older population, following the trends already observed among younger and mid-life groups. Furthermore, more women and men will *enter* older age as unmarried persons due to divorce, the death of a spouse, or lifelong singlehood (Markides 1989b; Uhlenberg, Cooney, and Boyd 1990).

These trends have particular significance for older divorced and widow/ered persons who are less likely to remarry and consequently are at increased risk for poverty. Older women are less likely to remarry than older men, and older persons of color are less likely to do so than older whites. Older women of color have the lowest rates of remarriage and the greatest risks for poverty (Morgan 1991; Uhlenberg et al. 1990). Trends toward higher rates of divorce within the older population and lower rates of remarriage almost certainly mean that members of these groups will face greater risks for poverty in the future than they do now.

What of Other Types of Intimate Relationships?

The study of how men and women respond to the loss of an intimate relationship—whether through death or divorce—has focused upon heterosexual relationships. If divorced women and men are afforded less social support than widows and widowers, partners in same-sex couples encounter even greater challenges. Gay and lesbian communities can provide a critical source of support (e.g., Friend 1990), but the termination (or existence) of a committed homosexual relationship may not be acknowledged in the wider community. Furthermore, surviving same-sex partners may encounter conflict with the deceased partner's family.

> "If I was effectively nonexistent to them before," one surviving mate said, "I really vanished after my partner died. For years, they denied our commitment to each other; now they acted as if they could completely erase me! They claimed everything: the body, our home, and seemingly, my right to grieve." (DeSpelder and Strickland 1992:323)

The lack of institutionalized support compounds the difficulties faced by surviving same-sex partners. Although there are serious shortcomings in Social Security benefit levels and eligibility criteria for surviving spouses who were married—and although divorced partners receive fewer benefits compared to those who lose a spouse through death—no benefits are available for surviving partners in homosexual relationships. Other benefits routinely extended to heterosexual married couples are anything but routine for same-sex couples, including the ability to make health-care and end-of-life decisions for ill partners. These issues will grow even more salient with the continued aging of the population.

CHAPTER
5

Adaptation to Retirement

The dominant view of retirement from paid labor has been that it is a stressful, problematic experience, especially for men. Retirement continues to be viewed as a "major life transition" and a "stressor," requiring social and psychological adjustment (e.g., Gradman 1994; Richardson and Kilty 1991; Sagy and Antonovsky 1992; Solomon and Szwabo 1994). However, the bulk of empirical studies on this topic shows that retirement in itself does not bring poor health or decreased well-being to most retirees.

In contrast to the literatures I have reviewed thus far, research on retirement shows a temporal pattern in the gender difference arguments that have been made. From the 1950s through 1970s, most scholars viewed retirement as problematic for men's adaptation but not for women's. Feminist scholars objected to the assumption that women's paid work and retirement were unimportant, and beginning in the 1970s works were published which took the opposite point of view—that women resisted retirement more than men and experienced greater difficulties in adapting to retired life. Due to a lack of evidence for deleterious consequences of retirement, the question of "which gender suffers more" in retirement receded in the research literature by the late 1980s/early 90s (but has not disappeared altogether from the research scene). Subsequent gender difference research has focused more on the reasons why women and men retire and how gendered pathways to retirement may be linked with problems of adaptation.

This chapter examines how and why retirement has been viewed in gendered terms, and explores how this experience can be placed in life course perspective. A continuing gender role theme is evident in the retirement literature, despite the fact that diverse arguments concerning gender differences have been made over the years. Structural arguments focusing on differences in women's and men's retirement incomes and access to pensions also are prominent, however. Consistent with the previous chapters, I argue that a gender difference focus overlooks important sources of variation in women's and men's retirement, and that a life course perspective provides an effective framework to investigate sources of similarity as well as difference in women's and men's pathways to retirement and subsequent experiences.

In the following section, I examine the gender difference arguments that have been made concerning adaptation to retirement. Retirement adaptation is a broad concept, encompassing individuals' attitudes toward retirement and retired life as well as their social relationships, health, and emotional well-being as retirees.

EXPLANATIONS FOR GENDER DIFFERENCES IN ADAPTATION TO RETIREMENT

A large portion of the retirement picture portrays retirement as a more difficult experience for men than for women. Many writers have argued that men are more reluctant to retire than women, that they are less satisfied with their lives in retirement, and that men's retirement eventuates in mental and physical health problems, if not premature death. These arguments were made most vigorously and pervasively during the 1950s through 1970s, but variations on this theme continue to emerge in contemporary writings (e.g., Gradman 1994; Solomon and Szwabo 1994).

Gender Role Explanations

Men Suffer More

Although some early writers believed that gender differences in retirement attitudes and adjustment were due in part to differential labor force experiences (Kutner et al. 1956; Lehr and Dreher 1969), most assumed that men and women would experience retirement differently and would hold different attitudes toward retirement due to salient characteristics of the male and female primary roles. Early studies of retirement concluded that the withdrawal from working life brings about a serious crisis for men due to the male's traditional role as breadwinner (Beck 1982; Lehr and Dreher 1969). Ralph Turner (1970) is representative of these writers when he states,

> In American society it is well-nigh impossible to be a man without having an occupation, and how much of a man and what kind of a man one is are to be measured largely by the nature of the occupation and the success with which it is pursued (1970:255).

According to this reasoning, the work role is critical to a man because it is the major source of influence on his self-identity (Cavan 1962). Occupations tie men to the larger social structure and place them in status hierarchies in the larger society and in their communities (Parsons 1954). Occupations also link men to their family roles of husband and father due to their activities as economic providers (Turner 1970). Withdrawal from the labor force is thus seen as a severe loss for a man since his identity and his status are defined by work.

The loss of men's worker role was thought to be greatly exacerbated by the fact that society has not clearly defined the parameters for the role of retiree. Writing in 1960, Donahue, Orbach, and Pollak contrast retirement with other role changes an individual typically undergoes. They claim that many other stages of social life are delineated by fairly clear social rules and behavioral expectations, and provide gradual transitions with formal and informal preparation for other new roles. This is not true for retirement. Retirement, they say, is a new form of social life that has yet to achieve any specific institutional integration. The "challenge of retirement" for contemporary society is

> to successfully create and clearly define a meaningful social role for the retired which will provide the individual with a sense of function and value and to integrate this role into the fabric of our industrial civilization (Donahue et al. 1960: 336).

Problems of ambiguity and lack of clarity characterizing the (male) retirement role have been cited by various writers since the 1950s (Blau 1973; Burgess 1960; Kroeger 1982; Parsons 1954; Sheppard 1976). Role ambiguity has been linked to negative retirement attitudes and to poor adjustment on the part of the male retiree, who is likely to be beset by feelings of insecurity, loneliness, and uselessness (Blau 1973; Bradford 1979; Burgess 1960; Parsons 1954).

Thus, the general consensus in the early retirement literature was that the average, healthy, American male will perceive retirement as aversive and hence will resist it because of the meanings retirement has acquired for men in western societies. Retirement deprives a man of the status and identity which are integral parts of the male role. Further, there are no clear-cut expectations available for the retirement role that may replace those of the worker role.

Men's occupational status and commitment to work—The negative consequences early writers associated with retirement were said to be more profound for men with a strong commitment to work (see Atchley 1971). Greater identification with the work role was assumed to produce greater resistance to retirement and poorer adjustment to it (Donahue et al. 1960; Fillenbaum 1971). A distinction was made by some writers, however, between commitment to work based on *intrinsic* versus *extrinsic* attributes of the job. Men who stress intrinsic rewards of work such as identity and self-esteem were thought to fare more poorly than men who stress the extrinsic rewards of status and prestige (see Quadagno 1978). Men in higher-status occupations (i.e., professional and upper white-collar workers) were expected to develop a strong commitment to work and to stress intrinsic meanings of their work. These men were therefore also expected to show greater resistance to retirement than men in lower-status occupations, who presumably had lower work commitment.

Women's roles—The distinctions researchers made between men of varying occupational statuses and work commitments are not nearly as sharp as those made between men and women. According to many early writers, retirement is not important for women because paid employment has little significance for them (Blau 1973; Cavan 1962; Cumming and Henry 1961; Donahue et al. 1960; Lowenthal, Thurnher, and Chiriboga 1976; Palmore 1965). A statement made by Cumming and Henry (1961:144) underscores this assumption:

> Retirement is not an important problem for women because . . . working seems to make little difference to them. It is as though they add work to their lives, the way they would add a club membership.

Women were expected to work only temporarily and to willingly give up work in the labor force so they could return full-time to their family roles (Donahue et al. 1960; Palmore 1965). Whereas retirement deprives men of their central source of identity and self-esteem and offers instead an ambiguous role devoid of meaning, it has been thought to have little impact on women because society offers them an equally acceptable, if not more acceptable, role in the position of full-time housewife (see Hatch 1987; Szinovacz 1982a).

Also, in contrast to the abrupt changes that retirement brings to a man (Blau 1973), this transition is considered to be more gradual for a woman, "cushioned by the necessity to continue with her household routine and accustomed responsibilities" (Heyman and Jeffers 1968:488). Although women have usually already experienced a type of retirement with regard to their familial roles when the children leave home, their household duties, albeit reduced in scope, still continue. Women's roles have been thought to remain essentially unchanged from girlhood to death (Cumming and Henry 1961) and this continuity, according to early writers, makes retirement from the labor force easier for them. Retirement from paid labor therefore does not result in a loss of self-identity for women. It also does not result in a loss of status for women since they can continue to perform their "primary" roles and since they derive social status from their husbands (Parsons 1954). Thus, women were thought to hold positive or neutral views toward retirement and to be affected minimally, if at all, by withdrawal from work in the labor force.

Although the early retirement literature did not make distinctions among women based on their occupational status and commitment to work (see Price-Bonham and Johnson 1982), some writers distinguished between women who had careers and those who did not (Cumming and Henry 1961; Palmore 1965; Gysbers, Johnston, and Gust 1968). Erdman Palmore notes that career women "to whom work is more important than any other role" represent an exception to the basic principle that the roles of wife, mother, and housewife are women's primary roles (1965:7). In addition, the paid work role was considered to be more important for women who did not, in fact, occupy the roles of wife or mother (Palmore

1965). Based on their review of literature, Keating and Jeffrey (1983) stated that most women who were approaching retirement age viewed paid work primarily as a means to fill the time before leaving their family of orientation and entering a family of procreation. "For some, this gap became a lifelong pattern, and the never married spinster was then expected to commit herself seriously to work in lieu of a family" (p. 417). However, the case of the noncareer, married woman was implicitly assumed in early arguments concerning how women and men are differentially affected by retirement.

Traditional gender roles: A continuing theme—The dominance of structural-functionalism in the 1950s and 60s helps to explain the emphasis on men's breadwinning roles and women's family roles in the retirement literature. As I discussed in Chapter 2, functionalists have contended that a gendered division of labor, both within and outside the home, promotes the smooth functioning of families as well as the larger society. Women's lower rates of labor force participation compared to those of men have been used to buttress this argument (e.g., Palmore 1965), overlooking the fact that high proportions of poor and working-class women have always been employed (Jones 1985; Kessler-Harris 1981).

This argument is made far less frequently in contemporary writings, but has not disappeared altogether. In their study of retirement attitudes in Israel, Aaron Antonovsky and colleagues wonder whether women may hold more positive attitudes toward retirement than men because "work is relatively less significant in their lives" (Antonovsky et al. 1990:62). On the other hand, these authors posit that employment may be as significant for older women as for men because most of these women "no longer had a major household and mother role" (p. 62). Each of these alternative conjectures revolve around the assumption of women's and men's separate spheres in family and paid work. The authors cite cultural and historical factors as reasons why paid work is not a central role for Israeli women, even though their rates of labor force participation have increased greatly in recent years. Conceding that the presumed lower significance of paid work for women has not been substantiated, the authors conclude ultimately that no clear hypothesis regarding gender and retirement attitudes can be formulated.

Other retirement researchers have not claimed that paid work is less important for women than men, but echo earlier writers' views that women's roles make retirement an easier experience for them (e.g., Aiken 1989; Elwell and Maltbie-Crannell 1981; Palmore, Fillenbaum, and George 1984). Continuity of women's family and household roles is often cited. A related argument, discussed in Chapter 3, is that women experience a number of roles and transitions throughout their lives, which provides them with greater role flexibility and ultimately a smoother adjustment to retirement and other life changes (e.g., Kline 1975; Markson 1995; Stevens 1995).

Women Suffer More

Beginning in the 1970s, feminist concerns were reflected in critiques of the retirement literature (Gratton and Haug 1983). Though the contention that men suffer more from retirement has continued to emerge in the literature, retirement scholars began to make the opposite argument more frequently. Many took issue with the claim that work and retirement are important for men but not for women (Atchley 1976a; Block 1982; Fox 1977; Jaslow 1976; Newman, Sherman, and Higgins 1982; Szinovacz 1982a). However, some of the same writers who objected to the assumption that paid work is central for men's identity and well-being, but not for women's, seemed to overlook the fact that these assumptions had not been substantiated for men (Gratton and Haug 1983). Furthermore, these investigations were based upon a "male model" of retirement (see Calasanti 1996), utilizing factors which predicted (white, middle-class) men's retirement more adequately than women's retirement.

Also interesting is the fact that traditional gender roles continued to be invoked to explain why women should have greater retirement-related problems than men. Several of these gender role explanations rest on the assumption that women are more expressive and sociable than men. For example, the loss of contacts with co-workers was seen as a greater problem for women than for men "since women's emotional well-being seems to be more contingent than men's on the maintenance of social contacts outside the family" (Szinovacz 1982a:19). From this view, women resist retirement because they do not wish to terminate social relationships afforded by the workplace (Martin Matthews and Brown 1988; Szinovacz 1982a, 1983). Along these lines, Maximiliane Szinovacz (1983:111-112) suggests that women's disadvantages in retirement include the fact that they "often lack socialization for leisure activities and depend more on social contacts than men." A related explanation, based on the assumption of gender differences in expressiveness, is that "women are more expressive of their discontent" (Johnson and Williamson 1980:80). Elizabeth Johnson and John Williamson propose that although women and men "suffer equally from retirement," women are more likely to voice their suffering (p. 80).

These authors also propose an interesting twist to the argument that men's identity and self-esteem suffer when they take on the "roleless role" of retirement, suggesting that women, not men, are more vulnerable on this score. In their words, "because of the lesser importance attached by society to the work role for women, women who retire may experience confusion over who they are or were" (Johnson and Williamson 1980:71). Thus, gender role explanations have been used regardless of the direction of reported (or presumed) gender differences in retirement.

Resource Explanations

Women Suffer More

What of social structural influences on women's and men's orientations to retirement and adaptation to retired life? Most frequently noted are gender differences in pension availability and income (Atchley 1982; Block 1982; Hatch 1987; Jaslow 1976; Seccombe and Lee 1986; Slevin and Wingrove 1995), which are expected to promote less favorable orientations toward retirement among women. As a group, women are less likely than men to work in jobs and industries offering pension benefits. Due to absences from the labor force earlier in the life course, women who do have access to private pension programs often must work longer than men to be vested (Schulz 1995). More generally, women, as a group, have greater vulnerability than men to economic problems in retirement, especially those who are not married (Burkhauser 1994; Older Women's League 1999), and for this reason can be expected to look less favorably upon retirement and to experience greater problems in retired life.

Many writers who stress the importance of economic resources for retirement adaptation also stress women's and men's choices in paid work and family life (e.g., Jaslow 1976; Keith 1982), which have cumulative effects on their incomes in retirement. Gender role socialization often provides an implicit explanation for such "choices," thus linking the resource and gender role arguments. Simply put, valuing family roles over employment translates into economic vulnerabilities for women in retirement (e.g., Jaslow 1976). Other retirement scholars take a more explicitly structural approach to the issue, citing constraints on individuals' work and family decisions (Keith 1982) or factors beyond individuals' decision-making (such as gendered biases structured into public and private pension programs) (Arendell and Estes 1991; Harrington Meyer 1990, 1996; Quadagno 1988), which impact women's and men's economic status in retirement.

EVALUATING ADAPTATION TO RETIREMENT

I turn now from theoretical discussions of gender differences in retirement adaptation to empirical studies on this topic. Evaluation of this body of research is complicated by conceptual and methodological limitations of retirement studies, which are reviewed below. In particular, the ability to make comparisons across the studies is limited by the use of differing definitions of retirement, many of which are problematic assessments of women's retirement (also reviewed in Hatch 1998).

Measures of Retirement and the Exclusion of Women

Sampling Biases

Until the 1980s, few studies of retirement made empirical comparisons between women and men. Most studies of retirement were based on samples of men (Hatch 1987; Szinovacz 1982a). During the 1950s through 1970s, most retirement researchers did not address this limitation, and probably did not perceive it to be a problem. Some writers justified women's exclusion by averring that retirement was not a common experience for them, or that it was not an important experience for women (see Hatch 1987; Szinovacz 1986/87). The latter justification has been applied especially to married women. For example, the longitudinal Retirement History Study, conducted from 1969 through 1979, included unmarried women but explicitly excluded married women. According to Lola Irelan, preliminary field interviews "made it clear that for most women of this generation 'retirement' has little meaning apart from their husbands' stopping work" (1972:6). No information was provided to document the unimportance of retirement for married women beyond this statement. In fact, results from other studies do not support this notion, including studies conducted contemporaneously to the Retirement History Study (e.g., Streib and Schneider 1971).

Measurement Biases

The predominance of all-male samples also has been linked to the problem of operationalizing occupational retirement for women (Connidis 1986; Fox 1977). In everyday usage, retirement has implied the cessation of paid work after a lifetime of labor force participation (Donahue et al. 1960), but how long and how continuously must one have worked to be able to "retire?" Some studies have required respondents to have been employed throughout their adult lives in order to be classified as retired (see Donahue et al. 1960), a criterion that excludes many women. In other studies, the range of labor force history is so broad that the criterion is rendered virtually meaningless (Connidis 1986). For example, Philip Jaslow (1976) classified any woman as "retired" who was not currently in the labor force, but who had been employed for five or more years since the age of twenty-one. Thus, a woman who had been employed only between the ages of twenty-two and twenty-seven would be categorized as a labor force retiree. An even more extreme example is Majda Thurnher's (1974) category of "pre-retired" respondents, which included all women—regardless of their own employment histories—who were married to "pre-retired" men (see also Connidis 1986).

In addition to labor force history, other "objective" measures of retirement also are poor or biased reflections of women's retirement (see Hatch 1998). Measuring retirement as the complete withdrawal from labor force activity affects women's rates more than men's rates, because women are more likely to work part-time (Schulz 1995). Eligibility for private pensions also is a problematic criterion for retirement, since women are less often eligible for such pensions and are also less likely to work in jobs and industries offering employer-provided pension benefits (Arendell and Estes 1991).

Since most women and men who have been employed are eligible for Social Security benefits, receipt of income from this source may seem to be a reasonable measure of retirement (Holden 1989). However, women who are eligible for either spousal or earnings-related Social Security benefits typically take the former. (Although spousal benefits are only one-half those allocated to the primary earner, this one-half benefit has been higher than the benefits many women would obtain from their own earnings records) (Quadagno 1999; Schulz 1995). Thus, measuring retirement by the receipt of earnings-related Social Security benefits would exclude most married women, as well as many widowed and divorced women.

Additional problems associated with using Social Security benefits as a retirement criterion include the fact that labor force participation may have ceased many years before Social Security benefits are received. On the other hand, benefits may be received while individuals continue to be employed. Furthermore, some types of paid work are not always included in Social Security calculations. For example, domestic workers—almost all of whom are women—have been included in the Social Security program since 1951 (Rollins 1985). However, "employers and domestics both avoid paying 5.85 percent of domestic's wages that would be their share of the tax" (Rollins 1985:56). This problem is exacerbated when workers are not paid the legally mandated minimum wage—"most prevalent in the South and in situations involving immigrant workers" (p. 56) (see also Angel and Angel 1996; Hogan, Kim, and Perrucci 1997). Under these conditions, workers are unable to accumulate credits toward Social Security benefits, and thus are vulnerable to extreme poverty in retirement.

Self-identification of retirement status avoids these measurement problems because it allows individuals to report whether or not they consider themselves retired. This criterion has been widely used in the retirement literature (e.g., Beck 1983; Block 1982; Ekerdt, Bossé, and Levkoff 1985; Fox 1977). However, research suggests that retirement has different meanings across gender groups, calling into question the generalizability of this measure as well. Using data from the Retirement History Study, I found that a substantial proportion of older women who reported themselves as "workers" when they were employed did not subsequently view themselves as "retired" when they were no longer employed. Instead, they identified themselves as "keeping house," even though they were no longer married or had never been married, and even though most of them lived alone (Hatch 1992). Findings from Ingrid Connidis' study (1986) suggest that older women's self-defined status reflects their work histories. Connidis found that women are more likely to consider themselves as retirees rather than homemakers when they have been employed for longer periods, when they have been employed later in life, and when they have worked in full-time rather than part-time jobs (see also Szinovacz and DeViney 1999).

Other Methodological Limitations of Studies Comparing Women and Men

In addition to measurement difficulties, studies of gender differences in retirement often suffer from other methodological problems. Many have been based on small samples (Jewson 1982; Kutner et al. 1956; Lowenthal et al. 1976; Quadagno 1978; Thurnher 1974; Tuckman and Lorge 1953), nonrandomly selected samples (Jewson 1982; Tuckman and Lorge 1953), or samples not considered representative of workers or retirees in the population (Crook and Heinstein 1958; Jewson 1982; Keith 1982; Kutner et al. 1956; Levy 1978, 1980/81; Lowenthal et al. 1976; Thurnher 1974).

A more serious methodological problem for studies of potential gender differences is the use of noncomparable subsamples of women and men. Many of the researchers who have reported gender differences in retirement attitudes and adaptation have compared groups of women and men who differ on many dimensions in addition to gender, including their occupational status, income, age, marital status, labor force history, and length of time since retirement (e.g, Jacobson 1974; Kutner et al. 1956; Lowenthal et al. 1976; Newman et al. 1982; Streib and Schneider 1971; Thurnher 1974; Tuckman and Lorge 1953). Because these characteristics are correlated with measures of retirement adaptation (Atchley 1982; Atchley and Robinson 1982; Barfield and Morgan 1978; Beck 1982; Fillenbaum, George and Palmore 1985; Friedmann and Orbach 1974; Palmore et al. 1985), their effects must be taken into consideration before conclusions regarding gender differences can be reached. However, early studies of retirement that included samples of women seldom considered potentially spurious associations between gender and retirement responses. Some of the recent studies also have implemented rather limited statistical controls for alternative causes of gender differences.

"Male" and "Female" Models of Retirement

A related issue concerns the choice of independent variables to include in studies of retirement. When separate analyses have been performed for female and male subsamples, fewer variables have been found to predict the antecedents and outcomes of women's retirement compared to men's retirement. Such discrepancies have been attributed to a continuing reliance on male models of retirement (Calasanti 1996; George, Fillenbaum, and Palmore 1984; Gratton and Haug 1983; Martin Matthews and Brown 1988; Palmore et al. 1985; Szinovacz 1982a). An alternative "female model" has yet to be identified, but measures of family responsibilities and social involvements have been proposed as potentially important for understanding women's retirement. I return to this issue shortly in evaluating gendered pathways to retirement.

ADAPTATION TO RETIREMENT AND THE EMPIRICAL RECORD ON GENDER DIFFERENCES

How does retirement impact the adaptation of older adults? Many of the dimensions used to assess adaptation to retirement are parallel to those discussed in previous chapters—social relationships, mental health and coping, physical health and mortality. In addition, attitudes toward retirement and satisfaction with life in retirement have been utilized as measures of retirement adaptation (e.g., Block 1982; Calasanti 1996; Donahue et al. 1960; Seccombe and Lee 1986; Shanas 1970). The retirement literature reflects a hazy distinction between measures which focus specifically on adaptation to retirement and those which assess subjective well-being more broadly. Measures of adaptation to retirement have included whether retirement is viewed in positive or negative terms (e.g., Atchley 1976a, 1982; Barfield and Morgan 1978; Goudy et al. 1980; Jewson 1982; Kerckhoff 1966; Skoglund 1980); respondents' evaluations of retired life (Glamser 1981; McGee, Hall, and Lutes-Dunckley 1979; Seccombe and Lee 1986; Thompson 1958); and measures of life satisfaction, happiness, and morale (Beck 1982; Calasanti 1996; Dorfman, Kohout, and Heckert 1985; Martin Matthews and Brown 1988; Riddick 1982; Szinovacz 1982b; Thompson, Streib, and Kosa 1960), which may or may not focus on satisfaction with life *in retirement*, or satisfaction with life more broadly.

The following discussion examines these dimensions of adaptation to retirement, as well as studies of social relationships, health, and mortality following retirement. Due to the difficulties of disentangling retirement attitudes from life satisfaction in retirement and other elements of subjective well-being, these dimensions are examined together in a separate section.

Social Relationships

Studies to date indicate that intimate relationships and levels of social activity do not change substantially following retirement (Anderson 1992; Atchley 1992; Ekerdt and Vinick 1991; Keith, Wacker, and Schafer 1992; Lee and Shehan 1989; Palmore et al. 1985; Vinick and Ekerdt 1992; Wan and Odell 1983). This conclusion contrasts with expectations held by researchers and retirees alike that social relationships will change following retirement. Some writers have contended that retirees reduce their levels of social participation, either because of role changes or because of factors associated with retirement such as changes in income or health (Bradford 1979; Cumming and Henry 1961); others have suggested that retirement may enhance social relationships (see Wan and Odell 1983). A third group of writers has argued that retirees substitute work-based ties with other types of social contacts to maintain participation levels comparable to those experienced prior to retirement (see Kosloski, Ginsburg, and Backman 1984).

Most studies finding significant differences between workers and retirees in their levels of social participation have been cross-sectional in design. Using data from several longitudinal data sets, Erdman Palmore and his colleagues (1985) found few significant changes in social activity following retirement, and these effects were small in magnitude. Patterns established prior to retirement apparently have far greater influence on levels of social participation than the experience of retirement itself (Palmore et al. 1985; see also Wan and Odell 1983).

Retirees themselves anticipate that the leisure time afforded by retirement will bring significant changes in their relationships and activities. For example, married couples in Barbara Vinick and David Ekerdt's cross-sectional study (1992) anticipated that they would share more leisure activities together following retirement. However, couples who had already retired reported virtually no change in companionate activities. Married women who were still working also expected that retirement would bring a more egalitarian division of household labor, but married women who had retired continued to perform most of the household work. Other studies using quantitative methods have also failed to find significant effects of retirement on marital satisfaction (Atchley 1992; Lee and Shehan 1989), emotional support and confiding within marriage (Anderson 1992), marital complaints (Ekerdt and Vinick 1991), or perceptions of equity among spouses (Keith et al. 1992).

Robert Atchley's (1992) qualitative study of retirement and marital satisfaction generally supports the quantitative studies cited above: most spouses in his sample felt that their marital relationships had not changed as a result of retirement. However, as the following examples show, some spouses reported positive shifts in their marriages following retirement, while others felt that their relationships had suffered (pp. 153-155):

> We have more time together, more pursuing of mutual interests, more *loving*. (woman, age 64)

> I did not believe it was possible, but retirement has enhanced our marriage. We spend much more time together, have more time to share, more time to *do* for each other. (man, age 63)

> I found it to be more confusing, being with my husband 24 hours a day and giving up much of my privacy and quiet times. There are more meals to cook and more housework. (woman, age 66)

Since I retired, what I expect of my wife is sometimes unrealistic. I do not communicate with her like I should. When she comes home from work, I expect her to go places with me—places I want to go. (man, age 68)

Thus, although retirement is unlikely to bring drastic alterations in marital relationships, changes nonetheless can occur. Further research is needed to investigate the subtle ways in which retirement can affect social relationships. Research also is needed to examine the impact of retirement on intimate ties beyond the marital dyad.

Retirement can bring other life changes, which in turn can affect retirees' social networks and interaction (Brubaker and Brubaker 1992). For example, retirees with inadequate incomes are less likely to own or use automobiles, which in turn predicts lower levels of social participation (Atchley, Pignatiello, and Shaw 1979). In general, greater financial resources enable older persons to participate in a wider variety of social activities. In addition, social relationships will undergo change when older persons move to a different community after they retire. Retirees often move to places where they have friends or family; these relationships can be renewed or intensified (Cuba 1992).

Gender Differences

Although other bodies of literature reviewed in this book have emphasized that men are more vulnerable than women to social losses with aging, this argument is not prominent in the retirement literature—perhaps because it is assumed that retired men are married and hence retain the social and emotional support provided by their wives. Rather, arguments have been made that women attach greater importance to their workplace friendships than men do, and that women consequently resist retirement.

A study which has been cited as evidence for women's greater reluctance to leave their workplace friendships is Sandra Candy's article "What Do Women Use Friends For?" (1977) (e.g., Martin Matthews and Brown 1988; Szinovacz 1982a, 1983). This research could not possibly evaluate whether women were more reluctant to leave their co-workers than men: the study did not examine older workers, nor did it include a comparison group of men. My own study of retirement among unmarried women and men, based on data from the Retirement History Study, found that never married *men*, not women, expressed stronger reluctance to retire and leave their co-workers (Hatch 1992).

Health and Mortality

According to many of the early writers, men resist retirement and suffer ill effects from it because the work role is integral to male self-identity and status. The presumed negative effects of retirement on mental health and self-esteem, physical health, and mortality have not been substantiated for any cohort of retired men, although poor health may encourage or compel retirement (Bossé et al. 1991; Martin and Doran 1966; Parnes and Nestel 1981; Reitzes et al. 1996; Shanas 1970; Streib and Schneider 1971; Thompson and Streib 1958; Thompson et al. 1960). Nor have ill effects of retirement been substantiated for women's mental or physical health (Reitzes et al. 1996; Streib and Schneider 1971; Wan 1984), although this body of research is less extensive. The "crisis of retirement" has not been documented even for those who were strongly committed to their work (Atchley 1971; Bell 1978/1979; Fillenbaum 1971; Glamser 1976; Goudy, Powers, and Keith 1975; McGee et al. 1979). In fact, commitment to work is largely unrelated to retirement adaptation (Bell 1978/79; Glamser 1976, 1981; McGee et al. 1979).

Retirement Attitudes and Satisfaction

Studies also have shown that most workers do not resist retirement. Overall, older adults hold positive attitudes toward retirement, look forward to it, and report satisfaction with their lives following retirement (Atchley 1982; Beck 1982; Elwell and Maltbie-Crannell 1981; George et al. 1984; Gratton and Haug 1983; Jewson 1982; Parnes and Nestel 1981; Shanas 1970). Further contradicting claims that men—or women—abhor retirement, older workers often retire early when there are economic incentives to do so (Ruhm 1989; Schulz 1995).

Gender Differences

Most studies have found that both women and men hold generally positive attitudes toward retirement and are satisfied with retired life. Questions of gender differences arise with respect to relative differences between the groups. A range of studies have reported gender differences in retirement attitudes and adaptation, but many of these have been based on bivariate analyses, or have included rather limited control variables in the analyses. Some studies have found poorer retirement attitudes and satisfaction on the part of women (e.g., Barfield and Morgan 1978; Jacobson 1974; Newman et al. 1982); others have reported the reverse (e.g., Atchley 1982; Jewson 1982).

Other studies have not found gender differences. For example, Jill Quadagno (1978) examined groups of women and men with comparable labor force histories. Her sample was very small ($N = 20$ men and 20 women), but all respondents belonged to a single occupational category (that of physician), and all had similar patterns of labor force participation. The women did not have more career interruptions than the men, and although the women had spent longer periods of time away from work, this difference was small. No gender differences were found in either attitudes toward work or attitudes toward retirement. Using data from a larger, national sample of unmarried older adults (Hatch 1992), I found that gender differences in retirement attitudes were no longer significant when controls were introduced for variables including income, pension coverage, occupational status, and labor force history.

Similar patterns have been reported for retirement satisfaction. When Karen Seccombe and Gary Lee (1986) analyzed their data at the bivariate level, they found that women were less satisfied with retirement than men. The gender difference disappeared when controls for health, income, and marital status were introduced in the analyses. Richardson and Kilty (1991) also reported a lack of gender differences in retirees' well-being and morale when income, education, and occupational status was controlled. These findings lead to the conclusion that when women's material situations are less advantageous, they may be expected to anticipate retirement in less favorable terms, and to report greater problems following retirement. These conclusions are consistent with a resource explanation for gender differences.

In contrast, Toni Calasanti (1996) found higher life satisfaction in retirement among women rather than men. Gender differences in life satisfaction persisted following the introduction of controls for income, health, education, and marital status. Calasanti contends that these variables are more relevant to men's adjustment processes than to women's, explaining why the coefficient for gender remained significant in the multivariate analyses. In other words, variables drawn from the "male model" of retirement were unable to account for the effects of gender on life satisfaction. (Other researchers also have reported that fewer of these "male model" variables predict women's retirement than men's retirement (Martin Matthews and Brown 1988; Palmore et al. 1985).) In addition, statistical tests showed that the variables included in the analyses exerted different effects for the subsample of women compared to the subsample of men.[1]

I agree entirely that additional factors must be identified to specify retirement processes and outcomes for differing groups. However, other retirement studies I have reviewed here found that gender differences were not significant when health, income, and other "male model" variables were included in the analyses. These findings suggest that differences in women's and men's socioeconomic resources "explain" the gender differences observed for some retirement outcomes, at least at a broad level. This conclusion does not exclude the need to consider additional factors to understand the retirement of differing groups. It is not only the case that a male model of retirement may misspecify women's retirement. Not all men fit a male model of retirement either, an issue I explore further in discussing a life course approach.

---

[1] A significant interaction was found between gender and marital status, reflecting greater life satisfaction on the part of married men. In addition, results from the Chow test "revealed that gender significantly differentiates the process of life satisfaction in retirement" (Calasanti 1996:S27). The Chow test assesses whether sets of coefficients included in regression models differ significantly from one another.

Evaluating the Empirical Record

Structural explanations focusing on gender differences in retirement resources invariably have been applied *post hoc*, and thus have not been tested rigorously. However, gender role explanations are even further from empirical verification. Despite continuing scholarly arguments that men's occupations are central to their identities and well-being (e.g., Gradman 1994; Solomon and Szwabo 1994), a great deal of evidence shows that retirement, in itself, is not detrimental to men's health and well-being. Nor is there any compelling evidence for the contention that retirement is easier for women than men because they experience greater role continuity over their lifetimes, or because they have greater flexibility in adapting to different roles (see Chapter 3).

Nor does evidence support the gender role argument that women resist retirement because they are more sociable than men and thus reluctant to leave their co-workers. It is possible, however, that structural components of the workplace may produce stronger ties among workers in selected occupations. Clifford Mottaz (1986) found that women workers who occupied low-level jobs attached greater importance to the social rewards offered by their jobs than did women in higher-level jobs. When jobs offer fewer rewards in the form of salary, promotion, or autonomy, "there is a tendency to upgrade social rewards" offered by interaction with co-workers (Mottaz 1986:373). This finding supports a structural explanation, which focuses on how job structures impact workers' attitudes and behaviors (see Kanter 1977). Extending the structural argument to retirement, it is possible that interaction with co-workers in low-level occupations "may have a more important influence on life satisfaction for retirees from these occupations" (Calasanti 1996:S27). This thesis was not tested explicitly, however, for either women or men who retired from restricted occupations.

Gender roles clearly are inadequate to understand women's and men's attitudes and behaviors (Chapter 2). This does not mean, however, that gendered expectations and meanings do not impact people's lives, including their lives in retirement. Research on married retirees' perceptions of equity in their marriages helps to illustrate this point. Keith, Wacker, and Schafer (1992) found that retirees who agreed with traditional gender role attitudes were more likely to report an equitable division of labor in their marriages than those who reported non-traditional attitudes.[2] Wives and husbands who believe that they *should* be

---

[2] Different findings were reported for older employed respondents than for the retired. Among the retired, perceptions of equity were associated with respondents' gender-role attitudes (those with traditional attitudes were likely to say that their marital division of labor was equitable). For those who were employed, however, perceptions of equity were largely independent of their gender-role attitudes (those with traditional attitudes were no more likely to report marital equity than those holding non-traditional attitudes). The authors suggest that by virtue of being retired (and hence operating within women's "traditional" sphere of the home), retired women were able to act upon their traditional values, which may have contributed to perceptions of equity in their marital relationships.

responsible for different tasks are likely to perceive their division of labor as equitable or "fair," although the amount of time and effort partners expend in that labor is not necessarily equal.

Other studies have found that wives' household work exceeds that of husbands, even when men are unemployed or retired (e.g., Ade-Ridder and Brubaker 1988; Vinick and Ekerdt 1992).[3] Since perceived equity in household tasks apparently facilitates retirement well-being (see Dorfman 1992), married couples who agree that traditional gender roles are appropriate may fare better emotionally in retirement than those who do not. Support for this point comes from a study by Maximiliane Szinovacz (1996). She reports that older couples express greater satisfaction with their marriages when their behaviors are consistent with their gender role attitudes. For example, married women who agreed with traditional gender roles expressed lower satisfaction with their marriages when their husbands were retired but they were still employed—a pattern in conflict with the "male breadwinner" role which the women believed was appropriate. These "traditional" women expressed greater satisfaction with their marriages when their husbands were employed but they themselves were not.

Resource explanations for gender differences in retirement focus on differential access to pension coverage and income. Along with health, these factors are important to both women's and men's retirement. As noted, researchers have found that these predictors are not as robust for women as they are for (white, middle-class) men (Calasanti 1996; George et al. 1984; Martin Matthews and Brown 1988; Palmore et al. 1985).

The importance of health and income in shaping men's retirement decisions and responses was recognized by a number of the early writers (Kutner et al. 1956; Thompson 1958; Thompson and Streib 1958). However, this recognition was often eclipsed by the stress placed upon the meaning of the worker role and the problems assumed to be associated with the withdrawal of that role. Today, the general consensus of retirement researchers is represented by Francis Glamser's statement that retirement attitudes—on the part of both women and men—may be "better understood as resulting from the worker's realistic appraisal of the type of retirement experience which he [sic] can expect than as part of a general value orientation stressing the worker role" (1976:104).

The weight of evidence for gender differences in retirement attitudes and adaptation is on the side of resource/structural explanations. I have reviewed studies showing that gender differences are not statistically significant when health, income, and other resource variables are controlled. But how much does a structural approach contribute to an understanding of retirement adaptation for

---

[3] Some studies suggest that men increase their involvement in household tasks following retirement, but that they do not approximate the amount of household work done by women (see Dorfman 1992).

either gender? To say that women's and men's responses to retirement are comparable under certain conditions allows us to recognize that socioeconomic resources are important in shaping such responses. On the other hand, women and men typically do not occupy comparable labor force positions or have access to equivalent socioeconomic resources. It would also be difficult to locate women and men who occupy equivalent family roles and positions, given the highly gendered nature of parenting, caregiving, and household responsibilities (e.g., Pavalko and Artis 1997; Piotrkowski, Rapoport, and Rapoport 1987; Sanchez and Thompson 1997; Szinovacz 1989b). For these reasons, it seems useful to consider the *pathways* by which women and men approach retirement.

WOMEN'S AND MEN'S RETIREMENT PATHWAYS AND ADAPTATION

Beginning in the 1980s, the study of gender differences in retirement moved toward examining the factors which promote women's and men's retirement and how gendered pathways to retirement impact adaptation. Many of these studies have focused on specified groups of women and men, especially married persons. Thus, this body of literature considers some sources of diversity in women's and men's lives, rather than relying solely on dichotomous comparisons between men and women.

Studies have found that the retirement decisions of married women are more heavily contingent on their spouse's health and labor force status than are those of married men (O'Rand, Henretta, and Krecker 1992; Szinovacz 1989a). Research also indicates that women are far more likely than men to retire when a family member requires care (Henretta and O'Rand 1980; O'Rand et al. 1992; Szinovacz 1983, 1989a), although some married men reduce their hours of employment when their wives require care (Stone, Cafferata, and Sangl 1987).

Maximiliane Szinovacz (1989a) reports that women's adaptation to retirement, including feelings of well-being, is poorer when they retire in order to care for ill family members or because their spouse had retired. Few men reported retiring for these reasons. However, men showed lower retirement adaptation when their spouse was still employed. Szinovacz interprets this finding by suggesting that men "seem to resent the continued employment of their wives and the reversal in the provider role associated with this situation" (1989a:305). This interpretation is consistent with traditional gender role theory (and seems to be supported in her later study of marital satisfaction among retired couples, reviewed above) (Szinovacz 1996). A structural explanation for this finding also is possible, however. For example, the women married to these men may have been unable to retire for economic reasons (such as needing to work longer for pension vesting). The retirement experience of these couples may be less positive as a consequence.

A further study (Szinovacz and Washo 1992) examined gender differences in life events which surround the retirement transition and the effects of such experiences on men's and women's retirement adaptation. Possible life events included changes in marital status, the illness or death of a family member or friend, or change of residence. The number of life events experienced by women prior to their retirement was found to be greater than the number of events experienced by men. In addition, women's retirement adaptation (assessed by perceptions of job deprivation) seemed to be affected more strongly (and negatively) than men's when they experienced life changes within a two-year period after retirement. The authors conclude that women's greater apparent vulnerability to life events may be due to their greater involvement in social network crises—women may be called upon more frequently to provide support or they may be more emotionally involved than men (this argument was reviewed in Chapter 3). The authors' conclusions remain speculative, although it is true that women are more likely to be family caretakers than men and to be named as confidants of men as well as other women (Chapters 3 and 4). It should be noted that respondents selected life events from a fixed list (adapted from Holmes and Rahe's 1967 scale), which may not have included events of personal importance to them.

It is clear that women and men often follow different routes to retirement. However, diversity in retirement pathways and experiences also is found *within* gender groups, which a life course perspective helps to identify. The following section examines the timing of workers' retirement as well as their retirement attitudes and outcomes, using the life course framework advanced in the previous chapters.

BEYOND GENDER DIFFERENCES: ADAPTATION TO RETIREMENT IN LIFE COURSE PERSPECTIVE

A life course approach to retirement emphasizes individuals' histories of experience leading to retirement, including transitions between work and retirement, the timing of those transitions, and the long-term effects of earlier life events on retirement. After considering these factors, I examine the influence of workers' social locations and membership in social groups on their retirement experiences, trends in retirement across birth cohorts, and the broader societal context for retirement.

Employing the Multi-Level Life Course Model

Personal Histories

Diverse retirement pathways—Pathways to retirement include but are not limited to the traditionally recognized institutions of Social Security and private pensions (Henretta 1992). I have noted that women are more likely than men to retire for family caregiving reasons or in response to spouse's retirement.

Long-term effects of women's family and work experiences also have been documented by life course studies of retirement.

Angela O'Rand and Richard Landerman (1984) found that each child and each year of delay in women's full-time labor force participation reduced their occupational status and their opportunities for jobs offering pension benefits. These constraints, in turn, delayed the women's retirement and reduced their retirement income. The authors report that "significant family life cycle costs are present for women but not for men" (p. 38).

Marital transitions also influence women's pathways to retirement. Leslie Morgan (1992) found that women who were divorced or widowed between the ages of forty-five and fifty-nine planned to retire later than women who were married, or they expected never to retire at all. Compared to their married counterparts, the widowed and divorced women had substantially lower incomes and fewer expected to receive income from a private pension source. (Most of the married women expected that their retirement benefits would derive from their husbands' employment.) The type of marital dissolution also was important, with more divorced than widowed women expecting to receive retirement income from only one source (probably Social Security). On the other hand, women who experience divorce or widowhood earlier in the life course can anticipate a more favorable retirement scenario because they are better able to increase their involvement in the labor force at a younger age, and thus be better able to meet eligibility criteria for private pensions (when they are available) and to earn Social Security credits. Such resources can enable these women to retire "early" or on-time (Morgan 1992).

Though less well-recognized, unemployment and disability also are pathways to retirement (Ruhm 1989), especially for members of historically disadvantaged racial-ethnic groups. Rose Gibson (1986, 1987, 1988, 1991) reports that a substantial proportion of older African Americans—as many as 40 percent of those age fifty-five and older who are not employed—can be classified as the "unretired-retired." These are "individuals who appear and behave as if they were retired, but do not call themselves such" (Gibson 1986:362-363). According to Gibson, economic need, physical disability, and discontinuous work patterns produce a hazy line between "work" and "nonwork" for many African Americans. Women and men of other racial-ethnic minority groups also experience alternating periods of employment and unemployment over the life course (Zsembik and Singer 1990).

These studies illustrate several important points about measures of retirement. Men and women of color are likely to be excluded from research when traditional retirement measures are used, a feature shared with white women. The studies also suggest that gender differences in subjective retirement (self-definition of retiree status) are less likely to be observed among racial-ethnic minorities than among non-Hispanic whites. However, these findings may depend upon how questions of subjective retirement are phrased.

Based on her findings from a national survey of older African Americans, Rose Gibson (1987, 1988) has argued that gender is not important in the subjective retirement of this group. In contrast to current cohorts of older whites, African American women and men are both likely to have had lifetime work experience and to share discontinuous patterns of employment. Gibson believes that these factors account for the lack of gender differences in her sample: African Americans of both genders often fail to identify themselves as retired in their later years.

Barbara Zsembik and Audrey Singer (1990) also found that gender did not differentiate Mexican Americans' self-reports of being retired. However, when retirement was assessed somewhat differently—by asking what the respondent was "currently doing" rather than asking "are you retired?"—the women were more likely than the men to describe their current activity as "retired." The women were *less* likely than the men to be considered retired when other measures of retirement were used (receipt of public or private pensions or current employment status).

Thus, adequate study of retirement requires attention to work/retirement pathways and variations in retirement meanings across gender and racial-ethnic groups. Factors that emerge as important predictors of retirement adaptation often vary depending upon the specific retirement criterion that is used (a finding also reported for samples of white men) (e.g., Palmore et al. 1985). For any group, it is clear that the picture of retirement that emerges depends on how retirement is conceptualized and measured.

Life course continuities—Nonetheless, some central findings regarding retirement adaptation have been reported across studies. Adequate income and good health predict greater subjective well-being at all ages, as well as positive attitudes toward retirement and satisfaction with retired life (e.g., Bossé et al. 1991; Calasanti 1996; Levkoff et al. 1987; Rozzini et al. 1988). Continuity over the life course also is shown by longitudinal studies, which have found that attitudes held prior to retirement are among the strongest predictors of post-retirement attitudes and adaptation (e.g., McPherson and Guppy 1979; Streib and Schneider 1971). Similarly, feelings of self-esteem apparently do not change appreciably after retirement (Reitzes et al. 1996).

Retirement processes and changes—The knowledge that retirement is not a cataclysmic event, and that considerable continuity is shown over the life course, should not be taken to mean that retirement is void of any change. Previously, I discussed how some husbands and wives believe that retirement has impacted their marriage in positive ways, while others describe negative impacts of retirement (Atchley 1992).

Gerontologists have long argued that the transition from work to retirement involves a period of adaptation (Ekerdt et al. 1985; Kosloski et al. 1984). Most retirees experience some reduction of income (although these losses are more consequential for some retirees than others) (Schulz 1995). Changes also may be expected in self-identities following retirement, as well as the types of activities individuals spend their time doing (Cuba 1992; Kosloski et al. 1984; Szinovacz 1992; Vinick and Ekerdt 1992).

Adaptation to retirement usually has been considered part of the larger process of adaptation to aging. Each of the "classical theories" of adaptation—disengagement, activity, and continuity theory—has been applied to retirement (e.g., Cavan 1962; Kosloski et al. 1984; McGee et al. 1979; Neugarten and Havighurst 1969), as well as to aging more generally (Chapter 3).

In a framework developed specifically for retirement, Robert Atchley (1976b) has proposed that retirement adaptation consists of several possible phases. The first is a "pre-retirement period," in which individuals orient them-selves to leaving employment and develop fantasies of what retirement will be like. Realistic fantasies can help to smooth the process of retirement adaptation; unrealistic fantasies set up false expectations and can impede adaptation. Immediately following the event of retirement, a "honeymoon period" may be experienced, characterized by activity and euphoria. The honeymoon phase may be succeeded by a period of letdown or disappointment, which in turn may lead to a reorientation phase in which retirement is evaluated more realistically. The retiree has reached the "stability phase" of retirement when "he [sic] has mastered the retirement role" (p. 70) and has developed a predictable and satisfying lifestyle in retirement.

Atchley' retirement phases were suggested in a series of empirical studies (Atchley 1994), but were not tested systematically (Ekerdt et al. 1985). Ekerdt, Bossé, and Levkoff attempt to provide such a test, using a sample of Boston-area men born between 1884 and 1945. Results from this study provide tentative support for some aspects of Atchley's framework. Compared to men who had been retired for longer periods of time, men who had been retired for six or fewer months reported greater life satisfaction, optimism for the future, and involvement in physical activities. In general terms, these results support a "honeymoon phase." The notion that a subsequent period of disenchantment is succeeded by a more balanced appraisal of one's situation was also suggested by the results: men who had been retired for nineteen or more months had higher life satisfaction than those retired between thirteen and eighteen months.

Although these cross-sectional results provide some support for Atchley's framework, the process of retirement is not yet well understood even among the group most frequently studied by retirement researchers—white men. Atchley himself has cautioned that some people will not experience a honeymoon phase, either because they do not have a positive orientation toward retirement or because they lack adequate economic resources. He emphasizes that these phases are not intended as a rigid sequence that all retirees will experience, and in later writings (e.g., Atchley 1994) has provided a somewhat more detailed and flexible framework for retirement adaptation. The main contribution of the framework is that it calls attention to the importance of considering processual dimensions of retirement, rather than simply treating retirement as an act or event.

Social Location and Social Groups

I have discussed how individuals approach retirement via diverse routes, including partial retirement and multiple labor-force entries and exits. Diversity also has been found in how individuals perceive and evaluate retirement, and in the material conditions of their lives in retirement. In this section, I examine how social class and marital circumstances shape the retirement experience, including intersecting influences of gender and race-ethnicity.

Social class and the retirement experience—Many studies have examined the effects of income, pension coverage, and occupational status on retirement. These elements reflect aspects of social class, but their effects usually have been assessed separately from one another. Over the years, studies have documented that an adequate income and pension coverage predict more favorable retirement attitudes and retirement satisfaction (Atchley 1976c; Atchley and Robinson 1982; Beck 1983; Glamser 1976; Shanas 1970; Thompson and Streib 1958). Pension coverage and the expectation of an adequate retirement income also promote early retirement.

Occupational status is highly correlated with income, but its impact on retirement outcomes is far less clear. Some studies have suggested an inverse relationship between occupational status and retirement attitudes, with greater reluctance to retire and poorer adaptation among men in high-status occupations (Friedmann and Havighurst 1954; Stokes and Maddox 1967). Other studies indicate a positive relationship between occupational status and retirement attitudes and timing (Atchley 1982; McPherson and Guppy 1979; Streib and Schneider 1971). These studies show that workers with higher occupational status hold more favorable retirement attitudes and are more likely to plan early retirements. It is also possible that workers in higher-status occupations are more reluctant to retire, but that once retired, they report higher levels of satisfaction than retirees who occupied lower status occupations (Loether 1967; Stokes and Maddox 1967). A curvilinear relationship is yet another possibility: some studies have found that men occupying either high- or low-status occupations express less favorable retirement orientations, including a greater reluctance to retire (Simpson, Back, and McKinney 1966; see also Freidmann and Orbach 1974; Kasl 1980).

A more useful approach is to consider workers' abilities to control the timing and circumstances of their retirement. Such abilities more often characterize workers in higher-status occupations, but factors in addition to occupational status are also important. Specifically, workers' location in the economic structure affects the conditions under which retirement is likely to take place. In his study, Scott Beck (1983) used three indicators of position in the economic structure. In addition to occupational status, he considered whether workers were located in core versus peripheral industries and whether workers were self-employed. Those working in core industries share a number of the same advantages typically enjoyed by workers with higher occupational status: stable employment, fringe benefits, and better access to retirement planning information. Self-employed workers are better able than wage and salary workers to control the timing of their retirement, but they have had less access to retirement planning information.

Using the National Longitudinal Surveys of Mature Men (NLS), Beck found that men with higher-status occupations and those working in core industries were more likely to retire at or near their expected age of retirement. Although this data set did not include measures for retirement attitudes, other studies have found that having expected to retire predicts favorable retirement attitudes and life satisfaction in retirement (Beck 1982; Martin Matthews and Brown 1988).

In one of the few studies of retirement to investigate social class in a more holistic way, Toni Calasanti and Alessandro Bonanno (1992) examined returns to work among working-class retirees.[4] Using qualitative data, the authors described how some retirees returned to paid labor for purposes of economic survival, while others went back to work to preserve their social status or to improve the quality of their families' lives. Other retirees performed unpaid work to help improve the quality of life in their communities.

Calasanti and Bonanno argue that there are important implications for working-class retirees, as well as for the socioeconomic system, when retired persons return to work for economic survival. Older marginal workers provide a flexible source of labor to industry and receive low pay and few or no fringe benefits. The societal assumption that individuals voluntarily withdraw from labor when they retire is class-based in that this "dominant ideal" does not accord with the actual experiences of many working-class individuals.

This point can be made more broadly. What may appear to be a "voluntary retirement" may not be perceived as such by the actor involved. From their study of early retirement among auto workers, Melissa Hardy and Jill Quadagno report that "the rhetoric of choice is often inconsistent with [the workers'] constructions of why and how they retired" (1995:S228). These workers appeared to have chosen to retire due to the provision of an early retirement incentive package. Most of those who took early retirement expressed satisfaction with the timing of their retirements and their retirement experiences. Others, however, "were presented with limited options, limited time, and limited information" (p. S228), producing feelings of uncertainty and loss of control over the process.

Thus, retiring in response to proferred economic incentives is not necessarily the crucial element in promoting retirement satisfaction. A study which asked

---

[4] Following a neo-Marxian definition (Steinmetz and Wright 1989), the working class was defined as wage laborers, and excludes the self-employed, managers, and "experts" in professional or technical occupations.

specifically whether individuals had *wanted* to retire found that this element was "the strongest predictor of retirement having affected individuals 'a lot in a positive way' " (Martin Matthews and Brown 1988:563).

In general, those in professional occupations are better able than other workers to choose the timing and circumstances of their retirement (Beck 1983). Rose Gibson and Cheryl Burns (1992) detail the representation of racial-ethnic groups in this occupational category. While 28 percent of whites occupy professional and managerial jobs, only 16 percent of African Americans, 11 percent of Puerto Rican Americans, and 9 percent of Mexican Americans have these types of jobs. At the other end of the occupational ladder, 14 percent of whites are craftsmen, compared to 22 percent of African Americans, 25 percent of Puerto Rican Americans, 22 percent of Cuban Americans, and 31 percent of Mexican Americans.

Given these patterns, along with the knowledge that racial-ethnic minorities often leave paid labor due to health disabilities and typically have low incomes in retirement, it can only be supposed that their retirement satisfaction would be relatively low. However, Gibson (1986, 1991) argues that retirement can offer greater promise for happiness and security to racial-ethnic minorities than was possible during their pre-retired years. This is so because members of these groups often are restricted to low-level, unsatisfying employment which does not accommodate physical limitations. Although Social Security payments to members of racial-ethnic minority groups often are low (due to lower average earnings and less continuous work histories), this source of income can provide greater economic security than was previously available.

Marital status and retirement—Marital status has been consequential for women's and men's retirement incomes and experiences, as well as their pathways to retirement. Married men and women express more positive views about retirement compared to unmarried persons, and they express greater satisfaction with their lives in retirement (e.g., Seccombe and Lee 1986). These findings may reflect differences in the economic situations of married and unmarried individuals. Controlling for annual income or pension benefits in statistical analyses may not capture the full range of economic resources that may differentiate the married from the unmarried, such as home ownership and other assets, which in turn can promote feelings of life satisfaction. Married men also tend to express greater satisfaction with their lives in retirement compared to married women (e.g., Calasanti 1996). This finding is part of a broader pattern which reflects greater socioemotional and health benefits derived from marriage by men, which I explore further in the concluding chapter.

It is important to distinguish within the category of individuals classified as "unmarried." Evidence indicates that women who never married are more positively oriented toward retirement compared to women who married and subsequently became single (Hatch 1992; Keith 1985). Today's older never-married women are more likely to have had continuous labor-force histories than women who married, and thus more likely to anticipate a satisfactory economic situation at retirement compared to women who are divorced, separated, or widowed. Furthermore, employment has been found to have beneficial effects on women's happiness and mental health (Chapter 3), which can also help to explain why never-married women have been more favorably oriented toward retirement.

Patterns of employment and childbearing have been linked more closely for white women, especially those in the middle class. Married women in all racial-ethnic groups participate less in paid labor when they have young children, but due to economic pressures, women of color have been less able than white women to leave paid labor for extended periods to raise children (Smith and Tienda 1988; Spitze 1988). In addition, women's employment seems to be more accepted in African American communities. Elizabeth Higginbotham (1981) found that middle-class as well as working-class African American parents encouraged their daughters to pursue educational and career goals. Most of the mothers, who would be retirement age today, were themselves employed at the time of the study. These findings can help to explain why African American women have been as likely as African American men to identify themselves as retirees, rather than as homemakers (Gibson 1987, 1988).

Birth Cohort

Diversity in workforce experience is unlikely to decline. In fact, sporadic workforce experience is predicted to spread more pervasively throughout the population as a result of industrial dislocations and restructuring (Gibson 1986, 1991). Further contributing factors include increased opportunities for part-time work in older age and changes in Social Security provisions, which permit an increased amount of earned income without penalty to retirees' benefits (Mutchler et al. 1997).

Jan Mutchler and colleagues (1997) predict that future cohorts increasingly will experience a "blurred" retirement transition (characterized by a gradual or uneven transition between employment and retirement) rather than a "crisp" transition (in which a precise time point demarcates the transition to retirement). Not surprisingly, blurred transitions are more likely to be found among workers in low-wage jobs who lack pension benefits.

Trends in men's retirement attitudes—The fact that retirement was not yet an established social institution can explain in part the strong opposition to retirement reported among cohorts of men in the 1940s and early 1950s[5] (Donahue et al.

---

[5] Retirement emerged as a recognized social institution in the United States in the late 1930s when the federal Social Security System was introduced. See Jill Quadagno and Steve McClellan (1989) for an historical overview of how retirement evolved in the United States.

1960). (Because most of the early studies of retirement focused on men, comparable data for women are not available.) More materially, men's negative reactions to retirement can be traced to financial concerns (Friedmann and Orbach 1974). The expansion of private pensions and Social Security coverage in the United States during the 1950s and 1960s provided a degree of financial support for most labor force retirees, and by the middle of the 1960s American men were reporting more favorable attitudes toward retirement. Changes enacted in the Social Security system during the 1970s increased the value of Social Security benefits, which in turn has contributed to the trend toward early retirement (Clark 1988; DeViney and O'Rand 1988).

Trends in age at retirement—The average age at retirement has declined over the past four decades. Early retirement has been documented especially for white men (Clark 1988; DeViney and O'Rand 1988), but similar trends have been found for white women and for African American men and women (Gendell and Siegel 1996). These trends show an average decline of three to four and a half years in workers' average age at retirement since the 1950s. In 1955, the median age at retirement was 66.3 for African American women, 66.1 for white women, 64.7 for African American men, and 65.8 for white men. By 1990, the median retirement ages of these groups had declined to 61.7, 63.0, 61.7, and 62.6, respectively (Gendell and Siegel 1996).

Findings from this study also show that retirement often takes place before individuals are eligible for Social Security benefits. A gap between age at retirement and the receipt of benefits was found for all four race-gender groups, but larger gaps were found for African Americans. (This interval was "generally less than a year" (Gendell and Siegel 1996:S138) among whites, but approximately 1 to 2 years for African Americans.) These patterns were attributed to the higher disability levels of African Americans. Due to poor health, many African Americans "retire" before they are eligible for Social Security benefits. However, benefits may be available through Social Security disability programs. "Elderly African Americans have continued to be considerably more likely to be awarded Social Security disability benefits than elderly Whites" (Gendell and Siegel 1996:S138). Reflecting on this issue, Hayward, Friedman, and Chen argue that if disability programs were curtailed, "the necessity of working might well increase Blacks' levels of [labor force] attachment (while simultaneously lowering the overall health of older Black workers)" (1996:S9).

Private pension programs also have shown varying effects on the retirement of differing groups. Stanley DeViney and Angela O'Rand (1988) report cohort and gender differences in the impact of private pensions on retirement. The labor force participation rates for a cohort age fifty-five to sixty-four was compared with a group aged sixty-five and older, during the period between 1951 and 1984. Among men, the extension of private pensions was important in the retirement of both age groups across the period studied, but this was not the most important factor in the retirement of men age sixty-five and older. Rather, men in this age group had been "pushed" from the labor force due to declining demands for manufacturing skills. On the other hand, the extension of private pension benefits was the primary factor for retirement among the younger group of men. Although the data for white and non-white men were not exactly comparable, analyses suggested that similar patterns held for men in both race categories. DeViney and O'Rand conclude that growth in the numbers of retired men sixty-five and older led to "a need and a political demand for enhanced private and public pension benefits" (1988:536). Thus, policies developed in response to the retirement of the older age group (65 and older) led to the retirement of the younger age group. These patterns were not evident among women in either age group. Changes in private pension and Social Security programs apparently have not affected women's retirement as much as they have men's.

Other studies have shown that, in general, early retirees are composed of two disparate groups. One group consists of workers who will benefit economically from early retirement. As noted, pension incentives have strong effects on early retirements (Ruhm 1989; Schulz 1995), but these are more often offered to highly-paid workers (O'Rand and MacLean 1986). A second group of early retirees is composed of persons in less advantaged economic circumstances who are unemployed or in poor health (Beck 1983; Gibson 1986).

Societal Context

Thus, retirement patterns are framed by the social policies and institutions which regulate labor and allocate retirement resources. Just as is true during the years of employment, greater income in retirement is linked with lengthy and continuous labor force histories and by working in advantageous occupations and industries. The much-touted "three-legged stool" of retirement income—consisting of Social Security, employer-sponsored pensions, and savings/investment income—is a lopsided, often shaky structure for retirees whose employment histories do not match those criteria.

Social Security— Although Social Security utilizes a weighted benefit formula intended to favor workers with lower earnings (Schulz 1995), women and racial-ethnic minorities receive lower Social Security benefits on average than white men. Among retired workers, the benefits received by black men are 20 percent lower on average than those received by white men. Black women's average benefits are 20 percent lower than those received by black men, and 34 percent lower than those of white men. Gender comparisons within the white population show that women's Social Security benefits are 24 percent lower on average than those of men (Social Security Administration 1995, calculated from Table 5.A1). In addition to receiving lower average benefits, minorities and unmarried women often rely on Social Security as their principal—or only—source of income (Arendell and Estes 1991; Choi 1997).

Social Security has a dual-eligibility structure. Those who are currently or previously married can derive benefits either from their own workforce participation or from the earnings record of their spouse. Virtually all men receive Social Security benefits based on their own earnings record, but nearly all of those receiving spousal benefits are women (Harrington Meyer 1996). Spousal benefits are paid out at the rate of one-half the earner's (i.e., husband's) benefits. However, most women who are eligible for Social Security payments from their own labor force histories receive the spousal benefit because their own earnings-related benefits are even lower. Thus, the Social Security benefits these women receive are the same as if they had never been employed.

Non-traditional married couples are penalized by Social Security provisions. Burkhauser, Duncan, and Hauser (1994) illustrate why this is so. For a "traditional household," in which a husband's lifetime earnings are higher than the wife's earnings, the survivor benefit is two-thirds of the total benefits provided to the couple. On the other hand, if the wife's benefits as a wage earner exceed the benefits she would receive as a spouse—however small the difference may be—the survivor benefit will be lower. "In the extreme, when husband and wife have the same earning histories, the survivor benefit is one-half the couple's total benefit. Hence, a survivor benefit in the United States ranges between one-half and two-thirds the combined social security benefit of husband and wife while both are alive" (p. 157).

Put another way, employed husbands and wives are treated as "separate taxable units and consequently may collectively pay more social security taxes than a family with only a single worker earning the same amount." However, due to the eligibility structure of Social Security, outlined above, a spouse (usually the wife) in dual earner families "may pay social security taxes without adding to the family's retirement income" (Schulz 1995:131).

For those who are no longer married, the relative amount of spousal benefit depends upon how the marriage was terminated. When a marital partner dies, spousal benefits are calculated at two-thirds the couple's total Social Security benefit (for the "traditional households" described above), whereas divorced partners split the total benefit based on their own relative portions. Divorced husbands generally receive two-thirds of the couple's benefit and divorced wives one-third (Harrington Meyer 1990).

Whether widowed or divorced, displaced homemakers can be left without economic refuge following the end of their marriage. Since spousal benefits do not become available until age sixty, those whose marriages end before this age often experience a period of great economic insecurity (Older Women's League 1999). (For younger women, widows' benefits are available until the youngest child reaches the age of 16.) Furthermore, spousal benefits are not provided when marriages last less than ten years. According to Harrington Meyer (1996), the number of women who enter older age without a marriage lasting ten years will increase in the future, due to increases in cohabitation, a continuing high divorce rate, and declines in remarriage.

Women's risks for poverty could be reduced by altering the Social Security program to provide family caregiving credits. The replacement costs of unpaid family caregiving to older adults have been estimated at 9.6 billion per year in the United States (Dwyer and Coward 1992). By implementing family caregiving credits, those who leave paid labor to care for a family member could receive at least a minimum Social Security benefit when they reach the age of eligibility. Unpaid childcare—which, like eldercare, is performed primarily by women—also benefits the larger society and would be very costly if purchased in the market-place (Glazer 1987; Vanek 1984). However, proposals for eldercare, childcare, or homemaker credits have met with great controversy among social policy-makers. Inevitably, concerns about costs are at the forefront of debate, and there is disagreement about how much "credit" a family caregiver should receive (Burkhauser 1994; Schulz 1995). In the absence of such provisions, many women are penalized by the Social Security system.

Addressing the gendered biases of Social Security, Richard Burkhauser says "No one consciously 'planned' for social security to overprotect married couples and underprotect survivors, most of whom are women" (1994:148). He notes that "Social security policymaking has been dominated by traditional married men who have created a system that offers the greatest level of protection to traditional married men" (p. 148). Burkhauser does not say so, but racial inequities also are built into the Social Security system. Fewer minorities than whites live to the age of eligibility for Social Security benefits. For example, the life expectancies of African American men and women are 5.4 years and 4.9 years less, respectively, than white men and women (Novak 1997). A study of older men found that, proportionately, African American men spent *more* of their total lifetimes in the labor force than white men, and fewer years in retirement (Hayward et al. 1996). Life expectancies are expected to increase among racial-ethnic minorities in the future, but the minimum age for receipt of full benefits also will increase in the future (see the concluding section of this chapter).

Employer-sponsored pensions—Private pension programs do not com-pensate for the lower Social Security benefits received by vulnerable groups of older women and men. Pension income accounts for just 4 percent of the total income received by low-income elders (those with annual incomes of $10,752 or less). In comparison, pension income accounts for 39 percent of the total income received by middle-income older adults, and 57 percent of the income received by older adults in the high income bracket ($28,714 and over) (Reno 1993).

Among those who receive income from a pension, women's average benefits are slightly more than one-half (56%) those of men (U.S. Senate Special Com-mittee on Aging 1994:39). Women are also less likely to receive *any* income from a pension source. As of 1990, 32 percent of unmarried women compared to 41 percent of unmarried men received pension income. Furthermore, the median amount of pension income received by unmarried women is about one-half that received by unmarried men ($2,620 for women compared to $4,981 for men as of 1992) (Schulz 1995:18). Married couples fare better, with 57 percent receiving some pension income (Reno 1993). These aggregate figures mask the lower pension coverage and benefit levels of racial-ethnic minorities. In 1990, only about one-third of African American and Hispanic married couples received income from an employer-sponsored pension (Choi 1997).[6]

What happens when a spouse dies? Federal law requires that pension plans provide survivor benefits, but workers decide whether or not these benefits will be a part of their own benefit package. Pension plans without survivor benefits provide larger payouts during the worker's lifetime. Couples may "gamble" that the survivor benefit will not be needed (Schulz 1995). This is a large gamble indeed, since most married women survive their spouses. And until 1984, workers could reject the survivor benefit option without the consent or knowledge of their spouses. With passage of the Retirement Equity Act in 1984, employers must now obtain the spouse's consent in writing in order for a married worker to reject the survivor option. No doubt this legislation contributed to an increased proportion of retired married men who maintained both the joint and survivor annuity (from 65% in 1983 to 80% in 1988-89) (Schulz 1995).

Survivor benefits from private pensions are at most one-half the benefits of the wage-earning spouse. For couples who divorce, the allocation of private pension benefits depends upon the state in which they live. In many states, private pensions are considered the sole property of the wage-earner. In California and other states with community property laws, private pension benefits are more likely to be considered marital property and divided between the spouses (Harrington Meyer 1990).

In examining why women are less likely than men to receive pension income from their own employment, Jill Quadagno (1988) argues that women are penalized in indirect ways for their family involvements. Rather than focusing on irregular work histories as the reason for many women's failure to meet pension criteria, Quadagno contends that the central question concerns *why* criteria unfavorable to women were enacted. Her research showed that married women were less likely to participate in union politics due to conflicts with their family

---

[6] Income from savings and investments completes the presumed "three-legged stool" of U.S. retirement income. Assets are not a large component of most retirees' income, providing just $1,720 per year on average (Older Women's League 1999:311). As is true for other sources of retirement income, married couples, especially whites, have greater income from this source than other retirees. They also are able to rely more heavily upon assets as a portion of their total income, achieving a more stable "third leg" of the retirement income stool. In 1990, assets provided nearly 19 percent of the retirement income of white married couples, compared to 4 percent and 7 percent respectively for black and Hispanic married couples (Choi 1997:31; see also Hogan et al. 1997).

responsibilities, and thus had limited power in decision-making processes, including pension eligibility criteria.

In sum, it is not simply a matter of the family and paid work "choices" that women make throughout the life course that put them at an economic disadvantage in old age. Women are penalized by the ways in which old-age benefit programs are structured. Social Security as well as private pension programs continue to reflect traditional assumptions about gender and family, including the meaning of "productive" and "unproductive" (i.e., paid and unpaid) labor.

An Exemplar of Life Course Research: Married Couples' Retirement Pathways and the Family Life Course

Jill Quadagno's research highlights how married women's family responsibilities interweave with the political context in which pension decisions are made. Previously, this chapter addressed asymmetries in husbands' and wives' retirement pathways, including how married women's retirement reflects life course histories of childbearing and employment, and is responsive to family caregiving responsibilities.

The family context for retirement patterns and decisions encompasses more than these predictors, however. Beyond the fact that other types of families have been neglected in this body of research, a life course perspective emphasizes that individuals' life courses mesh with those of families (Chapter 2). How can we understand retirement in the context of a *family* life course? In this section, I discuss an exemplar of life course research which addresses this issue. This study also focuses on married couples, but rather than comparing the predictors of retirement for married women with those for married men, emphasis was placed on the *couple's* family, work, and retirement histories.

O'Rand, Henretta, and Krecker (1992:84) examined "mutually contingent work and family careers" among married couples. Data were obtained from interviews with married women who were sixty-two to seventy-two years of age in 1982. The specific focus of the study was on patterns of joint versus sequential retirement among married couples, and the life course factors which differentiate these patterns.

The results highlight the importance of "early family life-course patterns and their enduring effects" as well as "the intervening impact of late-life family conditions on retirement sequencing" (pp. 93-94). Joint retirement, in which marital partners retire at or near the same time, was more likely when both spouses had sustained attachment to the labor force (either in the presence or absence of children) and when the spouses had not been married previously. Compared to couples following the sequential pattern (one spouse retires, while the other continues to work), spouses who retired jointly were advantaged with respect to their economic and pension resources.

Less advantageous patterns were found for couples who retired sequentially. Couples in which which the wife continued to work after the husband retired were distinguished by larger and older households (the wives were older themselves, closer in age to their husbands) and were more likely than the jointly retiring couples to have children under the age of twenty-one living at home. The socio-economic status of these families also was substantially lower and the husband was more likely to have health limitations. This type of sequential retirement was less likely when female family members of the same or older generation (e.g., a sister or a mother) also were present in the household. The researchers interpret this latter finding as reflecting family caregiving demands within the household, concluding that "net of lifetime work and family history effects, wives work after their husbands retired (rather than retire with their husbands) when the household continues to be economically dependent on their work and when household caregiving demands do not override these economic requisites" (p. 96).

The second sequential pattern is when the wife retires prior to the husband. Like the first sequential pattern and in contrast to joint retirement, this pattern of retirement was characterized by older wives and husbands of similar ages and by the presence of dependent children in the household. "The work pathways variables condition these late-family effects" (p. 96): Marital partners tended to have lower education and occupational status, less favorable income histories, and less pension coverage. Thus, both patterns of sequential retirement reflected less advantaged circumstances compared to couples who retired jointly.

The authors conclude that differing life course factors distinguish joint and sequential retirements among married couples. Joint retirement "into relatively advantaged economic and household conditions" is enhanced when both partners have had long-term attachment to the labor force and have remained in the same marriage. In contrast, sequential retirements primarily "are responses to late-life family and health events" (p. 98). However, these late-life events also have roots in earlier family and work experiences, and in patterns of health and illness over the life course.

CONCLUSION

Empirical studies reveal that retirement is not a "crisis" event for either women or men. Responses to retirement are complex and multidimensional, characterized by positive as well as negative dimensions for both genders (George et al. 1984). However, the processes by which retirement is approached and experienced often differ greatly by gender, as well as by other sources of social differentiation and inequality, including race-ethnicity and social class. The family context for retirement also is important to consider. This latter research focus has centered rather narrowly upon the marital dyad, but the exemplar of life course research discussed above demonstrates well how retirement pathways and subsequent experiences must be considered within the social and temporal context of families' lives, as well as those of individuals (O'Rand et al. 1992). The use of a life course perspective focuses attention on these dimensions, as well as on the social-historical context for individual and family biographies.

Some Disquieting Trends

Gaps between women's and men's economic resources at retirement are expected to continue for the foreseeable future. In addition to persistent sex segregation in occupations and significantly lower incomes among women (Thornborrow and Sheldon 1995), women continue to have primary responsibility for household tasks, child care, and care to ill and disabled family members (Dwyer and Coward 1992; Pavalko and Artis 1997; Penrod et al. 1995). Younger as well as older women are more likely than men to reduce or terminate their employment to care for ill or disabled family members (Pavalko and Artis 1997; Stone et al. 1987; White-Means and Thornton 1990). Doing so reduces women's immediate income, as well as their long-term economic resources (Kingson and O'Grady-LeShane 1993). Furthermore, research suggests that women's feelings of well-being suffer when they retire to care for family members (Szinovacz 1989a), possibly due to economic and health strains which are often associated with intensive caregiving.

Fewer gender differences in retirement have been found among African Americans than among non-Hispanic whites. Although African American women and men do not differ in their self-evaluations of retired status, and are more likely than whites to retire for reasons of disability (Gibson 1991; Hayward et al. 1996), such findings do not address potentially gendered pathways to retirement. In a co-authored study (Hatch and Thompson 1992), we found that retirement is more likely for both African American and white women when a member of the household is ill or disabled and requires assistance.

Recent trends in U.S. society have the potential to transform the meaning and experience of retirement for future cohorts of older Americans. In response to industrial decline and restructuring, employers and labor unions have encouraged early retirement as a way to speed up the normal attrition of workers and thus regulate the supply of labor. Although mandatory retirement was eliminated in the United States in 1986 with the passage of amendments to the Age Discrimination in Employment Act, "it has become common practice for employers to encourage earlier retirement by setting the age of normal retirement specified by the pension plan below age 65" (Schulz 1995:79). The incentive to retire early is enhanced when workers are able to retire prior to the "normal retirement age" without sacrificing the size of their pension income. In fact, in some employment settings older workers who continue on the job are penalized economically (Kotlikoff and Wise 1989).

A different trend is being promoted in the public sector. In 1983, Congress approved a change in the Social Security program, to increase the age of eligibility for full benefits. (Early benefits will still be available, beginning at age 62. As is true now, taking advantage of the early retirement option will permanently reduce the level of benefits paid to beneficiaries and their survivors.) This change is intended to occur gradually, beginning in the year 2000. By the year 2027, workers must be age sixty-seven to receive full benefits, rather than age sixty-five (Leonesio 1993). However, some government officials would like to speed up this change, and some officials also favor further increases in the retirement age (U.S. Senate Special Committee on Aging 1997:19). For example, Senator Robert Kerrey and former Senator John Danforth have proposed that the age of "normal retirement" (the age at which full benefits are available) be gradually increased to seventy, and that the Social Security benefits formula also be modified. According to Eric Kingson and Jill Quadagno, the net result would be "a whopping 43 percent cut in Social Security benefits" (1999:351). Further, "the burden of the proposed change would fall most heavily on lower-income early retirees, most notably older workers in poor health, older workers who are functionally limited (but not totally disabled), minority older workers, unemployed older workers, and early retirees in 'downsizing' industries" (p. 351).

Thus, private and public sectors have been moving in *opposite directions* with respect to retirement policies. If changes in Social Security provisions are successful in raising the age of retirement, more industrial workers will face the prospect of layoffs. On the other hand, increased numbers of early retirees will challenge an already burdened Social Security system (Quadagno and McClellan 1989). Although questions of "Social Security reform" will continue to be debated in the years to come,[7] a number of analysts have argued that modest, incremental changes can be made in the existing program to maintain its basic structure and income protection functions (e.g., Chen 1989; Kingson and Quadagno 1999; Quadagno 1996; Schulz 1990).

Nonetheless, a likely scenario for the future is that more older persons will re-enter the labor force following their retirement, especially when "retirement" is realized through layoffs, unemployment, or in response to family caregiving needs. Changes in the labor market structure and Social Security provisions mean that more older persons in the future will experience the hazy line between work and retirement already familiar to many men and women of color. Although both genders and all racial-ethnic groups are affected by these societal changes, those who will have the greatest difficulty obtaining adequate post-retirement employment are also those who have had greatest difficulty obtaining adequate pre-retirement employment—women and racial-ethnic minorities (Couch 1988; Hardy 1991; Morgan 1991).

---

[7] See Kingson and Quadagno (1999) for a discussion of proposals to privatize Social Security and other options for Social Security reform.

CHAPTER
6

Conclusion

In light of the debates surrounding which gender adapts better or suffers more in aging, it is not surprising that arguments also have been made concerning whether women or men have been neglected in aging research. Elizabeth Markson argues that "until relatively recently, few gerontologists or others paid attention . . . to gender in old age" (1995:261), and that older women's problems and concerns have been neglected. Diane Beeson asserts that when older women have been included in research, their problems are evaluated as "less problematic, less traumatic, and their difficulties seen as more easily resolved" (1981:120).

Other writers have contended that older men, not women, have been over-looked in aging research (Kaye and Applegate 1994; Rubinstein 1986; Thompson 1994). Edward Thompson (1994) points out that some scholars have gone so far as to characterize older age as primarily a "women's concern" (e.g., Arber and Ginn 1991:vii). According to Thompson, the equation of women with aging is due not only to women's greater representation in the older population, but also because sociologists traditionally have paid greater attention to disadvantaged groups in society. "In this frame, the pernicious concept of 'the aged' is synonymous with a disadvantaged group and thus more synonymous with the providence of older women than older men" (Thompson 1994:7).

It is true that the study of gender has been equated with the study of women, and that research on men *as men* has been a less frequent focus. This is evident not only in the field of gerontology. Men of all ages have been viewed as "genderless" (Thompson 1994), representing the implicit model of human development and "normal" aging (Tavris 1992). I disagree with Thompson, however, that when gender is taken into consideration, older women have a much higher profile in gerontological research. Rather, this focus depends upon the specific issues under consideration. Some problems of aging *have* been characterized as "women's issues" because women are more likely to experience them. For example, Robert Hansson and his colleagues (1993:367) state that widowhood is "primarily a woman's issue" because women are more likely than men to undergo this experience. Poverty in old age also has been characterized as primarily a concern for women (Chapter 3). On the other hand, retirement more often has been viewed as a men's issue. "Male models" of retirement continue to be utilized, despite the fact that the variables included in these models do not predict women's retirement as effectively as they do retirement among (white, middle class) men (Chapter 5).

Furthermore, men—more often than women—have been viewed as experiencing problems in adapting to aging in general (Chapter 3), and in adapting to stressful life events in older age in particular. Despite the view of widowhood as primarily a "women's issue," men more often than women have been characterized as experiencing difficulties adapting to the death of a spouse (Chapter 4). It has also been commonly thought that men experience greater difficulties than women in adapting to retirement from paid labor (Chapter 5). This is not to say that opposing arguments are absent. Contradictory arguments—and evidence—are evident for virtually all of the gender difference questions examined in this book.

Older women tend to be in the forefront of concern where chronic health problems and economic strains and losses are concerned. Persistent health problems are not commonly viewed as a dimension of adaptation to aging, however. Rather, attention has focused on *changes* in outcome measures over time or changes in these measures following a stressful life event. Furthermore, economic status more often is utilized as a *predictor* of social and health functioning rather than a direct reflection of adaptation. Thus, while older women's economic problems have been accorded a good deal of attention in the gerontological literature, these do not always figure directly in the conclusions researchers draw about gender differences in adaptation to aging.

Men, more often than women, have been seen as experiencing losses in their social and health functioning with aging. These dimensions have been the central foci for studies of adaptation to aging, and they have been linked together. In particular, many writers have argued that men are dependent upon the social and emotional support provided by their wives, and hence that men who lose their spouses are vulnerable to mental and physical health problems (Chapters 3 and 4).

EVALUATING THEORIES OF GENDER DIFFERENCES IN ADAPTATION TO AGING

Gender Role Explanations

Consistent with its functionalist underpinnings, "traditional gender role theory" views women's and men's roles as complementary and equal. Women and men are thought to specialize in different tasks in the family and to make different contributions to it (Chapter 2). The loss of a spouse thus brings differing forms of stress and strain to surviving partners—women are vulnerable to economic stresses following the loss of their breadwinning spouse, while men lose the socioemotional support provided by their wives (Chapter 4).

In broad, simplified terms, these assertions are largely borne out in the research literature. It is true that women, as a group, are more likely than men to experience poverty following the death of a spouse, but men also are vulnerable to economic losses following bereavement. The gender role argument does not account for structural factors which help explain differential risks for poverty (e.g., labor force discrimination and inequality of opportunity), or the gendered biases built into social policies which allocate economic resources.

With regard to men's presumed dependence on their wives' socioemotional support, evidence does suggest that married men are likely to rely upon their spouse for emotional intimacy, and hence that widowers are vulnerable to the loss of their primary or sole intimate relationship. On the other hand, research also suggests that men underemphasize the extent to which they share their feelings with other men (Walker 1994). Further studies have documented interactional contexts which promote emotional intimacy among men (e.g., Elder and Clipp 1988), or which attest to men's abilities to take on the nurturing and caring behaviors which gender role theorists associate with women (e.g., Kaye and Applegate 1994).

This book has shown that for every gender role argument positing men's greater difficulties in adapting to aging and to life events in older age, the opposite argument has been made. For example, women's presumed socioemotional specialization has been thought to make adaptation to aging *more difficult*— not easier—for them. Arguments also have been made that women are socialized to be dependent and passive, hindering their abilities to adapt to new social roles—*or* that women's gender role socialization promotes their abilities to adapt to new roles in older age (Chapter 3). It is difficult to imagine a gender role argument that has not been made regarding adaptation to aging, and it is also difficult to find gender role arguments which do not directly contradict one another.

Traditional gender role theory was incorporated in the earliest models of adaptation to aging (Chapter 3); versions of this theory remain the central explanatory frameworks for examining gender issues in aging (Chapters 3 through 5). Beyond serious conceptual limitations associated with this approach to understanding gender (Chapter 2), "traditional gender role theory" simply has not been put to the empirical test in the literatures reviewed here. There are some exceptions to this conclusion, but they are few in number and provide limited support at best for the theory. Indeed, given the contradictory interpretations which have been linked with traditional gender roles, a clear set of hypotheses is difficult to derive from this approach.

"Blended" Gender Role Explanations

In contrast to "traditional" gender role theorists, other writers who take a gender role approach have argued that women's and men's roles are stratified rather than equal, and that wives and husbands derive unequal benefits from marriage (Chapter 2). These arguments "blend" traditional gender role theory with perspectives that emphasize women's and men's unequal resources and power in society and in interpersonal relationships. Jessie Bernard ([1972] 1978) was among the first to contend that power imbalances, rather than equality and complementarity, characterize women's and men's marital roles. According to Bernard, the marital institution is skewed in favor of husbands' power. Bernard and other writers taking this position have argued that the institution of marriage is beneficial to men's health and well-being, but harmful to women. Within this body of literature, Walter Gove and his colleagues (Gove 1972, 1978, 1979; Gove and Tudor 1973; Gove and Zeiss 1987) focused upon role stress and strain in women's family roles and the limited alternative sources of gratification available to women. Gove observed that women's work within the home has little prestige or recognition, and can be boring and repetitive. Married women who are also employed face stress and strain from performing dual jobs in the home and in the marketplace. On the other hand, married men's work is located in only one realm—the marketplace—and this work is a source of status and power in the family. For men, "the family itself provides men with daily care. More than for women it is likely to be the sole source of emotional sustenance" (Riessman and Gerstel 1985:628). From this line of reasoning, men gain more than women do from marriage, and, hence, stand to lose more when marriage ends.

A good deal of evidence indicates that married men are happier, more satisfied with their lives, and otherwise have better mental health compared to married women (Calasanti 1996; Gove 1972; Gove and Tudor 1973; Keith 1980; Rosenfield 1989; Steil and Turetsky 1987; see also Coombs 1991). Although contradictory studies can be found for this conclusion (Thoits 1986; Wood, Rhodes, and Whelan 1989), the weight of evidence has been supportive.

There is also some empirical support for the extension of this thesis to spousal bereavement—since men apparently benefit more from marriage, they also "have more to lose when their spouses die" (Lee et al. 1998:626). Some studies do suggest that men's mental health is impacted more than women's when a spouse dies (e.g., Lee et al. 1998; Umberson et al. 1992). Researchers also have reported that men are more likely than women to experience physical health problems and increased mortality risks when a spouse dies. The evidence is not particularly overwhelming, however, especially for gender differences in physical health and mortality following bereavement. A number of studies have found more gender *similarities* than differences in how surviving partners respond to the death of a spouse (Chapter 4).

The research record also provides contradictory evidence for the thesis that women's mental health is worse when they are married than when they are single (cf. Glenn 1975; Gove and Tudor 1973; Haring-Hidore et al. 1985; Zollar and Williams 1987). Most studies have shown that married persons—both women and men—have better mental and physical health, less distress, and greater well-being compared to women and men who are not married. Studies also have found greater marital benefits for men relative to women (e.g., Lee et al. 1998; Schone and Weinick 1998; Umberson et al. 1992). These patterns seem to be more true for unmarried persons who have previously been married, however, than for those who have never married (Williams, Takeuchi, and Adair 1992).

Resource and Structural Explanations

Explanations focusing upon women's and men's differential positions in the social structure—and consequent differences in their access to resources—also have been utilized in the literatures reviewed here. Resource-based explanations have been used especially when focus is placed on women's economic vulnerabilities and the health problems which may ensue from income inadequacy.

Resource explanations for gender differences provide a partial picture of women's and men's lives. Certainly, much research attests to the importance of social, economic, and health resources for well-being at all ages (Chapter 3). However, these explanations tend to focus on a single slice in time (although this need not be the case) (Chapter 2). They tend to neglect what has come before in individuals' lives, and broader social processes and institutions also are often overlooked. Usually, focus is placed on specific resources which are available to individuals—health, income, and social ties—with less attention to *how* and *why* differential resources are allocated to individuals and groups in society.

Sometimes, but less often, attention is placed explicitly upon women's and men's structural locations in society. Gender differences in industrial placement of workers' jobs and sex segregation in occupations are thought to impact adaptation to aging (e.g., Calasanti 1996). Some writers also have explored whether imbalanced sex ratios are helpful or harmful to older women's adaptation (Chapters 3 and 4). Little direct testing of these theses has been conducted, however, a feature shared in common with gender role perspectives on adaptation to aging.

EVALUATING THE EMPIRICAL EVIDENCE ON GENDER DIFFERENCES

This book has evaluated the empirical evidence as well as theoretical approaches to gender differences in adaptation to aging. Approaches which exaggerate group differences are subject to "alpha bias." In contrast, approaches which ignore or minimize disparities between women and men are subject to "beta bias," such as when differences in women's and men's power and resources are overlooked. I have argued that traditional gender role theory encompasses *both* of these forms of bias (Chapter 2). Alpha bias is reflected in the assumption of dichotomous, nonoverlapping gender roles. Beta bias is reflected in the assumption that gender roles are complementary and equal.

In practice, the line between underestimating and overestimating gender differences is difficult to draw. In this book, I have worked to avoid both forms of bias, evaluating the weight of evidence concerning gender differences—or the lack thereof—as well as the quality of research. For the dimensions of adaptation examined here, "gender differences" clearly are a matter of degree. Conclusions about gender differences depend greatly upon the substantive focus for research, the measures that are utilized, and also how "difference" is assessed. "Researchers may choose to emphasize the size of mean differences, or within-group variability, or the overlap of group distributions to support the argument that sex differences do or do not exist" (Turner 1994:9).[1]

For these reasons, a focus on the factors *underlying* women's and men's experiences seems a useful approach. In recent years, gerontologists have been moving in this direction by investigating gendered pathways to retirement, for example. Such an approach shifts the focus from examining gender differences in outcome measures toward examining the *context* for women's and men's lives. A life course perspective provides an explicit framework to accomplish this.

EVALUATING THE LIFE COURSE PERSPECTIVE

This book has advanced a multi-level life course model which is organized around four broad, intersecting levels of human experience: *personal biographies* (including previous life events and patterns of experience, personality, patterns of coping, and so forth); *social location* (social class, race-ethnicity, gender, sexuality, age) and *membership in social groups* (for example, families and households); *birth cohort*; and *the broader societal context* (including large-scale societal events and the social policies and programs in place at a given period in time).

I have emphasized elements within this framework which correspond more closely to sociological investigations than to some other fields of inquiry. Psychological dimensions of adaptation have been touched upon but not emphasized in this work. Nor has the environmental context for aging been a focus, although this is clearly important to consider. The health of older adults is linked with the region of the country in which they live, for example, and the degree to which their environment is rural or urban (e.g., James et al. 1992; Krout 1995).

Thus, there is no single "theory of the life course." The multi-level life course model presented here accords most closely with Eleanor Stoller and Rose Gibson's framework (1994), which in turn builds upon a long history of life course study (Chapter 2). I have modified and expanded Stoller and Gibson's framework to identify more closely the levels of experience which can aid our understanding of differentiation and similarity in women's and men's lives. In order to illustrate important intersections between and within these levels of experience, I have also discussed specific exemplars of life course research. Results from these life

---

[1] Barbar Turner cites Eagly (1987) for this point.

course studies challenge central assumptions embedded in gender-difference explanations for adaptation to aging and life events in older age (specifically, spousal bereavement and retirement from paid labor).

I have argued that a life course perspective can only be enhanced by eliminating vestigial elements of functionalism (Chapter 2). Functionalist assumptions are evident, in particular, in the life course concept of on-time/off-time events. While the timing of life events is important in shaping subsequent trajectories of experience, studies have shown that violations of "timing norms" do not necessarily bring negative consequences to individuals. Individuals do *perceive* that there are "best times" or "expected times" to have children or get married or retire, but events experienced "off-time" apparently do not bring decreased health or well-being (Chapter 3). Similarly, although the death of a spouse may be more expected among older adults, little evidence shows that bereavement is easier in later life and more difficult at younger ages (Chapter 4). How the event is experienced and given meaning is more important than simply whether it occurs earlier or later in life. A focus on individuals' perceptions is consistent with the social constructionist approach reviewed in Chapter 2, which subsequent chapters of the book have drawn upon. More specifically, such a focus is consistent with the theoretical perspective of symbolic interactionism.

THEORETICAL UNDERPINNINGS

Many explanatory frameworks are built upon theoretical assumptions which may not be identified explicitly, but which provide conceptual foundations for the framework. The criticism has been made that the life course perspective is not linked explicitly with sociological (or other) theories, and hence that it lacks explanatory power (Passuth and Bengtson 1988). However, as I have shown, functionalism has served as an implicit foundation for some versions of the life course perspective.[2] Symbolic interactionism also serves as an implicit foundation for the life course perspective. In contrast to functionalism, symbolic interactionism provides a useful and important theoretical foundation for the life course approach.

The following section examines the contributions of symbolic interactionism to a life course perspective. I also address benefits to be gained from utilizing assumptions drawn from a macro-level theoretical perspective—that of political economy—which also helps to address theoretical lacunae in the life course approach. In contrast to symbolic interactionism, the perspective of political economy focuses upon the social structural context of aging (Minkler

---

[2] Diverse versions of functionalism have been formulated (e.g., Alexander 1985). The version I have presented here reflects the theory's usage in the gender and aging literature, which is the focus of this book.

1991), rather than the micro-level of social interaction and actors' subjective interpretations. Although it is beyond the scope of this book to attempt formal theoretical integrations, I believe it is important to make explicit the underlying theoretical frameworks which have helped to inform the issues addressed in this book.

Symbolic Interactionism

Symbolic interactionism is a variety of social constructionism (Hilbert 1986), which has served as a general orienting framework for this work (Chapter 2). In comparison to other varieties of social constructionism,[3] symbolic interactionists focus more fully on *how* human actors create and convey meanings through interaction with one another. Beliefs and expectations concerning gender, age, race, and other phenomena defined as "real" and socially relevant can be reinforced or challenged through social interaction. In turn, expectations for identity and behavior shape subsequent interactions and the decisions that individuals make throughout their lives.

Herbert Blumer coined the term *symbolic interactionism* in 1937 to identify "a relatively distinct approach to the study of human group life and human conduct" (Blumer 1969:1). To develop his own approach, Blumer drew from a range of notable scholars who shared "a great similarity in the general way in which they viewed and studied human group life" (p. 1), but he was especially indebted to George Herbert Mead. Blumer contended that other approaches in psychology and sociology (including Parsonsian functionalism) were "too mechanistic and ignored the active process of interpretation involved in both individual and coordinated social conduct" (see Handel 1993:129).

Blumer proposed three fundamental premises of symbolic interactionism. The first premise is that "human beings act toward things on the basis of the meanings that the things have for them" (1969:2). Second, "the meaning of a thing for a person grows out of the ways in which other persons act toward the person with regard to the thing" (p. 4). And third, "the use of meanings by the actor occurs through *a process of interpretation*" (p. 5). The first two premises identify, respectively, the importance of meaning ("the meanings that things have for human beings are central in their own right") (p. 3) and the source of meaning. The third premise emphasizes that meanings reflect an active interpretive process. Blumer cautions that "interpretation should not be regarded as a mere automatic application of established meanings but as a formative process in which meanings are used and revised as instruments for the guidance and formation of action" (p. 5).

---

[3] These include symbolic interactionism, ethnomethodology, labelling theory, "all manner of existential and phenomenological sociology," dramaturgical sociology, "plus a variety of specialized expressions of the perspective" (Hilbert 1986:7).

Blumer was greatly influenced by Mead, but focused more fully than did Mead upon the emergent nature of social interaction, which in turn follows from how the "self" is conceptualized. It is through the development of a self that human action and interaction is possible. Mead postulated that the self consists of two central processes, which he termed the "I" and the "me." Blumer's approach emphasizes the "I," the creative, emergent dimension of the self. In contrast, other interpretations of Mead's work have stressed the "me," "the relatively fixed parts of the self that are internalized from social roles" (Collins 1988:268). Role theory has developed from this latter emphasis on the "me."

Blumer's approach is encapsulated well in the following statement by the theorist:

> It is ridiculous, for instance, to assert, as a number of eminent sociologists have done, that social interaction is an interaction between social roles. Social interaction is obviously an interaction between *people* and not between roles; the needs of the participants are to interpret and handle what confronts them—such as a topic of conversation or a problem—and not to give expression to their roles. It is only in highly ritualistic relations that the direction and content of conduct can be explained by roles. Usually, the direction and content are fashioned out of what people in interaction have to deal with (Blumer 1969:75).

Thus, Blumer argues against fixed structures imposed by social roles—including, presumably, gender roles. In Blumer's perspective "one is not trapped in a social role, since one can detach oneself through the process of interpretation. Different 'me's' can be imagined and tried out" (Collins 1988:269). Blumer's approach buttresses the critique of traditional gender role theory detailed in Chapter 2 and supports a focus on the *interactional context* in which gendered meanings may be created, reinforced, or challenged. More generally, Blumer's emphasis on an active interpretive process is "fundamentally incompatible with Parsons's view that action is based on rational conformity to shared and relatively stable values" (Handel 1993:138).

A symbolic interactionist perspective is implicit in many of the studies reviewed in this book. Studies of adaptation to aging often rely upon individuals' assessments of their life circumstances, including their life satisfaction, happiness, perceived health, income adequacy, etc. Despite the frequent use of outcome measures such as these, life course researchers have tended to focus upon how individuals are impacted by life events such as the death of a spouse, or by large-scale events such as the Great Depression, and have neglected the active decision-making and interpretive processes on the part of human actors (George 1996).

In contrast, studies which have considered individuals' subjective interpretations have found, for example, that:

- Role overload is not as important in predicting psychological symptoms among women, compared to the women's *perceptions* of role conflict. If women perceive their roles as conflicting with one another, they are likely to suffer psychological distress (Chapter 3).

- Women and men may perceive that others in their environment *expect* them to become "androgynous" in older age, taking on both "feminine" and "masculine" qualities. The death of a spouse may promote such expectations on the part of surviving spouses and the friends and family with whom they interact—surviving spouses must often take on responsibilities their partners had performed. Family contexts in which older husbands take on a spousal caregiving role apparently help to shape men's views of themselves as nurturing and caring (Chapter 3).

- The cohort of white, working-class widows and never-married women included in Katherine Allen's study (1989) perceived the roles of wife and mother to be more valuable than alternative roles associated with remaining single. The widows' perceptions of having led fulfilling and valuable lives apparently provided them with a source of well-being in older age that was not available to women who had not married (Chapter 4).

- Among current cohorts of older adults, gender differences in the meaning of retirement are apparent for some racial groups, but not for others. Retirement meanings also are interwoven with women's and men's employment histories and health status. Differing meanings of retirement—and the differing retirement pathways which underlie these meanings—are masked when respondents are simply asked whether or not they are retired (Chapter 5).

Incorporation of the life course perspective and symbolic interactionism is consistent with earlier roots of these theoretical perspectives, reaching back to the Chicago school of sociology. Furthermore, some contemporary life course researchers make explicit use of symbolic interactionism in their work. For example, Glen Elder (1985) emphasizes that individuals' definitions of the situation must be considered to understand the impact of life events. Katherine Allen and Victoria Chin-Sang (1990) make a theoretical linkage in studying how aging African American women define work and leisure experiences over their lifetimes.

Symbolic interactionism rightfully has been critiqued as ahistoric and as neglecting broader social structures and processes (e.g., Stryker 1980). Theoretical linkages with the life course perspective can provide these vital missing pieces. However, because it is not an explanatory theory in itself, the life course perspective does not help us to understand *why* social institutions and processes have developed in particular ways. For this understanding, we must turn to other theoretical frameworks.

Political Economy

A political economy perspective helps to fill these theoretical gaps. Political economy and other conflict paradigms challenge functionalist assumptions that shared norms and values formed through consensus are fundamental to society. Rather, the social order reflects the dominance of powerful groups.

All versions of political economy draw upon Marxian theory; most incorporate facets of Weberian theory. The version described here moves beyond a Marxian focus on work which is socially defined as productive (wage-earning labor) to also consider unpaid work such as family caregiving and housework. In addition, this approach expands the concept of class beyond Marx's definition to include the impact of age, gender, and race-ethnicity relations on the relations of production (and of reproduction). Thus, recent developments in political economy address feminist concerns more adequately than have traditional versions of this perspective. In this regard, Carroll Estes argues "Any comprehensive theory must articulate not only the relations between state and economy, but also those with the household" (1999:22). The dynamics which give rise to and sustain these forms of work differ profoundly, but are interrelated. For example, the fact that family caregiving is not socially recognized as work has promoted the economic dependence of women on male wage earners.

The state plays a central role in defining and regulating relations of dependency. Continuing with the example above, U.S. social policy reflects and also helps to promote the definition of wage labor as the only form of "productive" work. Social Security and other social policies do not recognize unpaid work performed within the home, though society in general and capitalism in particular benefit from such labor (Cowan 1987; DeVault 1987; Glazer 1987).

Capitalism and the state are interdependent. The state depends upon revenue generated through private profit and the accumulation of private wealth (e.g., through taxation) (Offe and Ronge 1982). Further, the state is held responsible for the success of the economy—"the state bears the brunt of public dissatisfaction for economic difficulties" (Estes 1999:21). Conversely, the growth of private property and capital reinvestment are dependent upon the state.

It is thus unsurprising that inequalities structured into the economy are mirrored in social policies. Capital benefits from low-wage workers who can be moved easily in and out of the labor force. Upon retirement, Social Security provisions are lower for these workers relative to those with higher earnings and continuous labor force histories. Furthermore, workers' positions in the economy interlock with other forms of stratification. Women and racial-ethnic minorities are disproportionately represented in the peripheral sector of the economy, where jobs provide low wages, few if any fringe benefits, and little security (Dressel 1988).

Although political economy has focused primarily upon linkages between capitalism and the state, contemporary political economists increasingly argue that interconnections with patriarchy and racism also must be considered (Dressel et al. 1999; Estes 1999; Wallace 1991). These interconnections have been broad-ened to include issues of aging and older age. For example, Terry Arendell and Carroll Estes (1991) have examined gendered biases of retirement and health care policies for older adults. Steven Wallace (1991) has explored the political economy of health care for older African Americans. Paula Dressel (1988) has shown that we must consider intersections between race, class, and gender in the political economy of the United States in order to understand old-age poverty (see also Dressel et al. 1999).

The impact of structured inequalities extend beyond material conditions into the subjective realm. "Social policy reflects the dominant ideologies and belief systems that enforce, bolster, and extend the structure of advantage and disadvantage in the larger economic, political, and social order" (Estes 1999:30). Ideologies give rise to hegemony when "people accept as legitimate the conditions that lead to their own exploitation" (Hendricks and Leedham 1991:55). Hegemony is evidenced when women accept unquestioningly the social policies which carry economic penalties for doing "women's work" in the family. Hegemony also is denoted when racial-ethnic minorities accept racist ideologies which justify their overrepresentation in the lower rungs of the socioeconomic ladder.

Dominant ideologies, while pervasive, also meet with challenge and resis-tance. Throughout history, members of disenfrancised groups have questioned dominant belief systems and structural arrangements, as have (less often) mem-bers of advantaged groups (Collins 1990; Okihiro 1986). However, while conflict and resistance are integral to a political economy perspective, the micro-level processes and interactions of human actors are not a focus of this perspective.

Partly for this reason, political economy has been criticized as overly determinis-tic (Passuth and Bengtson 1988). Although political economists have considered linkages between the social structure and the subjective worlds of human actors (Hendricks and Leedham 1991), determinism is implied in statements such as Carroll Estes' that the situation of aging is "the product of social structural forces" (1999:19).[4] Insights from symbolic interactionism can provide to political economy the necessary volitional elements of human actors' reality construction and decision-making.

Conversely, political economy can be used to address limitations of symbolic interactionism, by helping to explain patterns and regularities of meaning construc-tion. The meanings that are created and re-created in social interaction (e.g., the meaning of "gender" or "work") do not come out of thin air. Specifically, symbolic interactionism has been criticized as neglecting social inequalities and the impact of the broader social structure. These phenomena are focal points of political economy.

---

[4] Estes subsequently addresses micro-macro linkages in the aging experience, and reflects upon the symbolic interactionist argument that growing old "is neither immutable nor 'given' by the character of external reality" (1999:28).

This is not to imply that symbolic interactionism and political economy are entirely compatible theories. As suggested in the preceding paragraphs, a central difference concerns the way in which social structure is conceptualized. Symbolic interactionists view the social structure as accomplished through social interaction and formed through the patterning of micro-level social process. Blumer and other symbolic interactionists associated with the Chicago School take this processual view further in conceiving social organization as fluid and tenuous. Political economists' conceptualization of social structure depends upon the degree to which they lean more toward traditional Marxian analysis, which tends to view the social structure and macro-level social processes as material facts, or a more balanced melding of Marxian and Weberian approaches.

From a symbolic interactionist perspective, it is the *perception* of the opportunities which are available to ourselves and others which is key, rather than "objective" features of social stratification and inequality. The oft-quoted encapsulation of this perspective is "If men [sic] define situations as real, they are real in their consequences" (Thomas and Thomas 1928:572). However, it is difficult to deny that differing groups in society face different life chances in the form of economic resources, health, risks for unemployment, and so on, and that these structured inequalities impact the interactional realm.

I have addressed the need to integrate symbolic interactionist insights with a life course perspective. Political economy also meshes well with a life course perspective. First, both are historically-grounded approaches. Political economists retain, by and large, the historical materialism of marxian analysis, which links social and economic relationships to the mode of production in place at a given point in time. Second, both political economy and a life course perspective focus upon linkages between hierarchies of inequality. According to Meredith Minkler, "a major contribution of the political economy perspective it its ability to highlight the intersections of race, class, gender, and aging as they shape and determine the experience of growing old" (1991:10). This statement calls attention to a third point of comparison: Political economy has been turned to issues of the life course. The status, resources, and health available in older age, as well as the life course trajectories which lead to older age, are shaped by "one's location in the social structure and the relations generated by the economic mode of production and the gendered division of labor" (Estes 1999:19). However, political economy does not address the multiple levels of human experience which are encompassed by a life course perspective (which considers birth cohorts, individuals' histories of experience, and so forth).

Some of the central points made in this book which follow from a political economy perspective include:

Old age policies and programs perpetuate economic inequalities established prior to retirement. Political economy identifies "how social policy for the aged mirrors the structural arrangements of U.S. society and the distribution of material, political, and symbolic (e.g., ideological) resources within it" (Estes 1999:18).

- Women and racial-ethnic minorities are less likely to receive benefits from a private pension source, and these groups receive lower average benefits when they are eligible (Chapter 5). Social Security provides a measure of support for older adults who otherwise would lack virtually any economic sustenance. However, those who were economically vulnerable prior to retirement typically receive low Social Security benefits and are vulnerable to poverty in old age (Chapters 3 and 5).

Public and private pension policies simultaneously reflect and reinforce traditional assumptions about gender, work, and family life.

- Unpaid work performed within the home is not considered work, and is not incorporated in pension programs. Although it might be argued that spousal benefits implicitly recognize childcare, elder care, and domestic labor more generally, spousal benefits are just that—benefits provided to a spouse. "Women do not earn spousal benefits by performing reproductive labor but by maintaining a marital relationship" (Harrington Meyer 1990:556). Benefits are based on family status rather than unpaid household labor, and thus are subject to change when family status changes (Chapters 3 and 4).
- Private and public pension programs in the United States provide greatest benefits to men and women who maintain a traditional marriage (Chapter 4). Both women and men risk economic losses when marriage ends, but women's risks (within racial-ethnic groups) are greater due to their greater likelihood of economic dependence on a male breadwinner. "By ignoring that marriage ends for a large proportion of older women, pension plan and individual retirement account rule structures systematically penalize women as a group" (Harrington Meyer 1990:554).
- Family dependencies are reinforced in pension policies. This is literally the case in that the Social Security benefits which most married women receive are designated for "dependent spouses" of the primary wage-earner. Furthermore, spousal benefits from public as well as private sources are permanently reduced if the primary beneficiary retires early (Chapter 4).

Racial-ethnic biases also underlie U.S. social policies.

- For example, by ignoring the lower life expectancies of racial-ethnic minorities, and of poor people in particular, public and private pension programs also penalize these groups by setting universal ages for the initial receipt of benefits (Chapter 5).

According to this reasoning, it may be argued that women benefit unfairly from Social Security due to their longer life expectancies. However, women already live out their longer lives on typically low levels of benefits. And, as has been noted, "women's work" is not considered work in pension calculations, despite its value to society in general and capital in particular (e.g., Cowan 1987; DeVault 1987; Glazer 1987).

Together, political economy and symbolic interactionism provide explanatory elements missing from the life course perspective. Without political economy, we cannot explain why social policies unfavorable to older women and racial-ethnic minorities have been developed, for example. Without symbolic interaction, we cannot explain how women and men attach meanings to their life experiences, how they define themselves and others, and how they act upon those meanings. On the other hand, a life course perspective provides crucial elements which are missing or neglected in symbolic interactionism and political economy, and also provides a useful organizing framework for considering multiple dimensions of human experience.

These are not the only theoretical approaches which can be integrated with a life course perspective, of course. Scholars from diverse fields have examined the potential for cross-fertilization of the life course perspective with demography (Uhlenberg 1996), stress paradigms (Pearlin and Skaff 1996), and perspectives within social psychology (George 1996), for example. For each of these approaches, the use of a life course perspective can help to guide the conceptualization of research questions and methodologies and the interpretation of findings.

In sum, the life course perspective provides a flexible framework which can be integrated fruitfully with diverse theoretical approaches. A life course approach provides the temporal dimensions of experience absent or neglected in many theoretical perspectives. As reflected in the multi-level life course model advanced in this book, temporality is located at the micro level of personal biographies and at the macro social-historical level (for example, by considering the social policies and programs in place at particular points in time). Explicit micro-macro linkages are incorporated via the concepts of birth cohort and social location.

Modifying the Study of Adaptation to Aging

I have addressed the need to draw upon additional theoretical frameworks to enhance the focus and explanatory power of a life course perspective. The need to modify the study of adaptation to aging also is evident. The term itself is value-laden. We can take individuals' own assessments of their health, economic, and emotional well-being as the "litmus test" for adaptation, as suggested initially (Chapter 2) (an approach which is consistent with symbolic interactionism), but the implication remains that adaptation is something which is "good" or "bad."

Individuals adapt "well" to aging, or they adapt "poorly."[5] The focus—and often an implied judgment—centers upon individuals rather than the social and historical contexts which help to frame opportunities and constraints for individuals and groups over the life course.[6]

Throughout the book, I have raised questions regarding functionalist elements in the study of aging. Functionalist assumptions are embodied in the life course concept of on-time/off-time life events, as well as in traditional gender role theory, which continues to be utilized in many studies of aging. Functionalist concerns also are reflected in the assumption that spousal bereavement and retirement constitute "role losses" which require extensive adaptive efforts on the part of individuals. The implicit assumption that individuals must adapt to these changes in order to regain equilibrium derives directly from functionalism, as does the assumption that equilibrium or a steady state characterized the individual's life prior to a stressful life event.

The notion that one "recovers" and returns to "normal" seems especially incongruous in the context of bereavement. Hansson, Carpenter, and Fairchild (1993) point out that bereaved persons never really "recover," but rather "are forever changed in certain ways" (p. 68). For this reason, measures reflecting "recovery to baseline" following spousal bereavement are not as useful as a focus upon coping processes. These writers define coping as a "process as combating the problem rather than good outcome" (1993:68). This definition is helpful in moving beyond outcome measures (and implied value judgments). Leonard Pearlin and Marilyn Skaff (1996:242) provide a necessary temporal dimension for the concept: coping can be understood "as the evolving and selective use of adaptive skills as one moves across the life course" (see Kahana 1992). A *meaning* component to coping also is incorporated. As people grow older, they "tend increasingly to rely on the management of meaning of difficult situations rather than the management or change of the situations themselves" (Pearlin and Skaff 1996:242). The authors propose that a shift toward the management of meaning occurs as an accommodation to increasing constraints of older age. Although

---

[5] In recent years, there has been some movement away from "adaptation" terminology toward alternatives such as "productive aging" and "successful aging." For example, Rose Gibson defines productive aging as "engagements over a lifetime in paid or unpaid activities that produce valued goods or services" (1995:279). Successful aging is defined as "reaching one's potential and arriving at a level of physical, social, and psychological well-being in old age that is pleasing to both self and others" (p. 279). Gibson's emphasis on unpaid as well as paid "productive" activities over the life course and upon self-evaluation of "success" in aging seems useful, though considerable ambiguity remains in this terminology (e.g., who are the "others" who evaluate the "pleasing aspects" of one's aging?). For other definitions of successful aging, see Baltes and Baltes (1990); Ikels et al. (1995); Moen, Dempster-McClain, and Williams (1992); Rowe and Kahn (1997).

[6] More specifically, the literature on adaptation to aging may reflect race and class biases. Dressel, Minkler, and Yen point out that concepts such as "'adjustment to old age' may have little relevance among groups such as African Americans for whom aging may be experienced not as a series of adjustments but as a process of survival" (1999:280).

fewer studies of adaptation to aging have examined *processes* of coping—as opposed to presumed outcomes of coping—progress is being made in this direction.

In addition, scholars of aging increasingly consider sources of *chronic strain* over the life course, moving from a primary focus on stressful life events in older age (e.g., Krause 1995; Pearlin and Skaff 1996). Most studies of stressful life events have found only modest associations with mental health (Wheaton 1990). Instead of being detrimental to health, some life events may offer relief from a chronically stressful situation. A focus on sources of stress which extend over time is consistent with the central tenets and goals of a life course perspective (e.g., Elder et al. 1996; Pearlin and Skaff 1996).

Leonard Pearlin and Marilyn McKean Skaff identify three types of chronic stressors "that arise more insidiously and that are more persistent than eruptive events" (1996:241). The likelihood that individuals will experience a particular chronic stress and the way in which the stressor is experienced and interpreted are influenced by the life course dimensions discussed in this book—personal histories of experience, individuals' placement in society and access to resources, and the socio-historical context for aging experienced by successive birth cohorts.

One type of chronic stressor identified by the authors is role strain, which is linked with institutional roles, particularly those involving the family. Pearlin and Skaff authors note that family-related conflicts may "arise early and continue to smolder across the entirety of the life course" (p. 241). Whether short-term or of long duration, family conflicts can be a source of great distress. The authors link health and financial problems with role strains because these problems can hinder the ability to fulfill role expectations.[7]

Ambient strains stem from conditions experienced in one's community and neighborhood. As individuals grow older (and contingent upon other life course dimensions), feelings of vulnerability and perceived threats to one's safety and well-being may increase. Changes in once-familiar neighborhoods can be stressful for long-time residents. Difficulties in accessing transportation, health care, and other services and amenities bring additional sources of chronic hardships.

Quotidian strains are the third source of chronic stress addressed by Pearlin and Skaff, referring to the ability to perform daily tasks and activities. These are "closely related to physical capacities and, therefore, exposure to them typically begins in young-old age and accelerates with the approach of old-old age" (p. 242). Such difficulties are potentially wide-ranging, including such things as climbing stairs, preparing meals, using the bathtub or shower, and so on. Although these activities generally are taken for granted for those who can perform them

---

[7] Other researchers focus directly on the effects of chronic health or financial strains, and do not ground these in role theory (e.g., Krause 1995).

readily, "they can emerge as the outstanding challenges of daily life" (p. 242). Just as exposure to these and other stressors varies across the life course, so does the availability of resources to cope with stressful conditions.

A further development in the study of adaptation to aging is the increasing recognition that gerontologists must move beyond a traditional focus on losses and decrements with aging. Powell Lawton argues that gerontology published "more bad-news reports in its earlier years" (1997:192) when the discipline was developing, but that more attention has been paid in recent years to "positive aspects" of aging, including personal growth, environmental mastery, satisfying relationships with others, and productivity among older people. Because retirement and widow/erhood have been central to theories and research on gender differences in aging, these life events have served as foci for this book. Rather than viewing these events primarily as "role losses," some researchers have emphasized that these events can bring positive as well as negative changes to individuals and families (e.g., Atchley 1992; Lopata 1996; Lund et al. 1986b) (Chapters 4 and 5).

Building Bridges: A Concluding Note

A primary goal of this book has been to show that cross-fertilization between gender studies and aging studies can be facilitated through the use of a life course perspective. This perspective provides, in my view, an effective framework to investigate sources of similarity as well as difference between—and among— women and men, across time and social space. Much remains to be done to refine the life course perspective, including developing theoretical linkages which enhance its explanatory power. By building such bridges, we can move further in attaining deeper, more satisfying insights about gender and aging.

References

Achenbaum, W. Andrew and Vern L. Bengtson. 1994. Re-engaging the disengagement theory of aging: On the history and assessment of theory development in gerontology. *The Gerontologist* 34(6):756-763.

Adams, Rebecca G. 1994. Older men's friendship patterns. In *Older Men's Lives*, edited by Edward H. Thompson, Jr. (pp. 159-177). Thousand Oaks, CA: Sage.

Ade-Ridder, Linda and Timothy H. Brubaker. 1988. Expected and reported division of responsibility of household tasks among older wives in two residential settings. *Journal of Consumer Studies and Home Economics* 12(1):59-70.

Adelman, Marcy. 1991. Stigma, gay lifestyles, and adjustment to aging: A study of later-life gay men and lesbians. *Journal of Homosexuality* 20(3/4):7-32.

Adelmann, Pamela K. 1994. Multiple roles and physical health among older adults: Gender and ethnic comparisons. *Research on Aging* 16(2):142-166.

Aiken, Lewis R. 1989. *Later Life.* 3rd ed. Hillsdale, NJ: Lawrence Erlbaum Associates.

Aiken, Lewis R. 1991. *Dying, Death, and Bereavement.* 2nd ed. Boston: Allyn and Bacon.

Aiken, Lewis R. 1995. *Aging: An Introduction to Gerontology.* Thousand Oaks, CA: Sage.

Akiyama, Hiroko, Kathryn Elliott, and Toni C. Antonucci. 1996. Same-sex and cross-sex relationships. *Journal of Gerontology* 51B(6):P374-P382.

Alexander, Jeffrey C., ed. 1985. *Neofunctionalism.* Newbury Park, CA: Sage.

Allen, Katherine R. 1989. *Single Women/Family Ties.* Newbury Park, CA: Sage.

Allen, Katherine R. 1995. Opening the classroom closet: Sexual orientation and self-disclosure. *Family Relations* 44(2):136-141.

Allen, Katherine R. and Victoria Chin-Sang. 1990. A lifetime of work: The context and meanings of leisure for aging black women. *The Gerontologist* 30(6):734-740.

Allen, Katherine R. and Robert S. Pickett. 1987. Forgotten streams in the family life course: Utilization of qualitative retrospective interviews in the analysis of lifelong single women's family careers. *Journal of Marriage and the Family* 49(3):517-526.

Altergott, Karen. 1985. Marriage, gender, and social relations in late life. In *Social Bonds in Later Life: Aging and Interdependence,* edited by Warren A. Peterson and Jill Quadagno (pp. 51-70). Beverly Hills, CA: Sage.

Amato, Paul R. and Sonia Partridge. 1987. Widows and divorcees with dependent children: Material, personal, family, and social well-being. *Family Relations* 36(3):316-320.

Anderson, Karen. 1988. A history of women's work in the United States. In *Women Working,* 2nd ed., edited by Ann Helton Stromberg and Shirley Harkess (pp. 25-41). Mountain View, CA: Mayfield.

Anderson, Kathryn H., Richard V. Burkhauser, and Joseph F. Quinn. 1983. Do retirement dreams come true? The effect of unexpected events on retirement age. *Discussion Paper 750-84*, Madison, WI: Institute for Research on Poverty, University of Wisconsin-Madison.

Anderson, Trudy B. 1992. Conjugal support among working-wife and retired-wife couples. In *Families and Retirement*, edited by Maximiliane Szinovacz, David J. Ekerdt, and Barbara H. Vinick (pp. 174-188). Newbury Park, CA: Sage.

Aneshensel, Carol S., Carolyn M. Rutter, and Peter A. Lachenbruch. 1991. Social structure, stress, and mental health: Competing conceptual and analytic models. *American Sociological Review* 56(2):166-178.

Angel, Jacqueline Lowe and Dennis P. Hogan. 1992. The demography of minority aging populations. *Journal of Family History* 17(1):95-115.

Angel, Ronald J. and Jacqueline L. Angel. 1996. The extent of private and public health insurance coverage among adult Hispanics. *The Gerontologist* 36(3):332-340.

Antonovsky, Aaron, Shifra Sagy, Israel Adler, and Rimona Visel. 1990. Attitudes toward retirement in an Israeli cohort. *International Journal of Aging and Human Development* 31(1):57-77.

Antonucci, Toni C. 1991. Attachment, social support, and coping with negative life events in mature adulthood. In *Life-Span Developmental Psychology*, edited by E. Mark Cummings, Anita L. Greene, and Katherine H. Karraker (pp. 261-276). Hillsdale, NJ: Lawrence Erlbaum Associates.

Antonucci, Toni C. and Hiroko Akiyama. 1987a. An examination of sex differences in social support among older men and women. *Sex Roles* 17(11/12):737-749.

Antonucci, Toni C. and Hiroko Akiyama. 1987b. Social networks in adult life and a preliminary examination of the convoy model. *Journal of Gerontology* 42(5):519-527.

Arber, Sara and Jay Ginn. 1991. *Gender and Later Life: A Sociological Analysis of Resources and Constraints*. London: Sage.

Arber, Sara and Jay Ginn. 1995. Connecting gender and ageing: A new beginning? In *Connecting Gender & Ageing: A Sociological Approach*, edited by Sara Arber and Jay Ginn (pp. 173-178). Buckingham, England: Open University Press.

Arbuckle, Nancy Weber and Brian de Vries. 1995. The long-term effects of later life spousal and parental bereavement on personal functioning. *The Gerontologist* 35(5):637-647.

Arendell, Terry J. 1987. Women and the economics of divorce in the contemporary United States. *Signs: Journal of Women in Culture and Society* 13(1):121-135.

Arendell, Terry and Carroll L. Estes. 1991. Older women in the post-Reagan era. In *Critical Perspectives on Aging: Toward a Political and Moral Economy of Aging*, edited by Meredith Minkler and Carroll L. Estes (pp. 209-226). Amityville, NY: Baywood.

Arens, Diana Antos. 1982/83. Widowhood and well-being: An examination of sex differences within a causal model. *International Journal of Aging and Human Development* 15(1):27-40.

Aries, Philippe. 1974. *Western Attitudes Toward DEATH: From the Middle Ages to the Present*. Baltimore, MD: Johns Hopkins University Press.

Arling, Greg. 1976. The elderly widow and her family, neighbors, and friends. *Journal of Marriage and the Family* 38(4):757-768.

Atchley, Robert C. 1971. Disengagement among professors. *Journal of Gerontology* 26(4): 476-480.

Atchely, Robert C. 1972. *The Social Forces in Later Life: An Introduction to Social Gerontology.* Belmont, CA: Wadsworth.

Atchely, Robert C. 1975. Dimensions of widowhood in later life. *The Gerontologist* 15(2):176-178.

Atchely, Robert C. 1976a. Selected social and psychological differences between men and women in later life. *Journal of Gerontology* 31(2):204-211.

Atchely, Robert C. 1976b. *The Sociology of Retirement.* New York: John Wiley and Sons.

Atchely, Robert C. 1976c. Orientation toward the job and retirement adjustment among women. In *Time, Roles, and Self in Old Age,* edited by Jaber F. Gubrium (pp. 199-208). New York: Human Sciences Press.

Atchely, Robert C. 1982. The process of retirement: Comparing women and men. In *Women's Retirement: Policy Implications for Recent Research,* edited by Maximiliane Szinovacz (pp. 153-168). Beverly Hills: Sage.

Atchely, Robert C. 1989. A continuity theory of normal aging. *The Gerontologist* 29(2):183-190.

Atchely, Robert C. 1992. Retirement and marital satisfaction. In *Families and Retirement,* edited by Maximiliane Szinovacz, David J. Ekerdt, and Barbara H. Vinick (pp. 145-158). Newbury Park, CA: Sage.

Atchely, Robert C. 1994. *Social Forces & Aging: An Introduction to Social Gerontology.* 7th ed. Belmont, CA: Wadsworth.

Atchley, Robert C., Linda Pignatiello, and Ellen C. Shaw. 1979. Interactions with family and friends: Marital status and occupational differences among older women. *Research on Aging* 1(1):83-95.

Atchley, Robert C. and Judith L. Robinson. 1982. Attitudes toward retirement and distance from the event. *Research on Aging* 4(3):299-313.

Babchuk, Nicholas and Trudy B. Anderson. 1989. Older widows and married women: Their intimates and confidants. *International Journal of Aging and Human Development* 28(1):21-35.

Babchuk, Nicholas and Alan Booth. 1969. Voluntary association membership: A longitudinal analysis. *American Sociological Review* 34(1):31-45.

Baldassare, Mark, Sarah Rosenfield, and Karen Rook. 1984. The types of social relations predicting elderly well-being. *Research on Aging* 6(4):549-559.

Balkwell, Carolyn. 1985. An attitudinal correlate of the timing of a major life event: The case of morale in widowhood. *Family Relations* 34(4):577-581.

Ball, Justine F. 1977. Widow's grief: The impact of age and mode of death. *Omega: The Journal of Death and Dying* 7(4):307-333.

Baltes, Paul B. 1987. Theoretical propositions of life-span developmental psychology: On the dynamics between growth and decline. *Developmental Psychology* 23(5):611-626.

Baltes, Paul B. and Margret M. Baltes. 1990. Psychological perspectives on successful aging: The model of selective optimization with compensation. In *Successful Aging: Perspectives from the Behavioral Sciences,* edited by Paul B. Baltes and Margret M. Baltes (pp. 1-34). Cambridge: Cambridge University Press.

Bankoff, Elizabeth A. 1983. Social support and adaptation to widowhood. *Journal of Marriage and the Family* 45(4):827-839.

Barer, Barbara M. 1994. Men and women aging differently. *International Journal of Aging and Human Development* 38(1):29-40.

Barfield, Richard E. and James N. Morgan. 1978. Trends in satisfaction with retirement. *The Gerontologist* 18(1):19-23.

Barnett, Rosalind C. and Grace K. Baruch. 1985. Women's involvement in multiple roles and psychological distress. *Journal of Personality and Social Psychology* 49(1): 135-145.

Barnett, Rosalind C., Nancy L. Marshall, and Joseph H. Pleck. 1992. Men's multiple roles and their relationship to men's psychological distress. *Journal of Marriage and the Family* 54(2):358-367.

Barrow, Georgia M. 1989. *Aging, the Individual, and Society.* 4th ed. St. Paul, MN: West.

Barry, Herbert, III, Margaret K. Bacon, and Irvin L. Child. 1957. A cross-cultural survey of some sex differences in socialization. *Journal of Abnormal and Social Psychology* 55(3):327-332.

Baruch, Grace K. 1984. The psychological well-being of women in the middle years. In *Women in Midlife,* edited by Grace Baruch and Jeanne Brooks-Gunn (pp. 161-180). New York: Plenum Press.

Bastida, Elena. 1987. Sex-typed age norms among older Hispanics. *The Gerontologist* 27(1):59-65.

Baur, Patricia A. and Morris A. Okun. 1983. Stability of life satisfaction in late life. *The Gerontologist* 23(3):261-265.

Bearon, Lucille B. 1989. No great expectations: The underpinnings of life satisfaction for older women. *The Gerontologist* 29(6):772-778.

Beck, Scott H. 1982. Adjustment to and satisfaction with retirement. *Journal of Gerontology* 37(5):616-624.

Beck, Scott H. 1983. Position in the economic structure and unexpected retirement. *Research on Aging* 5(2):197-216.

Beecher, Maureen Ursenbach, Carol Cornwall Madsen, and Lavinia Fielding Anderson. 1988. Widowhood among the Mormons: The personal accounts. In *On Their Own: Widows and Widowhood in the American Southwest 1848-1939,* edited by Arlene Scadron (pp. 117-139). Chicago, IL: University of Illinois Press.

Beeson, Diane. 1981. Women in aging studies: A critique and suggestions. In *Controversial Issues in Gerontology,* edited by Harold J. Wershow (pp. 120-126). New York: Springer.

Bell, Bill D. 1978/79. Life satisfaction and occupational retirement: Beyond the impact year. *International Journal of Aging and Human Development* 9(1):31-50.

Belsky, Janet. 1999. *The Psychology of Aging: Theory, Research, and Interventions,* 3rd ed. Pacific Grove, CA: Brooks/Cole.

Bem, Sandra Lipsitz. 1977. On the utility of alternative procedures for assessing psychological androgyny. *Journal of Consulting and Clinical Psychology* 45(2): 196-205.

Bem, Sandra Lipsitz. 1978. Beyond androgyny: Some presumptuous prescriptions for a liberated sexual identity. In *The Psychology of Women: Future Directions in Research,* edited by Julia A. Sherman and Florence L. Denmark (pp. 1-23). New York: Psychological Dimensions.

Bengtson, Vern L. and Leslie A. Morgan. 1987. Ethnicity and aging: A comparison of three ethnic groups. In *Growing Old in Different Societies: Cross-Cultural Perspectives,* edited by Jay Sokolovsky (pp. 157-167). Acton, MA: Copley.

Bennett, Neil G., David E. Bloom, and Cynthia K. Miller. 1995. The influence of nonmarital childbearing on the formation of first marriages. *Demography* 32(1): 47-62.

Berardo, Felix M. 1970. Survivorship and social isolation: The case of the aged widower. *The Family Coordinator* 19(1):11-25.

Berger, Raymond M. 1982. The unseen minority: Older gays and lesbians. *Social Work* 27(3):236-242.

Bernard, Jessie. [1972] 1978. *The Future of Marriage.* New York: Bantam.

Bielby, William T. and Denise D. Bielby. 1989. Family ties: Balancing commitments to work and family in dual earner households. *American Sociological Review* 54(5): 776-789.

Blair, Sampson Lee and Michael P. Johnson. 1992. Wives' perceptions of the fairness of the division of household labor: The intersection of housework and ideology. *Journal of Marriage and the Family* 54(3):570-581.

Blau, Peter M. 1977. *Inequality and Heterogeneity: A Primitive Theory of Social Structure.* New York: The Free Press.

Blau, Zena Smith. 1961. Structural constraints on friendships in old age. *American Sociological Review* 26(3):429-439.

Blau, Zena Smith. 1973. *Old Age in a Changing Society.* New York: New Viewpoints.

Block, Jeanne H. 1976. Debatable conclusions about sex differences. *Contemporary Psychology* 21:517-522.

Block, Marilyn R. 1982. Professional women: Work pattern as a correlate of retirement satisfaction. In *Women's Retirement: Policy Implications of Recent Research,* edited by Maximiliane Szinovacz (pp. 183-194). Newbury Park, CA: Sage.

Blom, Ida. 1991. The history of widowhood: A bibliographic overview. *Journal of Family History* 16(2):191-210.

Blumer, Herbert. 1969. *Symbolic Interactionism: Perspective and Method.* Englewood Cliffs, NJ: Prentice-Hall, Inc.

Booth, Alan. 1972. Sex and social participation. *American Sociological Review* 37(2): 183-192.

Borgatta, Edgar F. and Rhonda J. V. Montgomery. 1986. Plausible theories and the development of scientific theory: The case of aging research. *Research on Aging* 8(4):586-608.

Bornstein, Philipp E., Paula J. Clayton, James A. Halikas, William L. Maurice, and Eli Robins. 1973. The depression of widowhood after thirteen months. *British Journal of Psychiatry* 122:561-566.

Bossé, Raymond, Carolyn M. Aldwin, Michael R. Levenson, and Kathryn Workman-Daniels. 1991. How stressful is retirement? Findings from the Normative Aging Study. *Journal of Gerontology* 46(1):P9-14.

Bosworth, Hayden B. and K. Warner Schaie. 1997. The relationship of social environment, social networks, and health outcomes in The Seattle Longitudinal Study: Two analytical approaches. *Journal of Gerontology* 52B(5):P197-P205.

Bould, Sally, Beverly Sanborn, and Laura Reif. 1989. *Eighty-Five Plus: The Oldest Old.* Belmont, CA: Wadsworth.

Bound, John, Greg J. Duncan, Deborah S. Laren, and Lewis Oleinick. 1991. Poverty dynamics in widowhood. *Journal of Gerontology* 46(3):S115-124.

Bound, John, Michael Schoenbaum, and Timothy Waidmann. 1996. Race differences in labor force status and disability status. *The Gerontologist* 36(3):311-321.

Bowlby, John. 1960. Separation anxiety. *The International Journal of Psycho-analysis* 41(2-3):89-113.

Bowling, Ann. 1987. Mortality after bereavement: A review of the literature on survival periods and factors affecting survival. *Social Science and Medicine* 24(2): 117-124.

Bradford, Leland P. 1979. Emotional problems in retirement and what can be done. *Group & Organization Studies* 4(4):429-439.

Brehm, Sharon S. 1992. *Intimate Relationships,* 2nd ed. New York: McGraw-Hill.

Brim, Orville G., Jr. 1980. Type of life events. *Journal of Social Issues* 36(1):148-157.

Britton, Dana M. 1997. Gendered organizational logic: Policy and practice in men's and women's prisons. *Gender & Society* 11(6):796-818.

Brody, Elaine M. 1985. Parent care as a normative family stress. *The Gerontologist* 25(1):19-29.

Brody, Elaine M. and Claire B. Schoonover. 1986. Patterns of parent-care when adult daughters work and when they do not. *The Gerontologist* 26(4):372-381.

Brody, Elaine M., Morton H. Kleban, Pauline T. Johnsen, Christine Hoffman, and Claire B. Schoonover. 1987. Work status and parent care: A comparison of four groups of women. *The Gerontologist* 27(2):201-208.

Brokenleg, Martin and David Middleton. 1993. Native Americans: Adapting, yet retaining. In *Ethnic Variations in Dying, Death, and Grief: Diversity in Universality,* edited by Donald P. Irish, Kathleen F. Lundquist, and Vivian Jenkins Nelsen (pp. 101-112). Washington, DC: Taylor & Francis.

Broverman, Inge K., Donald M. Broverman, Frank E. Clarkson, Paul S. Rosenkrantz, and Susan R. Vogel. 1970. Sex-role stereotypes and clinical judgments of mental health. *Journal of Consulting and Clinical Psychology* 34(1):1-7.

Brubaker, Ellie and Timothy H. Brubaker. 1992. The context of retired women as caregivers. In *Families and Retirement,* edited by Maximiliane Szinovacz, David J. Ekerdt, and Barbara H. Vinick (pp. 222-235). Newbury Park, CA: Sage.

Bugen, Larry A. 1977. Human grief: A model for prediction and intervention. *American Journal of Orthopsychiatry* 47(2):196-206.

Bulcroft, Kris A. and Richard A. Bulcroft. 1991. The timing of divorce: Effects on parent-child relationships in later life. *Research on Aging* 13(2):226-243.

Burgess, Ernest W. 1960. Family structure and relationships. In *Aging in Western Societies,* edited by Ernest W. Burgess (pp. 271-298). Chicago, IL: University of Chicago Press.

Burkhauser, Richard V. 1994. Protecting the most vulnerable: A proposal to improve Social Security Insurance for older women. *The Gerontologist* 34(2):148-149.

Burkhauser, Richard V., Karen C. Holden, and Daniel Feaster. 1988. Incidence, timing, and events associated with poverty: A dynamic view of poverty in retirement. *Journal of Gerontology* 43(2):S46-52.

Burkhauser, Richard V., J. S. Butler, and Karen C. Holden. 1991. How the death of a spouse affects economic well-being after retirement: A hazard model approach. *Social Science Quarterly* 72(3):504-519.

Burkhauser, Richard V., Greg J. Duncan, and Richard Hauser. 1994. Sharing prosperity across the age distribution: A comparison of the United States and Germany in the 1980s. *The Gerontologist* 34(2):150-160.

Burnham, Linda. 1985. Has poverty been feminized in Black America? *The Black Scholar* 16(2):14-24.

Burr, Jeffrey A. 1992. Household status and headship among unmarried Asian Indian women in later life: Availability, feasability, and desirability factors. *Research on Aging* 14(2):199-225.

Cafferata, Gail Lee. 1987. Marital status, living arrangements, and the use of health services by elderly persons. *Journal of Gerontology* 42(6):613-618.

Cahill, Spencer E. 1986. Childhood socialization as a recruitment process: some lessons from the study of gender development. In *Sociological Studies of Child Development: A Research Annual,* edited by Patricia A. Adler, Peter Adler, and Nancy Mandell (pp. 163-186). Greenwich, CT: JAI Press.

Calasanti, Toni M. 1992. Theorizing about gender and aging: Beginning with the voices of women. *The Gerontologist* 32(2):280-282.

Calasanti, Toni M. 1996. Gender and life satisfaction in retirement: An assessment of the male model. *Journal of Gerontology* 51B(1):S18-S29.

Calasanti, Toni M. and Alessandro Bonanno. 1992. Working "over-time": Economic restructuring and retirement of a class. *The Sociological Quarterly* 33(1):135-152.

Calasanti, Toni M. and Anna M. Zajicek. 1993. A socialist-feminist approach to aging: Embracing diversity. *Journal of Aging Studies* 7(2):117-131.

Caldwell, Mayta A. and Letitia Anne Peplau. 1982. Sex differences in same-sex friendship. *Sex Roles* 8(7):721-732.

Candy, Sandra E. Gibbs. 1977. What do women use friends for? In *Looking Ahead,* edited by Lillian E. Troll (pp. 106-111). Englewood Cliffs, NJ: Prentice-Hall.

Carey, Ramond G. 1979. Weathering widowhood: Problems and adjustment of the widowed during the first year. *Omega: The Journal of Death and Dying* 10(2):163-174.

Cavan, Ruth Shonle. 1962. Self and role in adjustment during old age. In *Human Behavior and Social Processes,* edited by A. M. Rose (pp. 526-536). Boston, MA: Houghton Mifflin.

Cavan, Ruth Shonle, Ernest W. Burgess, Robert J. Havighurst, and Herbert Goldhamer. 1949. *Personal Adjustment in Old Age.* Chicago, IL: Science Research Associates, Inc.

Chafetz, Janet Saltzman. 1974. *Masculine/Feminine or Human? An Overview of the Sociology of Sex Roles.* Itasca, IL: F.E. Peacock.

Chappell, Neena L. 1995. Informal social support. In *Promoting Successful and Productive Aging,* edited by Lynne A. Bond, Stephen J. Cutler, and Armin Grams (pp. 171-185). Thousand Oaks, CA: Sage.

Chappell, Neena L. and Mark Badger. 1989. Social isolation and well-being. *Journal of Gerontology* 44(5):S169-176.

Chatters, Linda M., Robert Joseph Taylor, and James S. Jackson. 1985. Size and composition of the informal helper networks of elderly blacks. *Journal of Gerontology* 40(5):605-614.

Chen, Yung-Ping. 1989. Low confidence in Social Security is not warranted. In *Aging and the Family,* edited by Stephen J. Bahr and Evan T. Peterson (pp. 285-304). Lexington, MA: Lexington Books.

Choi, Namkee G. 1991. Racial differences in the determinants of living arrangements of widowed and divorced elderly women. *The Gerontologist* 31(4):496-504.

Choi, Namkee G. 1997. Racial differences in retirement income: The roles of public and private income sources. *Journal of Aging & Social Policy* 9(3):21-42.

Clark, Robert L. 1988. The future of work and retirement. *Research on Aging* 10(2): 169-193.

Clayton, Paula J. 1974. Mortality and morbidity in the first year of widowhood. *Archives of General Psychiatry* 30(6):747-750.

Cleiren, Marc. 1993. *Bereavement and Adaptation: A Comparative Study of the Aftermath of Death.* Washington, DC: Hemisphere Publishing.

Cockburn, Cynthia. 1983. *Brothers: Male Dominance and Technological Change.* London: Pluto Press.

Cockerham, W., K. Sharp, and J. Wilcox. 1983. Aging and perceived health status. *Journal of Gerontology* 38:349-355.

Cohler, Bertram J. 1991. Life-course perspectives on the study of adversity, stress, and coping: Discussion of papers from the West Virginia Conference. In *Life-Span Developmental Psychology: Perspectives on Stress and Coping,* edited by E. Mark Cummings, Anita L. Greene, and Katherine H. Karraker (pp. 297-326). Hillsdale, NJ: Lawrence Erlbaum Associates.

Coleman, Lerita M., Toni C. Antonucci, and Pamela K. Adelmann. 1987. Role involvement, gender, and well-being. In *Spouse, Parent, Worker: On Gender and Multiple Roles,* edited by Faye J. Crosby (pp. 138-153). New Haven, CT: Yale University Press.

Coll, Blanche D. 1969. *Perspectives in Public Welfare: A History.* Washington, DC: U.S. Department of Health, Education, and Welfare.

Collins, Patricia Hill. 1990. *Black Feminist Thought: Knowledge, Consciousness, and the Politics of Empowerment.* New York: Routledge.

Collins, Randall. 1988. *Theoretical Sociology.* San Diego, CA: Harcourt Brace Jovanovich.

Connell, R. W. 1985. Theorising gender. *Sociology* 19(2):260-271.

Connidis, Ingrid. 1986. The relationship of work history to self-definition of employment status among older women. *Work and Occupations* 13(3):348-358.

Conway, Katherine. 1985/86. Coping with the stress of medical problems among black and white elderly. *International Journal of Aging and Human Development* 21(1): 39-48.

Coombs, Robert H. 1991. Marital status and personal well-being: A literature review. *Family Relations* 40(1):97-102.

Costa, Paul T., Jr., Alan B. Zonderman, and Robert R. McCrae. 1991. Personality, defense, coping, and adaptation in older adulthood. In *Life-Span Developmental Psychology: Perspectives on Stress and Coping,* edited by E. Mark Cummings, Anita L. Greene, and Katherine H. Karraker (pp. 277-293). Hillsdale, NJ: Lawrence Erlbaum Associates.

Couch, Kenneth A. 1988. Late life job displacement. *The Gerontologist* 38(1):7-17.

Coverman, Shelley. 1989. Role overload, role conflict, and stress: Addressing consequences of multiple role demands. *Social Forces* 67(4):965-982.

Covey, Herbert C. 1981. A reconceptualization of continuity theory: Some preliminary thoughts. *The Gerontologist* 21(6):628-633.

Cowan, Ruth Schwartz. 1987. Women's work, housework, and history: The historical roots of inequality in work-force participation. In *Families and Work,* edited by Naomi Gerstel and Harriet Engel Gross (pp. 164-177). Philadelphia, PA: Temple University.

Cox, Harold G. 1996. *Later Life: The Realities of Aging.* 4th ed. Upper Saddle River, NJ: Prentice Hall.

Cox, Peter R. and John R. Ford. 1964. The mortality of widows shortly after widowhood. *The Lancet* 1(Jan. 18):163-164.

Creecy, Robert F., William E. Berg, and Roosevelt Wright, Jr. 1985. Loneliness among the elderly: A causal approach. *Journal of Gerontology* 40(4):487-493.

Crimmins, Eileen M., Mark D. Hayward, and Yasuhiko Saito. 1996. Differentials in active life expectancy in the older population of the United States. *Journal of Gerontology* 51B(3):S111-S120.

Crook, G. Hamilton and Martin Heinstein. 1958. *The Older Worker in Industry: A Study of the Attitudes of Industrial Workers Toward Aging and Retirement.* Berkeley: Institute of Industrial Relations, University of California.

Cruikshank, Margaret. 1990. Lavender and gray: A brief survey of lesbian and gay aging studies. *Journal of Homosexuality* 20(3/4):77-87.

Crystal, Stephen and Dennis Shea. 1990. Cumulative advantage, cumulative disadvantage, and inequality among elderly people. *The Gerontologist* 30(4):437-443.

Cuba, Lee. 1992. Family and retirement in the context of elderly migration. In *Families and Retirement,* edited by Maximiliane Szinovacz, David J. Ekerdt, and Barbara H. Vinick (pp. 205-221). Newbury Park, CA: Sage.

Cumming, Elaine. 1963. Further thoughts on the theory of disengagement. *International Social Science Journal* 15(3):377-393.

Cumming, Elaine, Lois R. Dean, David S. Newell, and Isabel McCaffrey. 1960. Disengagement—A tentative theory of aging. *Sociometry* 23(1):23-35.

Cumming, Elaine and William E. Henry. 1961. *Growing Old: The Process of Disengagement.* New York: Basic Books.

Cunningham, Walter R. and John W. Brookbank. 1988. *Gerontology: The Psychology, Biology, and Sociology of Aging.* New York: Harper & Row.

Cutler, Stephen J. and Nicholas L. Danigelis. 1993. Organized contexts of activity. In *Activity and Aging: Staying Involved in Later Life,* edited by John R. Kelly (pp. 146-163). Newbury Park, CA: Sage.

Cytron, Barry D. 1993. To honor the dead and comfort the mourners: Traditions in Judaism. In *Ethnic Variations in Dying, Death, and Grief: Diversity in Universality,* edited by Donald P. Irish, Kathleen F. Lundquist, and Vivian Jenkins Nelsen (pp. 113-124). Washington, DC: Taylor & Francis.

Deaux, Kay and Brenda Major. 1987. Putting gender into context: An interactive model of gender-related behavior. *Psychological Review* 94(3):369-389.

Deaux, Kay and Mary E. Kite. 1987. Thinking about gender. In *Analyzing Gender: A Handbook of Social Science Research,* edited by Beth B. Hess and Myra Marx Ferree (pp. 92-117). Newbury Park, CA: Sage.

Dellinger, Kirsten and Christine L. Williams. 1997. Makeup at work: Negotiating appearance rules in the workplace. *Gender & Society* 11(2):151-177.

Depner, Charlene and Berit Ingersoll. 1982. Employment status and social support: The experience of the mature woman. In *Women's Retirement: Policy Implications of Recent Research,* edited by Maximiliane Szinovacz (pp. 61-76). Beverly Hills, CA: Sage.

DeSpelder, Lynne Ann and Albert Lee Strickland. 1992. *The Last Dance: Encountering Death and Dying.* 3rd ed. Mountain View, CA: Mayfield.

DeVault, Marjorie L. 1987. Doing housework: Feeding and family life. In *Families and Work,* edited by Naomi Gerstel and Harriet Engel Gross (pp. 178-191). Philadelphia, PA: Temple University Press.

deVaus, David and Ian McAllister. 1987. Gender differences in religion: A test of the structural location theory. *American Sociological Review* 52(4):472-481.

DeViney, Stanley and Angela M. O'Rand. 1988. Gender-cohort succession and retirement among older men and women, 1951 to 1984. *The Sociological Quarterly* 29(4): 525-540.

Dimond, Margaret, Dale A. Lund, and Michael S. Caserta. 1987. The role of social support in the first two years of bereavement in an elderly sample. *The Gerontologist* 27(5):599-604.

DiPrete, Thomas A. and K. Lynn Nonnemaker. 1997. Structural change and labor market outcomes. *American Sociological Review* 62(3):386-404.

Donahue, Wilma, Harold L. Orbach, and Otto Pollak. 1960. Retirement: The emerging social pattern. In *Handbook of Social Gerontology,* edited by Clarke Tibbits (pp. 330-406). Chicago: University of Chicago Press.

Dorfman, Lorraine T. 1992. Couples in retirement: Division of household work. In *Families and Retirement,* edited by Maximiliane Szinovacz, David J. Ekerdt, and Barbara H. Vinick (pp. 159-173). Newbury Park, CA: Sage.

Dorfman, Lorraine T., Frank J. Kohout, and D. Alex Heckert. 1985. Retirement satisfaction in the rural elderly. *Research on Aging* 7(4):577-599.

Doyle, Daniel and Marilyn J. Forehand. 1984. Life satisfaction and old age: A reexamination. *Research on Aging* 6(3):432-448.

Dressel, Paula L. 1988. Gender, race, and class: Beyond the feminization of poverty in later life. *The Gerontologist* 28(2):177-180.

Dressel, Paula, Meredith Minkler, and Irene Yen. 1999. Gender, race, class, and aging: Advances and opportunities. In *Critical Gerontology: Perspectives from Political and Moral Economy,* edited by Meredith Minkler and Carroll L. Estes (pp. 275-294). Amityville, NY: Baywood.

Duncan, Greg J. and Saul D. Hoffman. 1985. Economic consequences of marital instability. In *Horizontal Equity, Uncertainty, and Economic Well-Being,* edited by Martin David and Timothy Smeeding (pp. 427-470). Chicago: University of Chicago Press.

Durkheim, Emile. [1897] 1951. *Suicide.* New York: Free Press.

Dwyer, Jeffrey W. and Raymond T. Coward. 1992. Gender, family, and long-term care of the elderly. In *Gender, Families, and Elder Care,* edited by Jeffrey W. Dwyer and Raymond T. Coward (pp. 3-17). Newbury Park, CA: Sage.

Eagly, Alice H. 1987. *Sex Differences in Social Behavior: A Social Role Interpretation.* Hillsdale, NJ: Lawrence Erlbaum Associates.

Easterlin, Richard A. 1961. The American baby boom in historical perspective. *American Economic Review* 51(5):869-911.

Eckenrode, John and Elaine Wethington. 1990. The process and outcome of mobilizing social support. In *Personal Relationships and Social Support,* edited by Steve Duck and Roxane Cohen Silver (pp. 83-103). London: Sage.

Eglit, Howard. 1989. Agism in the work place: An elusive quarry. *Generations* 13(2):31-35.

Eitzen, D. Stanley and Maxine Baca Zinn. 1989. Structural transformation and systems of inequality. In *The Reshaping of America: Social Consequences of the Changing Economy,* edited by D. Stanley Eitzen and Maxine Baca Zinn (pp. 131-143). Englewood Cliffs, NJ: Prentice-Hall.

Ekerdt, David J., Raymond Bossé, and Sue Levkoff. 1985. An empirical test for phases of retirement: Findings from the Normative Aging Study. *Journal of Gerontology* 40(1):95-101.

Ekerdt, David J. and Barbara H. Vinick. 1991. Marital complaints in husband-working and husband-retired couples. *Research on Aging* 13(3):364-382.

Elder, Glen H., Jr. 1974. *Children of the Great Depression: Social Change in Life Experience.* Chicago, IL: University of Chicago Press.

Elder, Glen H., Jr. 1978. Family history and the life course. In *Transitions: The Family and the Life Course in Historical Perspective,* edited by Tamara K. Hareven (pp. 17-64). New York: Academic Press.

Elder, Glen H., Jr. 1985. Perspectives on the life course. In *Life Course Dynamics: Trajectories and Transitions, 1968-1980,* edited by Glen H. Elder, Jr. (pp. 23-49). Ithaca, NY: Cornell University Press.

Elder, Glen H., Jr. and Elizabeth Colerick Clipp. 1988. War experiences and social ties: Influences across 40 years in men's lives. In *Social Structures and Human Lives,* edited by Matilda White Riley (pp. 306-327). Newbury Park, CA: Sage.

Elder, Glen H., Jr., Geraldine Downey, and Catherine E. Cross. 1986. Family ties and life chances: Hard times and hard choices in women's lives since the 1930s. In *Life-Span Developmental Psychology: Intergenerational Relations,* edited by Nancy Datan, Anita L. Greene, and Hayne W. Reese (pp. 151-183). Hillsdale, NJ: Lawrence Erhlbaum Associates.

Elder, Glen H., Jr., Linda K. George, and Michael J. Shanahan. 1996. Psychosocial stress over the life course. In *Psychosocial Stress: Perspectives on Structure, Theory, Life-Course, and Methods,* edited by Howard B. Kaplan (pp. 247-292). San Diego: Academic Press.

Elder, Glen H., Jr. and Jeffrey K. Liker. 1982. Hard times in women's lives: Historical influences across forty years. *American Journal of Sociology* 88(2):241-269.

Elder, Glen H., Jr. and Richard C. Rockwell. 1979. Economic depression and postwar opportunity in men's lives: A study of life patterns and health. In *Research in Community and Mental Health, Volume 1,* edited by Roberta G. Simmons (pp. 249-303). Greenwich, CT: JAI.

Elwell, F. and Alice D. Maltbie-Crannell. 1981. The impact of role loss upon coping resources and life satisfaction of the elderly. *Journal of Gerontology* 36(2): 223-232.

Engle, Veronica F. and Marshall J. Graney. 1985/86. Self-assessed and functional health of older women. *International Journal of Aging and Human Development* 22(4): 301-313.

Epstein, Cynthia Fuchs. 1988. *Deceptive Distinctions: Sex, Gender, and the Social Order.* New Haven/New York: Yale University Press and Russell Sage Foundation.

Estes, Carroll L. 1999. Critical gerontology and the new political economy of aging. In *Critical Gerontology: Perspectives on Political and Moral Economy,* edited by Meredith Minkler and Carroll L. Estes (pp. 17-35). Amityville, NY: Baywood.

Estes, Carroll L., Elizabeth A. Binney, and Richard A. Culbertson. 1992. The gerontological imagination: Social influences on the development of gerontology, 1945-present. *International Journal of Aging and Human Development* 35(1):49-65.

Faletti, Martin V., Jeanne M. Gibbs, M. Cherie Clark, Rachel A. Pruchno, and Elizabeth A. Berman. 1989. Longitudinal course of bereavement in older adults. In *Older Bereaved Spouses: Research With Practical Applications,* edited by Dale A. Lund (pp. 37-51). New York: Hemisphere.

Fausto-Sterling, Anne. 1992. *Myths of Gender: Biological Theories About Women and Men,* 2nd ed. New York: Basic Books.

Feinson, Marjorie Chary. 1987. Mental health and aging: Are there gender differences? *The Gerontologist* 27(6):703-711.

Feinson, Marjorie Chary. 1990. The distribution of distress by age and gender: Examining data from community surveys. In *The Legacy of Longevity: Health and Health Care in Later Life,* edited by Sidney M. Stahl (pp. 115-139). Newbury Park, CA: Sage.

Fengler, Alfred P. and Nicholas Danigelis. 1982. Residence, the elderly widow, and life satisfaction. *Research on Aging* 4(1):113-135.

Fenwick, Rudy and Charles M. Barresi. 1981. Health consequences of marital-status change among the elderly: A comparison of cross-sectional and longitudinal analyses. *Journal of Health and Social Behavior* 22(2):106-116.

Fernandez, Maria E., Elizabeth J. Mutran, and Donald C. Reitzes. 1998. Moderating the effects of stress on depressive symptoms. *Research on Aging* 20(2):163-182.

Ferraro, Kenneth F. 1984. Widowhood and social participation in later life: Isolation or compensation? *Research on Aging* 6(4):451-468.

Ferraro, Kenneth F. 1985/86. The effect of widowhood on the health status of older persons. *International Journal of Aging and Human Development* 21(1):9-25.

Ferraro, Kenneth F. 1987. Double jeopardy to health for Black older adults? *Journal of Gerontology* 42(5):528-533.

Ferraro, Kenneth F. 1989a. Reexamining the double jeopardy to health thesis. *Journal of Gerontology* 44(1):S14-16.

Ferraro, Kenneth F. 1989b. Widowhood and health. In *Aging, Stress, and Health,* edited by Kyriakos S. Markides and Cary L. Cooper (pp. 69-83). New York: John Wiley & Sons.

Ferraro, Kenneth F. and Charles M. Barresi. 1982. The impact of widowhood on the social relations of older persons. *Research on Aging* 4(2):227-247.

Ferraro, Kenneth F., Elizabeth Mutran, and Charles M. Barresi. 1984. Widowhood, health, and friendship support in later life. *Journal of Health and Social Behavior* 25(3): 246-259.

Ferree, Myra Marx. 1990. Beyond separate spheres: Feminism and family research. *Journal of Marriage and the Family* 52(Nov.):866-884.

Ferree, Myra Marx and Beth B. Hess. 1987. Introduction. In *Analyzing Gender: A Handbook of Social Science Research,* edited by Beth B. Hess and Myra Marx Ferree (pp. 9-30). Newbury Park, CA: Sage.

Fillenbaum, Gerda G. 1971. On the relation between attitude to work and attitude to retirement. *Journal of Gerontology* 26(2):244-248.

Fillenbaum, Gerda G., Linda K. George, and Erdman B. Palmore. 1985. Determinants and consequences of retirement among men of different races and economic levels. *Journal of Gerontology* 40(1):85-94.

Finley, Nancy J. 1989. Theories of family labor as applied to gender differences in caregiving for elderly parents. *Journal of Marriage and the Family* 51(1):79-86.

Fischer, Anita Kassen, Janos Marton, E. Joel Millman, and Leo Srole. 1979. Long-range influences on adult mental health: The Midtown Manhattan Longitudinal Study, 1954-1974. In *Research in Community and Mental Health, Vol. 1*, edited by Roberta G. Simmons (pp. 305-333). Greenwich, CT: JAI.

Fischer, Claude S. and Stacey J. Oliker. 1983. A research note on friendship, gender, and the life cycle. *Social Forces* 62(1):124-133.

Fisher, Gordon M. 1992. The development and history of the poverty thresholds. *Social Security Bulletin* 55(4):3-14.

Fitting, Melinda, Peter Rabins, M. Jane Lucas, and James Eastham. 1986. Caregivers for dementia patients: A comparison of husbands and wives. *The Gerontologist* 26(3): 248-252.

Folkman, Susan. 1991. Coping across the life span: Theoretical issues. In *Life-Span Developmental Psychology: Perspectives on Stress and Coping,* edited by E. Mark Cummings, Anita L. Greene, and Katherine H. Karraker (pp. 3-19). Hillsdale, NJ: Lawrence Erlbaum Associates.

Folkman, Susan and Richard S. Lazarus. 1980. An analysis of coping in a middle-aged community sample. *Journal of Health and Social Behavior* 21(3):219-239.

Foner, Anne. 1996. Age norms and the structure of consciousness: Some final comments. *The Gerontologist* 36(2):221-223.

Ford, Amasa B., Marie R. Haug, Paul K. Jones, Ann W. Roy, and Steven J. Folmar. 1990. Race-related differences among elderly urban residents: A cohort study, 1975-1984. *Journal of Gerontology* 45(4):S163-171.

Fox, Judith H. 1981/82. Perspectives on the continuity perspective. *International Journal of Aging and Human Development* 14(2):97-115.

Fox, Judith Huff. 1977. Effects of retirement and former work life on women's adaptation in old age. *Journal of Gerontology* 32(2):196-202.

Frank, Susan J., Patricia A. Towell, and Margaret Huyck. 1985. The effects of sex-role traits on three aspects of psychological well-being in a sample of middle-aged women. *Sex Roles* 12(9/10):1073-1087.

Franks, Melissa M. and Mary Ann Parris Stephens. 1992. Multiple roles of middle-generation caregivers: Contextual effects and psychological mechanisms. *Journal of Gerontology* 47(3):S123-129.

Freedman, Vicki A. 1996. Family structure and the risk of nursing home admission. *Journal of Gerontology* 51B(2):S61-S69.

Freudiger, Patricia. 1983. Life satisfaction among three categories of married women. *Journal of Marriage and the Family* 45(1):213-219.

Friedan, Betty. 1993. *The Fountain of Age.* New York: Simon & Schuster.

Friedmann, Eugene A. and Robert J. Havighurst. 1954. *The Meaning of Work and Retirement.* Chicago: University of Chicago Press.

Friedmann, Eugene A. and Harold L. Orbach. 1974. Adjustment to retirement. In *American Handbook of Psychiatry, Vol. 1: The Foundations of Psychiatry,* edited by Silvano Arieti (pp. 611-645). New York: Basic Books.

Friend, Richard A. 1990. Older lesbian and gay people: A theory of successful aging. *Journal of Homosexuality* 23(3/4):99-118.

Frieze, Irene H., Jacquelynne E. Parsons, Paula B. Johnson, Diane N. Ruble, and Gail L. Zellman. 1978. *Women and Sex Roles: A Social Psychological Perspective.* New York: W.W. Norton & Co.

Frodi, Ann, Jacqueline Macaulay, and Pauline Ropert Thome. 1977. Are women always less aggressive than men? A review of the experimental literature. *Psychological Bulletin* 84(4):634-660.

Gallagher, Dolores E., James N. Breckenridge, Larry W. Thompson, and James A. Peterson. 1983. Effects of bereavement on indicators of mental health in elderly widows and widowers. *Journal of Gerontology* 38(5):565-571.

Gallagher, Dolores, Steven Lovett, Patricia Hanley-Dunn, and Larry W. Thompson. 1989. Use of select coping strategies during late-life spousal bereavement. In *Older Bereaved Spouses: Research With Practical Applications,* edited by Dale A. Lund (pp. 111-121). New York: Hemisphere.

Gallagher, Dolores E., Larry W. Thompson, and James A. Peterson. 1982. Psychosocial factors affecting adaptation to bereavement in the elderly. *International Journal of Aging and Human Development* 14(2):79-95.

Gallagher-Thompson, Dolores, Andrew Futterman, Norman Farberow, Larry W. Thompson, and James Peterson. 1993. The impact of spousal bereavement on older widows and widowers. In *Handbook of Bereavement: Theory, Research, and Intervention,* edited by Margaret S. Stroebe, Wolfgang Stroebe, and Robert O. Hansson (pp. 227-239). Cambridge: Cambridge University Press.

Gass, Kathleen A. 1989. Appraisal, coping, and resources: Markers associated with the health of aged widows and widowers. In *Older Bereaved Spouses: Research With Practical Applications,* edited by Dale A. Lund (pp. 79-94). New York: Hemisphere.

Gendell, Murray and Jacob S. Siegel. 1996. Trends in retirement age in the United States, 1955-1993, by sex and race. *Journal of Gerontology* 51B(3):S132-139.

Gentry, Margaret and Arthur D. Shulman. 1988. Remarriage as a coping response for widowhood. *Psychology and Aging* 3(2):191-196.

George, Linda K. 1980. *Role Transitions in Later Life.* Monterey, CA: Brooks/Cole.

George, Linda K. 1987. Adaptation. In *The Encyclopedia of Aging,* edited by George L. Maddox, Robert C. Atchley, Leonard W. Poon, George S. Roth, Ilene C. Siegler, and Raymond M. Steinberg (pp. 5-7). New York: Springer.

George, Linda K. 1989. Stress, social support, and depression over the life-course. In *Aging, Stress and Health,* edited by Kyriakos S. Markides and Cary L. Cooper (pp. 241-267). New York: John Wiley & Sons.

George, Linda K. 1992. Social factors and the onset and outcome of depression. In *Aging, Health Behaviors, and Health Outcomes,* edited by K. Warner Schaie, Dan Blazer, and James S. House (pp. 137-159). Hillsdale, NJ: Lawrence Erlbaum Associates.

George, Linda K. 1993. Sociological perspectives on life transitions. In *Annual Review of Sociology, Vol. 19,* edited by Judith Blake and John Hagen (pp. 353-373). Palo Alto, CA: Annual Reviews, Inc.

George, Linda K. 1996. Missing links: The case for a social psychology of the life course. *The Gerontologist* 36(2):248-255.

George, Linda K., Gerda G. Fillenbaum, and Erdman Palmore. 1984. Sex differences in the antecedents and consequences of retirement. *Journal of Gerontology* 39(3): 364-371.

George, Linda K. and Lisa P. Gwyther. 1986. Caregiver well-being: A multidimensional examination of family caregivers of demented adults. *The Gerontologist* 26(3): 253-259.

German, Pearl S. 1995. Prevention and chronic disease in older individuals. In *Promoting Successful and Productive Aging,* edited by Lynne A. Bond, Stedphen J. Cutler, and Armin Grams (pp. 95-108). Thousand Oaks, CA: Sage.

Gerson, Judith M. 1985. Women returning to school: The consequences of multiple roles. *Sex Roles* 13(1/2):77-91.

Gerstel, Naomi. 1989. Divorce and kin ties: The importance of gender. *Journal of Marriage and the Family* 50(1):209-219.

Gibson, Rose C. 1982. Blacks at middle and later life: Resources and coping. *The Annals of the American Academy* 464(Nov.):79-90.

Gibson, Rose C. 1986. Blacks in an Aging society. *Daedalus* 115(1):349-371.

Gibson, Rose C. 1987. Reconceptualizing retirement for Black Americans. *The Gerontologist* 27(6):691-698.

Gibson, Rose C. 1988. The work, retirement, and disability of older Black Americans. In *The Black American Elderly,* edited by James S. Jackson, Patricia Newton, Adrian Otfield, Daniel Savage, and Edward L. Schneider (pp. 304-324). New York: Springer.

Gibson, Rose C. 1991. The subjective retirement of Black Americans. *Journal of Gerontology* 46(4):S204-209.

Gibson, Rose C. 1995. Promoting successful and productive aging in minority populations. In *Promoting Successful and Productive Aging,* edited by Lynne A. Bond, Stephen J. Cutler, and Armin Grams (pp. 279-288). Thousand Oaks, CA: Sage.

Gibson, Rose C. and Cheryl J. Burns. 1992. The health, labor force, and retirement experiences of aging minorities. In *Diversity: New Approaches to Ethnic Minority Aging,* edited by E. Percil Stanford and Fernando M. Torres-Gil (pp. 53-71). Amityville, NY: Baywood.

Gilanshah, Farah. 1993. Islamic customs regarding death. In *Ethnic Variations in Dying, Death, and Grief,* edited by Donald P. Irish, Kathleen F. Lundquist, and Vivian Jenkins Nelsen (pp. 137-145). Washington, DC: Taylor & Francis.

Gilligan, Carol. 1982. *In a Different Voice: Psychological Theory and Women's Development.* Cambridge, MA: Harvard University Press.

Glamser, Francis D. 1976. Determinants of a positive attitude toward retirement. *Journal of Gerontology* 31(1):104-107.

Glamser, Francis D. 1981. Predictors of retirement attitudes. *Aging and Work* 4(1):23-29.

Glazer, Nona Y. 1987. Servants to capital: Unpaid domestic labor and paid work. In *Families and Work,* edited by Naomi Gerstel and Harriet Engel Gross (pp. 236-255). Philadelphia, PA: Temple University Press.

Glenn, Evelyn Nakano. 1985. Racial ethnic women's labor: The intersection of race, gender and class oppression. *Review of Radical Political Economics* 17(3):86-108.

Glenn, Evelyn Nakano. 1987. Gender and the family. In *Analyzing Gender: A Handbook of Social Science Research,* edited by Beth B. Hess and Myra Marx Ferree (pp. 348-380). Newbury Park, CA: Sage.

Glenn, Norval D. 1975. The contribution of marriage to the psychological well-being of males and females. *Journal of Marriage and the Family* 37(3):594-601.

Glenn, Norval D. and Sara McLanahan. 1981. The effects of offspring on the psychological well-being of older adults. *Journal of Marriage and the Family* 43(2):409-421.

Glick, Paul C. 1977. Updating the life cycle of the family. *Journal of Marriage and the Family* 39(1):5-13.

Glick, Paul C. and Sung-Ling Lin. 1986. Recent changes in divorce and remarriage. *Journal of Marriage and the Family* 48(4):737-747.

Glick, Ira O., Robert S. Weiss, and C. Murray Parkes. 1974. *The First Year of Bereavement.* New York: John Wiley & Sons.

Goldberg, Steven. 1974. *The Inevitability of Patriarchy.* New York: William Morrow.

Goldscheider, Frances K. 1990. The aging of the gender revolution: What do we know and what do we need to know? *Research on Aging* 12(4):531-545.

Gore, Susan and Thomas W. Mangione. 1983. Social roles, sex roles, and psychological distress: Additive and interactive models of sex differences. *Journal of Health and Social Behavior* 24(4):300-312.

Goudy, Willis J., Edward A. Powers, and Patricia Keith. 1975. Work and retirement: A test of attitudinal relationships. *Journal of Gerontology* 30(2):193-198.

Goudy, Willis J., Edward A. Powers, Patricia M. Keith, and Richard A. Reger. 1980. Changes in attitudes toward retirement: Evidence from a panel study of older males. *Journal of Gerontology* 35(6):942-948.

Gove, Walter R. 1972. The relationship between sex roles, marital status, and mental illness. *Social Forces* 51(1):34-44.

Gove, Walter R. 1978. Sex differences in mental illness among adult men and women: An evaluation of four questions raised regarding the evidence on the higher rates of women. *Social Science and Medicine* 12B(3):187-198.

Gove, Walter R. 1979. Sex, marital status, and mortality. *American Journal of Sociology* 79(1):45-67.

Gove, Walter R. and Jeanette F. Tudor. 1973. Adult sex roles and mental illness. *American Journal of Sociology* 78(4):812-835.

Gove, Walter R. and Carol Zeiss. 1987. Multiple roles and happiness. In *Spouse, Parent, Worker: On Gender and Multiple Roles,* edited by Faye J. Crosby (pp. 125-137). New Haven, CT: Yale University Press.

Gradman, Theodore J. 1994. Masculine identity from work to retirement. In *Older Men's Lives,* edited by Edward H. Thompson, Jr. (pp. 104-121). Thousand Oaks, CA: Sage.

Gratton, Brian and Marie R. Haug. 1983. Decision and adaptation: Research on female retirement. *Research on Aging* 5(1):59-76.

Greene, Vernon L. and Jan I. Ondrich. 1990. Risk factors for nursing home admissions and exits: A discrete-time hazard function approach. *Journal of Gerontology* 45(6): S250-S258.

Griffith, Janet D., Helen P. Koo, and C. M Suchindran. 1985. Childbearing and family in remarriage. *Demography* 22(1):73-88.

Gutmann, David. 1994. *Reclaimed Powers: Men and Women in Later Life.* 2nd ed. Evanston, IL: Northwestern University Press.

Gutmann, David. 1997. *The Human Elder in Nature, Culture, and Society.* Boulder, CO: Westview.

Gutmann, David and Margaret Hellie Huyck. 1994. Development and pathology in postparental men: A community study. In *Older Men's Lives,* edited by Edward H. Thompson, Jr. (pp. 65-84). Thousand Oaks, CA: Sage.

Guttentag, Marcia and Paul F. Secord. 1983. *Too Many Women? The Sex Ratio Question.* Beverly Hills, CA: Sage.

Gysbers, Norman C., Joseph A. Johnston, and Tim Gust. 1968. Characteristics of homemaker- and career-oriented women. *Journal of Counseling Psychology* 15(6): 541-546.

Hägestad, Gunhild O. 1988. Demographic change and the life course: Some emerging trends in the family realm. *Family Relations* 37(4):405-410.

Handel, Warren H. 1993. *Contemporary Sociological Theory.* Englewood Cliffs, NJ: Prentice Hall.

Hansson, Robert O., Warren H. Jones, Bruce N. Carpenter, and Jacqueline H. Remondet. 1986/87. Loneliness and adjustment to old age. *International Journal of Aging and Human Development* 24(1):41-53.

Hansson, Robert O., Bruce N. Carpenter, and Sharon K. Fairchild. 1993. Measurement issues in bereavement. In *Handbook of Bereavement: Theory, Research and Intervention,* edited by Margaret S. Stroebe, Wolfgang Stroebe, and Robert O. Hansson (pp. 62-74). Cambridge: Cambridge University Press.

Hansson, Robert O., Jacqueline H. Remondet, and Marlene Galusha. 1993. Old age and widowhood: Issues of personal control and independence. In *Handbook of Bereavement: Theory, Research, and Intervention,* edited by Margaret S. Stroebe, Wolfgang Stroebe, and Robert O. Hansson (pp. 367-380). Cambridge: Cambridge University Press.

Hardy, Melissa A. 1991. Employment after retirement: Who gets back in? *Research on Aging* 13(3):267-288.

Hardy, Melissa A. and Lawrence E. Hazelrigg. 1993. The gender of poverty in an aging population. *Research on Aging* 15(3):243-278.

Hardy, Melissa A. and Jill Quadagno. 1995. Satisfaction with early retirement: Making choices in the auto industry. *Journal of Gerontology* 50B(4):S217-S228.

Hare-Mustin, Rachel T. and Jeanne Maracek. 1990a. On making a difference. In *Making a Difference: Psychology and the Construction of Gender,* edited by Rachel T. Hare-Mustin and Jeanne Maracek (pp. 1-21). New Haven: Yale University Press.

Hare-Mustin, Rachel T. and Jeanne Maracek. 1990b. Gender and the meaning of difference: Postmodernism and psychology. In *Making a Difference: Psychology and the Construction of Gender,* edited by Rachel T. Hare-Mustin and Jeanne Maracek (pp. 22-64). New Haven, CT: Yale University Press.

Harel, Zev and Gary Deimling. 1984. Social resources and mental health: An empirical refinement. *Journal of Gerontology* 39(6):747-752.

Harel, Zev, Robert N. Sollod, and Bela J. Bognar. 1982. Predictors of mental health among semi-rural aged. *The Gerontologist* 22(6):499-504.

Hareven, Tamara K. 1978. Introduction: The historical study of the life course. In *Transitions: The Family and the Life Course in Historical Perspective,* edited by Tamara K. Hareven (pp. 1-16). New York: Academic Press.

Hareven, Tamara K. 1980. The life course and aging in historical perspective. In *Life Course: Integrative Theories and Exemplary Populations,* edited by Kurt W. Back (pp. 9-25). Boulder, CO: Westview Press.

Haring-Hidore, Marilyn, William A. Stock, Morris A. Okun, and Robert A. Witter. 1985. Marital status and subjective well-being: A research synthesis. *Journal of Marriage and the Family* 47(4):947-953.

Harrington Meyer, Madonna. 1990. Family status and poverty among older women: The gendered distribution of retirement income in the United States. *Social Problems* 37(4):551-563.

Harrington Meyer, Madonna. 1996. Making claims as workers or wives: The distribution of Social Security benefits. *American Sociological Review* 61(3):449-465.

Hartmann, Heidi. 1981. The unhappy marriage of Marxism and Feminism: Towards a more progressive union. In *Women and Revolution: A Discussion of the Unhappy Marriage of Marxism and Feminism,* edited by Lydia Sargent (pp. 1-41). Boston, MA: South End Press.

Hatch, Laurie Russell. 1987. Research on men's and women's retirement attitudes: Implications for retirement policy. In *Critical Issues in Aging Policy: Linking Research and Values,* edited by E. F. Borgatta and R. J. V. Montgomery (pp. 127-160). Newbury Park, CA: Sage.

Hatch, Laurie Russell. 1991. Informal support patterns of older African-American and white women: Examining effects of family, paid work, and religious participation. *Research on Aging* 13(2):144-170.

Hatch, Laurie Russell. 1992. Gender differences in orientation toward retirement from paid labor. *Gender & Society* 6(1):66-85.

Hatch, Laurie Russell. 1998. Women's and men's retirement: Plural pathways, diverse destinations. In *Social Gerontology,* edited by David E. Redburn and Robert P. McNamara (pp. 125-141). Westport, CT: Auburn House.

Hatch, Laurie Russell and Kris Bulcroft. 1992. Contact with friends in later life: Disentangling the effects of gender and marital status. *Journal of Marriage and the Family* 54(1):222-232.

Hatch, Laurie Russell and Aaron Thompson. 1992. Family responsibilities and women's retirement. In *Families and Retirement,* edited by Maximiliane Szinovacz, David J. Ekerdt, and Barbara H. Vinick (pp. 99-113). Newbury Park, CA: Sage.

Havighurst, Robert J. and Ruth Albrecht. 1953. *Older People.* New York: Longmans, Green and Co.

Havighurst, Robert J., Bernice L. Neugarten, and Sheldon S. Tobin. 1968. Disengagement and patterns of aging. In *Middle Age and Aging: A Reader in Social Psychology,* edited by Bernice L. Neugarten (pp. 161-172). Chicago, IL: University of Chicago Press.

Hays, Judith C., Lawrence R. Landerman, Linda K George, Elizabeth P. Flint, Harold G. Koenig, Kenneth C. Land, and Dan G. Blazer. 1998. Social correlates of the dimensions of depression in the elderly. *Journal of Gerontology* 53B(1):P31-P39.

Hayward, Mark D., Samantha Friedman, and Hsinmu Chen. 1996. Race inequities in men's retirement. *Journal of Gerontology* 51B(1):S1-S10.

Hayward, Mark D. and Mei-Chun Liu. 1992. Men and women in their retirement years: A demographic profile. In *Families and Retirement*, edited by Maximiliane Szinovacz, David J. Ekerdt, and Barbara H. Vinick (pp. 23-50). Newbury Park, CA: Sage.

Heilbrun, Carolyn G. 1997. *The Last Gift of Time: Life Beyond Sixty*. New York: Dial Press.

Heinemann, Gloria D. and Patricia L. Evans. 1990. Widowhood: Loss, change, and adaptation. In *Family Relationships in Later Life*, 2nd ed., edited by Timothy H. Brubaker (pp. 142-168). Newbury Park, CA: Sage.

Helsing, Knud J. and Moyses Szklo. 1981. Mortality after bereavement. *American Journal of Epidemiology* 114(1):41-52.

Helsing, Knud J., Moyses Szklo, and George W. Comstock. 1981. Factors associated with mortality after widowhood. *American Journal of Public Health* 71(8):802-809.

Hendricks, Jon and Laurie Russell Hatch. 1993. Federal policy and family life of older Americans. In *The Remainder of Their Days: Domestic Policy and Older Families in the United States and Canada*, edited by Jon Hendricks and Carolyn J. Rosenthal (pp. 49-73). New York: Garland.

Hendricks, Jon, Laurie Russell Hatch, and Steven J. Cutler. 1999. Entitlements, social compacts, and the trend toward retrenchment in U.S. old-age programs. *Hallym International Journal of Aging* 1(1):14-32.

Hendricks, Jon and C. Davis Hendricks. 1986. *Aging in Mass Society: Myths and Realities.* 3rd ed. Boston, MA: Little, Brown.

Hendricks, Jon and Cynthia A. Leedham. 1991. Dependency or empowerment? Toward a Moral and Political Economy of Aging. In *Critical Perspectives on Aging: The Political and Moral Economy of Growing Old*, edited by Meredith Minkler and Carroll L. Estes (pp. 51-64). Amityville, NY: Baywood.

Hendricks, Jon and Howard B. Turner. 1995. Social dimensions of mental illness among rural elderly populations. In *Health and Health Care Utilization in Later Life*, edited by Jon Hendricks (pp. 109-129). Amityville, NY: Baywood.

Henretta, John C. 1992. Uniformity and diversity: Life course institutionalization and late-life work exit. *The Sociological Quarterly* 33(2):265-279.

Henretta, John C. and Angela M. O'Rand. 1980. Labor force participation of older married women. *Social Security Bulletin* 43(8):10-15.

Henry, William E. 1965. Engagement and disengagement: Toward a theory of adult development. In *Contributions to the Psychobiology of Aging*, edited by Robert Kastenbaum (pp. 19-35). New York: Springer.

Herzog, A. Regula. 1989. Methodological issues in research on older women. In *Health & Economic Status of Older Women*, edited by A. Regula Herzog, Karen C. Holden, and Mildred M. Seltzer (pp. 133-148). Amityville, NY: Baywood.

Hess, Beth B. 1986. Antidiscrimination policies today and the life chances of older women tomorrow. *The Gerontologist* 26(2):132-135.

Hewlett, Barry S. 1997. The cultural nexus of Aka father-infant bonding. In *Gender in Cross-Cultural Perspective*, 2nd ed., edited by Caroline B. Brettell and Carolyn F. Sargent (pp. 42-53). Upper Saddle River, NJ: Prentice Hall.

Heyman, Dorothy K. and Daniel T. Gianturco. 1973. Long-term adaptation by the elderly to bereavement. *Journal of Gerontology* 28(3):359-362.

Heyman, Dorothy K. and Frances C. Jeffers. 1968. Wives and retirement: A pilot study. *Journal of Gerontology* 23(4):488-496.

Higginbotham, Elizabeth. 1981. Is marriage a priority? Class differences in marital options of educated black women. In *Single Life,* edited by Peter J. Stein (pp. 259-267). New York: St. Martin's Press.

Higginbotham, Elizabeth. 1997. Introduction. In *Women and Work: Exploring Race,* Ethnicity, and Class, edited by Elizabeth Higginbotham and Mary Romero. Thousand Oaks, CA: Sage

Hilbert, Richard A. 1986. Anomie and the moral regulation of reality: The Durkheimian tradition in modern relief. *Sociological Theory* 4(1):1-19.

Hill, Connie Dessonville, Larry W. Thompson, and Dolores Gallagher. 1988. The role of anticipatory bereavement in older women's adjustment to widowhood. *The Gerontologist* 28(6):792-796.

Hill, Reuben. 1968a. *Family Development in Three Generations.* Cambridge, MA: Schenkman.

Hill, Reuben. 1968b. Decision making and the family life cycle. In *Middle Age and Aging: A Reader in Social Psychology,* edited by Bernice L. Neugarten (pp. 286-295). Chicago: University of Chicago Press.

Hill, Reuben. 1970. *Family Development in Three Generations.* Cambridge, MA: Schenkman.

Hill, Reuben and Roy H. Rodgers. 1964. The developmental approach. In *Handbook of Marriage and the Family,* edited by Harold T. Christensen (pp. 171-211). Chicago: Rand McNally.

Himes, Christine L., Dennis P. Hogan, and David J. Eggebeen. 1996. Living arrangements of minority elders. *Journal of Gerontology* 51B(1):S42-S48.

Hochschild, Arlie Russell. 1975. Disengagement theory: A critique and proposal. *American Sociological Review* 40(5):553-569.

Holden, Karen C. 1989. Economic status of older women: A summary of selected research issues. In *Health & Economic Status of Older Women,* edited by A. Regula Herzog, Karen C. Holden, and Mildred M. Seltzer (pp. 24-32). Amityville, NY: Baywood.

Holden, Karen C., Richard V. Burkhauser, and Daniel A. Myers. 1986. Income transitions at older stages of life: The dynamics of poverty. *The Gerontologist* 26(3):292-297.

Holden, Karen C. and Disang-Hui Daphne Kuo. 1996. Complex marital histories and economic well-being: The continuing legacy of divorce and widowhood as the HRS cohort approaches retirement. *The Gerontologist* 36(3):383-390.

Hogan, Richard, Meesook Kim, and Carolyn C. Perrucci. 1997. Racial inequality in men's employment and retirement earnings. *The Sociological Quarterly* 38(3):431-438.

Holloway, Clark and Stuart A. Youngblood. 1985/86. Survival after retirement. *International Journal of Aging and Human Development* 22(1):45-54.

Holmes, Thomas H. and Richard H. Rahe. 1967. The social readjustment rating scale. *Journal of Psychosomatic Research* 11(1):213-218.

Holzer, III, Charles E., Philip J. Leaf, and Myra M. Weissman. 1985. Living with depression. In *The Physical and Mental Health of Aged Women,* edited by Marie R. Haug, Amasa B. Ford, and Marian Sheafor (pp. 101-116). New York: Springer.

Homan, Sharon M., Cynthia Carter Haddock, Carol A. Winner, Rodney M. Coe, and Fredric D. Wolinsky. 1986. Widowhood, sex, labor force participation, and the use of physician services by elderly adults. *Journal of Gerontology* 41(6):793-796.

Hong, Lawrence K. and Robert W. Duff. 1994. Widows in retirement communities: The social context of subjective well-being. *The Gerontologist* 34(3):347-352.

Hooyman, Nancy R. 1992. Social policy and gender inequities in caregiving. In *Gender, Families, and Elder Care,* edited by Jeffrey W. Dwyer and Raymond T. Coward (pp. 181-201). Newbury Park, CA: Sage.

Hooyman, Nancy R. and H. Asuman Kiyak. 1995. *Social Gerontology: A Multidisciplinary Perspective,* 2nd ed. Boston: Allyn and Bacon.

Horn, John L. 1982. The theory of fluid and crystallized intelligence in relation to concepts of cognitive psychology and aging in adulthood. In *Aging and Cognitive Processes,* edited by F. I. M. Craik and Sandra Trehub (pp. 237-278). New York: Plenum Press.

House, James S., Ronald C. Kessler, A. Regula Herzog, Richard P. Mero, Ann M Kinney, and Martha J. Breslow. 1992. Social stratification, age, and health. In *Aging, Health Behaviors, and Health Outcomes,* edited by K. Warner Schaie, Dan Blazer, and James S. House (pp. 1-32). Hillsdale, NJ: Lawrence Erlbaum Associates.

Howard, Judith A. and Jocelyn Hollander. 1997. *Gendered Situations, Gendered Selves.* Thousand Oaks, CA: Sage.

Huyck, Margaret Hellie. 1994. The relevance of psychodynamic theories for understanding gender among older women. In *Women Growing Older: Psychological Perspectives,* edited by Barbara F. Turner and Lillian E. Troll (pp. 202-238). Thousand Oaks, CA: Sage.

Hyman, Herbert H. 1983. *Of Time and Widowhood: Nationwide Studies of Enduring Effects.* Durham, NC: Duke Press Policy Studies.

Ikels, Charlotte, Jeanette Dickerson-Putman, Patricia Draper, Christine L. Fry, Anthony Glascock, Henry Harpending, and Jennie Keith. 1995. Comparative perspectives on successful aging. In *Promoting Successful and Productive Aging,* edited by Lynne A. Bond, Stephen J. Cutler, and Armin Grams (pp. 304-323). Thousand Oaks, CA: Sage.

Ingersoll-Dayton, Berit, David Morgan, and Toni Antonucci. 1997. The effects of positive and negative social exchanges on aging adults. *Journals of Gerontology* 52B(4): S190-S199.

Irelan, Lola M. 1972. Retirement history study: Introduction. *Social Security Bulletin* 35(11):3-8.

Irish, Donald P. 1993. Memorial services among Quakers and Unitarians. In *Ethnic Variations in Dying, Death, and Grief: Diversity in Universality,* edited by Donald P. Irish, Kathleen F. Lundquist, and Vivian Jenkins Nelsen (pp. 147-159). Washington, DC: Taylor & Francis.

Jackson, Jacquelyne Johnson. 1985. Poverty and minority status. In *The Physical and Mental Health of Aged Women,* edited by Marie R. Haug, Amasa B. Ford, and Marian Sheafor (pp. 166-181). New York: Springer.

Jackson, James S. and Toni C. Antonucci. 1992. Social support processes in health and effective functioning of the elderly. In *Stress and Health Among the Elderly,* edited by May L. Wykle, Eva Kahana, and Jerome Kowal (pp. 72-95). New York: Springer.

Jackson, Maurice, Bohdan Kolody, and James L. Wood. 1982. To be old and black: The case for double jeopardy on income and health. In *Minority Aging: Sociological and Social Psychological Issues,* edited by Ron C. Manuel (pp. 77-82). Westport, CT: Greenwood Press.

Jacobson, Dan. 1974. Rejection of the retiree role: A study of female industrial workers in their 50's. *Human Relations* 27(5):477-492.

James, Sherman A., Nora L. Keenan, and Steve Browning. 1992. Socioeconomic status, health behaviors, and health status among Blacks. In *Aging, Health Behaviors, and Health Outcomes,* edited by K. Warner Schaie, Dan Blazer, and James S. House (pp. 39-57). Hillsdale, NJ: Lawrence Erlbaum Associates.

Jaslow, Philip. 1976. Employment, retirement, and morale among older women. *Journal of Gerontology* 31(2):212-218.

Jerrome, Dorothy. 1990. Intimate relationships. In *Aging in Society: An Introduction to Social Gerontology,* edited by John Bond and Peter Coleman (pp. 181-208). London: Sage.

Jewett, S. 1973. Longevity and the longevity syndrome. *The Gerontologist* 13:91-99.

Jewson, Ruth Hathaway. 1982. After retirement: An exploratory study of the professional woman. In *Women's Retirement: Policy Implications for Recent Research,* edited by Maximiliane Szinovacz (pp. 169-181). Newbury Park, CA: Sage.

Johnson, Colleen Leahy and Donald J. Catalano. 1983. A longitudinal study of family supports to impaired elderly. *The Gerontologist* 23(6):612-618.

Johnson, Elizabeth S. and John B. Williamson. 1980. *Growing Old: The Social Problems of Aging.* New York: Holt, Rinehart & Winston.

Johnson, Miriam M. 1989. Feminism and the theories of Talcott Parsons. In *Feminism and Sociological Theory,* edited by Ruth A. Wallace (pp. 101-118). Newbury Park, CA: Sage.

Johnson, Robert J. and Fredric D. Wolinsky. 1994. Gender, race, and health: The structure of health status among older adults. *The Gerontologist* 34(1):24-35.

Jones, Jacqueline. 1985. *Labor of Love, Labor of Sorrow: Black Women, Work and the Family, From Slavery to the Present.* New York: Vintage Books.

Kahana, Eva. 1992. Stress research and aging: Complexities, ambiguities, paradoxes, and promise. In *Stress and Health Among the Elderly,* edited by May L. Wykle, Eva Kahana, and Jerome Kowal (pp. 239-256). New York: Springer.

Kamo, Yoshinori and Min Zhou. 1994. Living arrangements of elderly Chinese and Japanese in the United States. *Journal of Marriage and the Family* 56(3):544-558.

Kanter, Rosabeth Moss. 1977. *Men and Women of the Corporation.* New York: Basic Books.

Kaplan, George A. 1992. Health and aging in the Alameda County Study. In *Aging, Health Behaviors, and Health Outcomes,* edited by K. Warner Schaie, Dan Blazer, and James S. House (pp. 69-88). Hillsdale, NJ: Lawrence Erlbaum Associates.

Kasl, Stanislav V. 1980. The impact of retirement. In *Current Concerns in Occupational Stress,* edited by Cary L. Cooper and Roy Payne (pp. 135-196). New York: Wiley.

Katz, Michael B. 1989. *The Undeserving Poor: From the War on Poverty to the War on Welfare.* New York: Pantheon Books.

Kavanaugh, Robert E. 1972. *Facing Death.* Los Angeles, CA: Nash.

Kaye, Lenard W. and Jeffrey S. Applegate. 1994. Older men and the family caregiving orientation. In *Older Men's Lives,* edited by Edward H. Thompson, Jr. (pp. 218-236). Thousand Oaks, CA: Sage.

Keating, Norah and Barbara Jeffrey. 1983. Work careers of ever married and never married retired women. *The Gerontologist* 23(4):416-421.

Keith, Jennie. 1977. *Old People, New Lives: Community Creation in a Retirement Residence.* Chicago: University of Chicago Press.

Keith, Pat M. 1980. Two models of singleness: Managing an atypical marital status. *International Journal of Sociology of the Family* 10(2):301-310.

Keith, Pat M. 1982. Working women versus homemakers: Retirement resources and correlates of well-being. In *Women's Retirement: Policy Implications of Recent Research,* edited by M. Szinovacz (pp. 77-91). Beverly Hills: Sage.

Keith, Pat M. 1983. A comparison of the resources of parents and childless men and women in very old age. *Family Relations* 32(3):403-409.

Keith, Pat M. 1985. Work, retirement, and well-being among unmarried men and women. *The Gerontologist* 25(4):410-416.

Keith, Pat M., Kathleen Hill, Willis J. Goudy, and Edward A. Powers. 1984. Confidants and well-being: A note on male friendship in old age. *The Gerontologist* 24(3): 318-320.

Keith, Pat M. and Robbyn R. Wacker. 1990. Sex roles in the older family. In *Family Relationships in Later Life,* 2nd ed., edited by T. H. Brubaker (pp. 115-141). Newbury Park, CA: Sage.

Keith, Pat M., Robbyn R. Wacker, and Robert B. Schafer. 1992. Equity in older families. In *Families and Retirement,* edited by Maximiliane Szinovacz, David J. Ekerdt, and Barbara H. Vinick (pp. 189-201). Newbury Park, CA: Sage.

Keith, Patricia M. and Robert B. Schafer. 1985. Equity, role strains, and depression among middle-aged and older men and women. In *Social Bonds in Later Life: Aging and Interdependence,* edited by Warren A. Peterson and Jill Quadagno (pp. 37-49). Beverly Hills, CA: Sage.

Kelly, John R., Ed. 1993. *Activity and Aging: Staying Involved in Later Life.* Newbury Park, CA: Sage.

Kerckhoff, Alan C. 1966. Husband-wife expectations and reactions to retirement. In *Social Aspects of Aging,* edited by I. Simpson and J. C. McKinney (pp. 510-516). Durham, NC: Duke University Press.

Kessler, Ronald C. and Jane D. McLeod. 1984. Sex differences in vulnerability to undesirable life events. *American Sociological Review* 49(5):620-631.

Kessler, Ronald C. and James A. McRae, Jr. 1982. The effect of wives' employment on the mental health of married men and women. *American Sociological Review* 47(2): 216-227.

Kessler, Suzanne J. and Wendy McKenna. 1978. *Gender: An Ethnomethodological Approach.* New York: Wiley.

Kessler-Harris, Alice. 1981. *Women Have Always Worked: A Historical Overview.* New York: The Feminist Press.

Kimmel, Douglas C. 1990. *Adulthood and Aging: An Interdisciplinary, Developmental View.* 3rd ed. New York: John Wiley.

Kimmel, Douglas C. 1995. Lesbians and gay men also grow old. In *Promoting successful and productive aging,* edited by Lynne A. Bond, Stephen J. Cutler, and Armin Grams (pp. 289-303). Thousand Oaks, CA: Sage.

Kimmel, Michael S. and Michael A. Messner. 1989. *Men's Lives.* New York: Macmillan.

King, Deborah K. 1988. Multiple jeopardy, multiple consciousness: The context of a black feminist ideology. *Signs: Journal of Women in Culture and Society* 14(1):42-72.

Kingson, Eric R., Barbara A. Hirshorn, and John M. Cornman. 1986. *Ties That Bind: The Interdependence of Generations.* Washington, DC: Seven Locks Press.

Kingson, Eric R. and Regina O'Grady-LeShane. 1993. The effects of caregiving on women's Social Security benefits. *The Gerontologist* 33(2):230-239.

Kingson, Eric and Jill Quadagno. 1999. Social Security: Marketing radical reform.*Critical Gerontology: Perspectives from Political and Moral Economy,* edited by Meredith Minkler and Carroll L. Estes. Amityville, NY: Baywood.

Kivett, Vira R. 1978. Loneliness and the rural widow. *The Family Coordinator* 27(4): 389-394.

Kline, Chrysee. 1975. The socialization process of women: Implications for a theory of successful aging. *The Gerontologist* 15(6):486-492.

Knapp, Martin R. J. 1977. The activity theory of aging: An examination of the English context. *The Gerontologist* 17(6):553-559.

Kohen, Janet A. 1983. Old but not alone: Informal social supports among the elderly by marital status and sex. *The Gerontologist* 23(1):57-63.

Koo, Helen P. and Barbara K. Janowitz. 1983. Interrelationships between fertility and marital dissolution: Results of a simultaneous, logit model. *Demography* 20(2):129-145.

Kosloski, Karl, Gerald Ginsburg, and Carl W. Backman. 1984. Retirement as a process of active role transition. In *Role Transitions: Explorations and Explanations,* edited by V. L. Allen and E. van de Vliert (pp. 331-341). New York: Plenum Press.

Kotlikoff, Laurence J. and David A. Wise. 1989. *The Wage Carrot and the Pension Stick: Retirement Benefits and Labor Force Participation.* Kalamazoo, MI: W. E. Upjohn Institute.

Kovach, Christine R. and Thomas R. Knapp. 1989. Age, cohort, and time-period confounds in aging research. *Journal of Gerontological Nursing* 15(3):11-15.

Kraus, Arthur S. and Abraham M. Lilienfeld. 1959. Some epidemiologic aspects of the high mortality rate in the young widowed group. *Journal of Chronic Diseases* 10(3):207-217.

Krause, Neal. 1995. Stress and well-being in later life: Using research findings to inform intervention design. In *Promoting Successful and Productive Aging,* edited by Lynne A. Bond, Stephen J. Cutler, and Armin Grams (pp. 203-219). Thousand Oaks, CA: Sage.

Krause, Neal and Gina Jay. 1991. Stress, social support, and negative interaction in later life. *Research on Aging* 13(3):333-363.

Krivo, Lauren J. and Jan E. Mutchler. 1989. Elderly persons living alone: The effect of community context on living arrangements. *Journal of Gerontology* 44(2):S54-62.

Kroeger, Naomi. 1982. Preretirement preparation: Sex differences in access, sources, and use. In *Women's Retirement: Policy Implications of Recent Research,* edited by Maximiliane Szinovacz (pp. 77-91). Newbury Park, CA: Sage.

Krout, John A. 1995. Rural versus urban differences in health dependence among the elderly population. In *Health and Health Care Utilization in Later Life,* edited by Jon Hendricks (pp. 93-107). Amityville, NY: Baywood.

Kübler-Ross, Elisabeth. 1969. *On Death and Dying.* London: Macmillan.

Kutner, Bernard, David Fanshel, Alice M. Togo, and Thomas S. Langner. 1956. *Five Hundred Over Sixty: A Community Survey on Aging.* New York: Russell Sage Foundation.

La Gaipa, John L. 1990. The negative effects of informal support system. In *Personal Relationships and Social Support,* edited by Steve Duck with Roxane Cohen Silver (pp. 122-139). London: Sage.

Labouvie-Vief, Gisela. 1985. Intelligence and cognition. In *Handbook of the Psychology of Aging,* 2nd ed., edited by James E. Birren and K. Warner Schaie (pp. 500-530). New York: van Nostrand Reinhold.

Lambert, Helen H. 1978. Biology and equality: A perspective on sex differences. *Signs: Journal of Women in Culture and Society* 4(1):97-117.

Lamphere, Louise. 1997. The domestic sphere of women and the public world of men: The strengths and limitations of an anthropological dichotomy. In *Gender in Cross-Cultural Perspective,* 2nd ed., edited by Caroline B. Brettell and Carolyn F. Sargent (pp. 82-92). Upper Saddle River, NJ: Prentice Hall.

Larson, Reed, Jiri Zuzanek, and Roger Mannell. 1985. Being alone versus being with people: Disengagement in the daily experience of older adults. *Journal of Gerontology* 40(3):375-381.

Lashbrook, Jeff. 1996. Promotional timetables: An exploratory investigation of age norms for promotional expectations and their association with job well-being. *The Gerontologist* 36(2):189-198.

Lawrence, Barbara S. 1996. Organizational age norms: Why is it so hard to know one when you see one? *The Gerontologist* 36(2):209-220.

Lawton, M. Powell. 1997. Is gerontology biased toward a negative view of the aging process and old age? In *Controversial Issues in Aging,* edited by Andrew E. Scharlach and Lenard W. Kaye (pp. 190-194). Boston, MA: Allyn and Bacon.

Lee, Gary R. and Eugene Ellithorpe. 1982. Intergenerational exchange and subjective well-being among the elderly. *Journal of Marriage and the Family* 44(1): 217-224.

Lee, Gary R. and Constance L. Shehan. 1989. Retirement and marital satisfaction. *Journal of Gerontology* 44(6):S226-230.

Lee, Gary R., Marion C. Willetts, and Karen Seccombe. 1998. Widowhood and depression: Gender differences. *Research on Aging* 20(5):611-630.

Lee, John Alan. 1987. What can homosexual aging studies contribute to theories of aging? *Journal of Homosexuality* 13(4):43-71.

Lee, John Alan. 1990. Foreword. *Journal of Homosexuality* 20(3/4):xiii-xix.

Lehr, Ursula and Gernot Dreher. 1969. Determinants of attitudes toward retirement. In *Adjustment to Retirement: A Cross-National Study,* edited by Robert J. Havighurst, Joep M. A. Munnichs, Bernice L. Neugarten, and Hans Thomae (pp. 116-137). Assen, The Netherlands: Koninklijke van Gorcum & Co.

Leibowitz, Arleen and Jacob Alex Klerman. 1995. Explaining changes in married mothers' employment over time. *Demography* 32(3):365-378.

Lemon, Bruce W., Vern L. Bengtson, and James A. Peterson. 1972. An exploration of the activity theory of aging: Activity types and life satisfaction among in-movers to a retirement community. *Journal of Gerontology* 27(4):511-523.

Lennon, Mary Clare. 1987. Sex differences in distress: The impact of gender and work roles. *Journal of Health and Social Behavior* 28(3):290-305.

Leonesio, Michael V. 1993. Social Security and older workers. *Social Security Bulletin* 56(2):47-57.

Levkoff, Sue E., Paul D. Cleary, and Terrie Wetle. 1987. Differences in the appraisal of health between aged and middle-aged adults. *Journal of Gerontology* 42(1):114-120.

Levy, Sandra M. 1978. Some determinants of temporal experience in the retired and its correlates. *Genetic Psychology Monographs* 98(2):181-202.

Levy, Sandra M. 1980/81. The adjustment of the older woman: Effects of chronic ill health and attitudes toward retirement. *International Journal of Aging and Human Development* 12(2):93-110.

Lewin-Epstein, Noah. 1986. Employment and ill-health among women in Israel. *Social Science and Medicine* 23(11):1171-1179.

Lewis, Charles E. and Mary Ann Lewis. 1977. The potential impact of sexual equality on health. *The New England Journal of Medicine* 297(16):863-869.

Libow, Judith A. 1985. Gender and sex role issues as family secrets. *Journal of Strategic and Systemic Therapies* 4(2):32-41.

Lieberman, Morton A. 1992. Limitations of psychological stress model: Studies of widowhood. In *Stress and Health Among the Elderly,* edited by May L. Wykle, Eva Kahana, and Jerome Kowal (pp. 133-150). New York: Springer.

Lin, Nan and Walter M. Ensel. 1989. Life stress and health: Stressors and resources. *American Sociological Review* 54(3):382-395.

Lin, Nan, Mary Woelfel, and Mary Y. Dumin. 1986. Gender of the confidant and depression. In *Social Support, Life Events, and Depression,* edited by Nan Lin, Alfred Dean, and Walter M. Ensel (pp. 283-306). Orlando, FL: Academic Press.

Lin, Nan, Mary W. Woelfel, and Stephen C. Light. 1985. The buffering effects of social support subsequent to an important life event. *Journal of Health and Social Behavior* 26(3):247-263.

Lindsey, Linda L. 1997. *Gender Roles: A Sociological Perspective.* 3rd ed. Upper Saddle River, NJ: Prentice Hall.

Lipman-Blumen, Jean. 1984. *Gender Roles and Power.* Englewood Cliffs, NJ: Prentice-Hall.

Lips, Hilary M. 1988. *Sex & Gender: An Introduction.* Mountain View, CA: Mayfield.

Livson, Florine B. 1983. Gender identity: A life-span view of sex-role development. In *Sexuality in the Later Years: Roles and Behavior,* edited by Ruth B. Weg (pp. 105-127). New York: Academic Press.

Loether, H. J. 1967. *Problems of Aging.* Belmont, CA: Dickenson Publishing.

Long, Judy and Karen L. Porter. 1984. Multiple roles of midlife women: A case for new directions in theory, research, and policy. In *Women in Midlife,* edited by Grace Baruch and Jeanne Brooks-Gun (pp. 109-159). New York: Plenum Press.

Longino, Charles F., Jr. and Cary S. Kart. 1982. Explicating activity theory: A formal replication. *Journal of Gerontology* 37(6):713-722.

Longino, Jr. Charles F. and Aaron Lipman. 1982. The married, the formerly married and the never married: Support system differentials of older women in planned retirement communities. *International Journal of Aging and Human Development* 15(4):285-297.

Longino, Charles F., Jr., George J. Warheit, and Julie Ann Green. 1989. Class, aging, and health. In *Aging and Health: Perspectives on Gender, Race, Ethnicity, and Class,* edited by K. S. Markides (pp. 79-109). Newbury Park, CA: Sage.

Lopata, Helena Znaniecki. 1973. Social relations of black and white widowed women in a northern metropolis. *American Journal of Sociology* 78(4):1003-1010.

Lopata, Helena Znaniecki. 1993. The support systems of American urban widows. In *Handbook of Bereavement: Theory, Research, and Intervention,* edited by Margaret S. Stroebe, Wolfgang Stroebe, and Robert O. Hansson (pp. 381-397). Cambridge: Cambridge University Press.

Lopata, Helena Znaniecki. 1996. *Current Widowhood: Myths & Realities.* Thousand Oaks, CA: Sage.

Lopata, Helena Znaniecka and Henry P. Brehm. 1986. *Widows and Dependent Wives: From Social Problem to Federal Program.* New York: Praeger.

Lopata, Helena Z. and Barrie Thorne. 1978. On the term "sex roles." *Signs: Journal of Women in Culture and Society* 3(3):718-721.

Lorber, Judith. 1994. *Paradoxes of Gender.* New Haven, CT: Yale University Press.

Lorber, Judith and Susan A. Farrell, eds. 1991. *The Social Construction of Gender.* Newbury Park, CA: Sage.

Loring, Marti and Brian Powell. 1988. Gender, race, and DSM-III: A study of the objectivity of psychiatric diagnostic behavior. *Journal of Health and Social Behavior* 29(1):1-22.

Lowenthal, Marjorie Fiske and Clayton Haven. 1968. Interaction and adaptation: Intimacy as a critical variable. *American Sociological Review* 33(1):20-30.

Lowenthal, Marjorie Fiske and Betsy Robinson. 1976. Social networks and isolation. In *Handbook of Aging and the Social Sciences,* edited by Robert H. Binstock and Ethel Shanas (pp. 432-456). New York: Van Nostrand Reinhold.

Lowenthal, Marjorie Fiske, Majda Thurnher, and David Chiriboga. 1976. *Four Stages of Life.* San Francisco: Jossey-Bass.

Lubinski, David, Auke Tellegen, and James N. Butcher. 1983. Masculinity, femininity, and androgyny viewed and assessed as distinct concepts. *Journal of Personality and Social Psychology* 44(2):428-439.

Luborsky, Mark R. and Robert L. Rubinstein. 1990. Ethnic identity and bereavement in later life: The case of older widowers. In *The Cultural Context of Aging: Worldwide Perspectives,* edited by Jay Sokolovsky (pp. 229-240). New York: Bergin & Garvey.

Lund, Dale A., ed. 1989a. *Older Bereaved Spouses: Research With Practical Applications.* New York: Hemisphere.

Lund, Dale A. 1989b. Conclusions about bereavement in later life and implications for interventions and future research. In *Older Bereaved Spouses: Research With Practical Applications,* edited by Dale A. Lund (pp. 217-231). New York: Hemisphere.

Lund, Dale A., Michael S. Caserta, and Margaret F. Dimond. 1986a. Gender differences through two years of bereavement among the elderly. *The Gerontologist* 26(3): 314-320.

Lund, Dale A., Michael S. Caserta, and Margaret F. Dimond. 1989. Impact of spousal bereavement on the subjective well-being of older adults. In *Older Bereaved Spouses: Research With Practical Implications,* edited by Dale A. Lund (pp. 3-15). New York: Hemisphere.

Lund, Dale A., Michael S. Caserta, and Margaret F. Dimond. 1993. The course of spousal bereavement in later life. In *Handbook of Bereavement: Theory, Research, and Intervention,* edited by Margaret S. Stroebe, Wolfgang Stroebe, and Robert O. Hansson (pp. 240-254). Cambridge: Cambridge University Press.

Lund, Dale A., Michael S. Caserta, Margaret F. Dimond, and Robert M. Gray. 1986b. Impact of bereavement on the self-conceptions of older surviving spouses. *Symbolic Interaction* 9(2):235-244.

Lund, Dale A., Michael S. Caserta, Margaret F. Dimond, and Susan K. Shaffer. 1989. Competencies, tasks of daily living, and adjustments to spousal bereavement in later life. In *Older Bereaved Spouses: Research With Practical Applications*, edited by Dale A. Lund (pp. 135-152). New York: Hemisphere.

Lund, Dale A., Michael S. Caserta, Jan van Pelt, and Kathleen A. Gass. 1990. Stability of social support networks after later-life spousal bereavement. *Death Studies* 14:53-73.

Lynch, Marty and Meredith Minkler. 1999. Impacts of the proposed restructuring of Medicare an dMedicaid: A conceptual framework and analysis. In *Critical Gerontology: Perspectives from Political and Moral Economy*, edited by Meredith Minkler and Carroll L. Estes (pp. 185-201). Amityville, NY: Baywood.

Maccoby, Eleanor E. and Carol N. Jacklin. 1974. *The Psychology of Sex Differences.* Stanford University Press: Stanford, CA.

Maddox, George L. 1963. Activity and morale: A longitudinal study of selected elderly subjects. *Social Forces* 42(2):195-204.

Maddox, George L., Jr. 1964. Disengagement theory: A critical evaluation. *The Gerontologist* 4(2):80-82.

Manuel, Ron C. and John Reid. 1982. A comparative demographic profile of minority and nonminority aged. In *Minority Aging: Sociological and Social Psychological Issues*, edited by Ron C. Reid (pp. 31-62). Westport, CT: Greenwood Press.

Maracek, Jeanne. 1979. Social change, positive mental health, and psychological androgyny. *Psychology of Women Quarterly* 3(3):241-247.

Marini, Margaret Mooney. 1984. Age and sequencing norms in the transition to adulthood. *Social Forces* 63(1):229-244.

Markides, Kyriakos S. 1989a. Aging, gender, race/ethnicity, class, and health: A conceptual overview. In *Aging and Health: Perspectives on Gender, Race, Ethnicity, and Class*, edited by K. S. Markides (pp. 9-21). Newbury Park, CA: Sage.

Markides, Kyriakos S. 1989b. Consequences of gender differentials in life expectancy for black and Hispanic Americans. *International Journal of Aging and Human Development* 29(2):95-102.

Markson, Elizabeth W. 1995. Issues affecting older women. In *Promoting Successful and Productive Aging*, edited by Lynne A. Bond, Stephen J. Cutler, and Armin Grams (pp. 261-278). Thousand Oaks, CA: Sage.

Marshall, Nancy L., Rosalind C. Barnett, Grace K. Baruch, and Joseph H. Pleck. 1990. Double jeopardy: The costs of caring at work and at home. In *Circles of Care: Work and Identity in Women's Lives*, edited by Emily K. Abel and Margaret K. Nelson (pp. 266-277). Albany, NY: State University of New York Press.

Marshall, Victor W. 1994. Sociology, psychology, and the theoretical legacy of the Kansas City Studies. *The Gerontologist* 34(6):768-774.

Martin, John and Ann Doran. 1966. Evidence concerning the relationship between health and retirement. *Sociological Review* 14(3):329-343.

Martin Matthews, Anne and Kathleen H. Brown. 1988. Retirement as a critical life event. *Research on Aging* 9(4):548-571.

Mastekaasa, Arne. 1992. Marriage and psychological well-being: Some evidence on selection into marriage. *Journal of Marriage and the Family* 54(4):901-911.

Matthews, Sarah H. 1986. *Friendships Through the Life Course.* Beverly Hills, CA: Sage.

May, Martha. 1987. The historical problem of the family wage: The Ford Motor Company and the five dollar day. In *Families and Work,* edited by Naomi Gerstel and Harriet Engel Gross (pp. 111-131). Philadelphia, PA: Temple University Press.

McCrae, Robert R. and Paul T. Costa, Jr. 1984. *Emerging Lives, Enduring Dispositions: Personality in Adulthood.* Boston, MA: Little, Brown.

McCrae, Robert R. and Paul T. Costa, Jr. 1993. Psychological resilience among widowed men and women: A 10-year follow-up of a national sample. In *Handbook of Bereavement: Theory, Research, and Intervention,* edited by Margaret S. Stroebe, Wolfgang Stroebe, and Robert O. Hansson (pp. 196-207). Cambridge: Cambridge University Press.

McFall, Stephanie and Baila H. Miller. 1992. Caregiver burden and nursing home admission of frail elderly persons. *Journal of Gerontology* 47(2):S73-79.

McGee, Jeanne and Kathleen Wells. 1982. Gender typing and androgyny in later life: New directions for theory and research. *Human Development* 25(12):116-139.

McGee, Mark G., James Hall, III, and Candida J. L. Lutes-Dunckley. 1979. Factors influencing attitude toward retirement. *Journal of Psychology* 101:15-18.

McKinlay, Sonia M., Randi S. Triant, John B. McKinlay, Donald J. Brambilla, and Matthew Ferdock. 1990. Multiple roles for middle-aged women and their impact on health. In *Gender, Health, and Longevity: Multidisciplinary Perspectives,* edited by Marcia G. Ory and Huber R. Warner (pp. 119-156). New York: Springer.

McLanahan, Sara S. and Aage B. Sørensen. 1985. Life events and psychological well-being over the life course. In *Life Course Dynamics: Trajectories and Transitions, 1968-1980,* edited by Glen H. Elder, Jr. (pp. 217-238). Ithaca, NY: Cornell University Press.

McPherson, Barry D. 1990. *Aging As a Social Process: An Introduction to Individual and Population Aging.* 2nd ed. Toronto: Butterworths.

McPherson, Barry and Neil Guppy. 1979. Pre-retirement life-style and the degree of planning for retirement. *Journal of Gerontology* 34(2):254-263.

Meeker, Barbara F. and Patricia A. Weitzell-O'Neill. 1985. Sex roles and interpersonal behavior in task-oriented groups. In *Status, Rewards, and Influence,* edited by Joseph Berger and Morris Zelditch, Jr. (pp. 379-405). San Francisco, CA: Jossey-Bass.

Miller, Baila. 1990. Gender differences in spousal caregiver strain: Socialization and role explanations. *Journal of Marriage and the Family* 52:311-321.

Miller, Joanne and Howard H. Garrison. 1982. Sex roles: The division of labor at home and in the workplace. *Annual Review of Sociology* 8:237-262.

Mineau, Geraldine P. 1988. Utah widowhood: A demographic profile. In *On Their Own: Widows and Widowhood in the American Southwest 1848-1939,* edited by Arlene Scadron (pp. 140-165). Urbana and Chicago: University of Illinois Press.

Minkler, Meredith. 1991. Overview. In *Critical Perspectives on Aging: The Political and Moral Economy of Growing Old,* edited by Meredith Minkler and Carroll L. Estes (pp. 3-17). Amityville, NY: Baywood.

Minkler, Meredith and Caroll Estes, eds. 1991. *Critical Perspectives on Aging: The Political and Moral Economy of Growing Old.* Amityville, NY: Baywood.

Minkler, Meredith and Carroll Estes, eds. 1999. *Critical Gerontology: Perspectives from Political and Moral Economy.* Amityville, NY: Baywood.

Minkler, Meredith and Robyn Stone. 1985. The feminization of poverty and older women. *The Gerontologist* 25(4):351-357.

Mirowsky, John and Catherine E. Ross. 1996. Fundamental analysis in research on well-being: Distress and the sense of control. *The Gerontologist* 36(5):584-594.

Mitchell, Juliet. 1971. *Woman's Estate.* New York: Random House.

Moen, Phyllis. 1995. A life course approach to postretirement roles and well-being. In *Promoting Successful and Productive Aging,* edited by Lynne A. Bond, Stephen J. Cutler, and Armin Grams (pp. 239-256). Thousand Oaks, CA: Sage.

Moen, Phyllis, Donna Dempster-McClain, and Robin M. Williams, Jr. 1992. Successful aging: A life-course perspective on women's multiple roles and health. *American Journal of Sociology* 97(6):1612-1638.

Moore, Gwen. 1990. Structural determinants of men's and women's personal networks. *American Sociological Review* 55(5):726-735.

Morawski, Jill G. 1990. Toward the unimagined: Feminism and epistemology in psychology. In *Making a Difference: Psychology and the Construction of Gender,* edited by Rachel T. Hare-Mustin and Jeanne Maracek (pp. 150-183). New Haven, CT: Yale University Press.

Morgan, Barbara A., Isaac F. Megbolugbe, and David W. Rasmussen. 1996. Reverse mortgages and the economic status of elderly women. *The Gerontologist* 36(3):400-405.

Morgan, Carolyn Stout, Marilyn Affleck, and Lisa R. Riggs. 1986. Gender, personality traits, and depression. *Social Science Quarterly* 67(1):69-83.

Morgan, David L. 1989. Adjusting to widowhood: Do social networks really make it easier? *The Gerontologist* 29(1):101-107.

Morgan, Leslie A. 1976. A re-examination of widowhood and morale. *Journal of Gerontology* 31(6):687-695.

Morgan, Leslie A. 1980. Work in widowhood: A viable option? *The Gerontologist* 20(5):581-587.

Morgan, Leslie A. 1981. Economic change at mid-life widowhood: A longitudinal analysis. *Journal of Marriage and the Family* 43(4):899-907.

Morgan, Leslie A. 1984a. Changes in family interaction following widowhood. *Journal of Marriage and the Family* 46(2):323-331.

Morgan, Leslie A. 1984b. Continuity and change in the labor force activity of recently widowed women. *The Gerontologist* 24(5):530-535.

Morgan, Leslie A. 1986. The financial experience of widowed women: Evidence from the LRHS. *The Gerontologist* 26(6):663-668.

Morgan, Leslie A. 1991. *After Marriage Ends: Economic Consequences for Midlife Women.* Newbury Park, CA: Sage.

Morgan, Leslie A. 1992. Marital status and retirement plans: Do widowhood and divorce make a difference? In *Families and Retirement,* edited by Maximiliane Szinovacz, David J. Ekerdt, and Barbara H. Vinick (pp. 114-126). Newbury Park, CA: Sage.

Mottaz, Clifford. 1986. Gender differences in work satisfaction, work-related rewards and values, and the determinants of work satisfaction. *Human Relations* 39(4): 359-377.

Mueller, Charles W., Elizabeth Mutran, and Elizabeth Hege Boyle. 1989. Age discrimination in earnings in a dual-economy market. *Research on Aging* 11(4):492-507.

Murrell, Stanley A., Samuel Himmelfarb, and James F. Phifer. 1995. Effects of bereavement/ loss and pre-event status on subsequent physical health in older adults. In *Health and Health Care Utilization in Later Life*, edited by Jon Hendricks (pp. 159-177). Amityville, NY: Baywood.

Mutchler, Jan E. 1990. Household composition among the nonmarried elderly: A comparison of black and white women. *Research on Aging* 12(4):487-506.

Mutchler, Jan E., Jeffrey A. Burr, Amy M. Pienta, and Michael P. Massagli. 1997. Pathways to labor force exit: Work transitions and work instability. *Journal of Gerontology* 52B(1):S4-S12.

Mutran, Elizabeth. 1985. Intergenerational family support among blacks and whites: Response to culture or to socioeconomic differences. *Journal of Gerontology* 40(3): 382-389.

Nathanson, Constance A. 1990. The gender-mortality differential in developed countries: Demographic and sociocultural dimensions. In *Gender, Health, and Longevity: Multidisciplinary perspectives,* edited by Marcia G. Ory and Huber R. Warner (pp. 3-23). New York: Springer.

Nelson, Sarah M. 1988. Widowhood and autonomy in the Native-American Southwest. In *On Their Own: Widows and Widowhood in the American Southwest 1848-1939,* edited by Arlene Scadron (pp. 22-41). Chicago, IL: University of Illinois Press.

Neugarten, Bernice L. and Robert J. Havighurst. 1969. Disengagement reconsidered in crossnational context. In *Adjustment to retirement,* edited by Robert J. Havighurst, Joep M. A. Munnichs, Bernice L. Neugarten, and Hans Thomae (pp. 138-146). Assen, The Netherlands: Van Gorcum.

Neugarten, Bernice L., Joan W. Moore, and John C. Lowe. 1965. Age norms, age constraints, and adult socialization. *American Journal of Sociology* 70(6):710-717.

Newman, Evelyn S., Susan R. Sherman, and Claire E. Higgins. 1982. Retirement expectations and plans: A comparison of professional men and women. In *Women's Retirement: Policy Implications of Recent Research,* edited by Maximiliane Szinovacz (pp. 113-122). Beverly Hills, CA: Sage.

Nielsen, Joyce McCarl. 1990. *Sex and Gender in Society: Perspectives on Stratification.* 2nd ed. Prospect Heights, IL: Waveland Press.

Novak, Mark. 1997. *Issues in Aging: An Introduction to Gerontology.* New York: Longman.

O'Bryant, Shirley L. 1988. Sibling support and older widows' well-being. *Journal of Marriage and the Family* 50(1):173-183.

O'Bryant, Shirley L. 1991. Older widows and independent lifestyles. *International Journal of Aging and Human Development* 32(1):41-51.

O'Bryant, Shirley L. and Leslie A. Morgan. 1990. Recent widows' kin support and orientations to self-sufficiency. *The Gerontologist* 30(3):391-398.

O'Rand, Angela M. 1996. The precious and the precocious: Understanding cumulative disadvantage and cumulative advantage over the life course. *The Gerontologist* 36(2):230-238.

O'Rand, Angela M., John C. Henretta, and Margaret L. Krecker. 1992. Family pathways to retirement. In *Families and Retirement,* edited by Maximiliane Szinovacz, David J. Ekerdt, and Barbara H. Vinick (pp. 81-98). Newbury Park, CA: Sage.

O'Rand, Angela M. and Richard Landerman. 1984. Women's and men's retirement income status: Early family role effects. *Research on Aging* 6(1):25-44.

O'Rand, Angela M. and Vicky M. MacLean. 1986. Labor market, pension rule structure and retirement benefit promise for long-term employees. *Social Forces* 65(1): 224-240.

Offe, Claus and Volker Ronge. 1982. Thesis on the theory of the state. In *Classes, Power and Conflict,* edited by Anthony Giddens and David Held (pp. 249-256). Berkeley, CA: University of California Press.

Okihiro, Gary Y., ed. 1986. *In Resistance: Studies in African, Caribbean, and Afro-American History.* Amherst, MA: University of Massachusetts Press.

Okun, Morris A. and Verna M. Keith. 1998. Effects of positive and negative social exchanges with various sources on depressive symptoms in younger and older adults. *Journal of Gerontology* 53B(1):P4-P20.

Okun, Morris A., William A. Stock, Marilyn J. Haring, and Robert A. Witter. 1984. The social activity/subjective well-being relation: A quantitative synthesis. *Research on Aging* 6(1):45-65.

Older Women's League. 1999. The path to poverty: An analysis of women's retirement income. In *Critical Gerontology: Perspectives from Political and Moral Economy,* edited by Meredith Minkler and Carroll L. Estes (pp. 299-313). Amityville, NY: Baywood.

Oliker, Stacey J. 1989. *Best Friends and Marriage: Exchange Among Women.* Berkeley, CA: University of California Press.

Palmore, Erdman B. 1965. Differences in the retirement patterns of men and women. *The Gerontologist* 5(1):4-8.

Palmore, Erdman B., Bruce M. Burchett, Gerda G. Fillenbaum, Linda K. George, and Laurence M. Wallman. 1985. *Retirement: Causes and Consequences.* New York: Springer.

Palmore, Erdman B., Gerda G. Fillenbaum, and Linda K. George. 1984. Consequences of retirement. *Journal of Gerontology* 39(1):109-116.

Parkes, C. Murray, B. Benjamin, and R. G. Fitzgerald. 1969. Broken heart: A statistical study of increased mortality among widowers. *British Medical Journal* 1(Mar.):740-743.

Parkes, C. Murray and R. J. Brown. 1972. Health after bereavement: A controlled study of young Boston widows and widowers. *Psychosomatic Medicine* 34(5):449-461.

Parkes, Colin Murray. 1993. Bereavement as a psychosocial transition: Processes of adaptation to change. In *Handbook of Bereavement: Theory, Research, and Intervention,* edited by Margaret S. Stroebe, Wolfgang Stroebe, and Robert O. Hansson (pp. 91-101). Cambridge: Cambridge University Press.

Parkes, Colin Murray and Robert S. Weiss. 1983. *Recovery From Bereavement.* New York: Basic Books.

Parnes, Herbert S. and Gilbert Nestel. 1981. The retirement experience. In *Work and Retirement: A Longitudinal Study of Men,* edited by Herbert S. Parnes (pp. 155-197). Cambridge, MA: MIT Press.

Parsons, Talcott. 1954. *Essays in Sociological Theory.* New York: Free Press.

Parsons, Talcott. 1955. Sex roles in the American kinship system. In *Family, Socialization, and Interaction Processes,* edited by Talcott Parsons and Robert F. Bales (pp. 324-328). New York: The Free Press.

Parsons, Talcott and Robert F. Bales. 1955. *Family, Socialization and Interaction Processes.* Glencoe, IL: The Free Press.

Passuth, Patricia M. and Vern L. Bengtson. 1988. Sociological theories of aging: Current perspectives and future directions. In *Emergent Theories of Aging,* edited by James E. Birren and Vern L. Bengtson (pp. 333-355). New York: Springer.

Pavalko, Eliza K. and Julie E. Artis. 1997. Women's caregiving and paid work: Causal relationships in late midlife. *Journal of Gerontology* 52B(4):S170-S179.

Pearlin, Leonard I. and Carmi Schooler. 1978. The structure of coping. *Journal of Health and Social Behavior* 19(1):2-21.

Pearlin, Leonard I. and Marilyn McKean Skaff. 1996. Stress and the life course: A paradigmatic alliance. *The Gerontologist* 36(2):239-247.

Penning, Margaret J. 1998. In the middle: Parental caregiving in the context of other roles. *Journal of Gerontology* 53B(4):S188-S197.

Penrod, Joan D., Rosalie A. Kane, Robert L. Kane, and Michael D. Finch. 1995. Who cares? The size, scope, and composition of the caregiver support system. *The Gerontologist* 35(4):489-497.

Perry, Hosea L. 1993. Mourning and funeral customs of African Americans. In *Ethnic Variations in Dying, Death, and Grief,* edited by Donald P. Irish, Kathleen F. Lundquist, and Vivian Jenkins Nelsen (pp. 51-65). Washington, DC: Taylor & Francis.

Peters, George R., Danny R. Hoyt, Nicholas Babchuk, Marvin Kaiser, and Yuko Iijima. 1987. Primary-group support systems of the aged. *Research on Aging* 9(3):392-416.

Peterson, Jane W. 1990. Age of wisdom: Elderly Black women in family and church. In *The Cultural Context of Aging: Worldwide Perspectives,* edited by Jay Sokolovsky (pp. 213-227). New York: Bergin & Garvey.

Petrowsky, Marc. 1976. Marital status, sex, and the social networks of the elderly. *Journal of Marriage and the Family* 46(2):323-331.

Phillips, Bernard S. 1957. A role theory approach to adjustment in old age. *American Sociological Review* 22(2):212-217.

Phillips, Derek L. and Bernard E. Segal. 1969. Sexual status and psychiatric symptoms. *American Sociological Review* 34(1):58-72.

Pihlblad, C. T. and David L. Adams. 1972. Widowhood, social participation, and life satisfaction. *Aging and Human Development* 3(4):323-330.

Piotrkowski, Chaya S., Robert N. Rapoport, and Rhona Rapoport. 1987. Families and work. In *Handbook of Marriage and the Family,* edited by Marvin B. Sussman and Suzanne K. Steinmetz (pp. 251-283). New York: Plenum.

Powers, Edward A. and Gordon L. Bultena. 1976. Sex differences in intimate friendships of old age. *Journal of Marriage and the Family* 38(4):739-747.

Pratt, Michael W. and Joan E. Norris. 1994. *The Social Psychology of Aging.* Blackwell: Cambridge, MA.

Price-Bonham, Sharon and Carolyn Kitchings Johnson. 1982. Attitudes toward retirement: A comparison of professional and nonprofessional married women. In *Women's Retirement: Policy Implications for Recent Research,* edited by Maximiliane Szinovacz (pp. 123-138). Newbury Park, CA: Sage.

Quadagno, Jill S. 1978. Career continuity and retirement plans of men and women physicians: The meaning of disorderly careers. *Sociology of Work and Occupations* 5(1):55-74.

Quadagno, Jill. 1988. Women's access to pensions and the structure of eligibility rules: Systems of production and reproduction. *The Sociological Quarterly* 29(4):541-558.

Quadagno, Jill. 1996. Social Security and the myth of the entitlement "crisis." *The Gerontologist* 36(3):391-399.

Quadagno, Jill. 1999. *Aging and the Life Course: An Introduction to Social Gerontology*. Boston, MA: McGraw-Hill.

Quadagno, Jill and Steve McClellan. 1989. The other functions of retirement. *Generations* 13(2):7-10.

Quam, Jean K. and Gary S. Whitford. 1992. Adaptation and age-related expectations of older gay and lesbian adults. *The Gerontologist* 32(3):367-374.

Radloff, Lenore. 1975. Sex differences in depression: The effects of occupation and marital status. *Sex Roles* 1(3):249-265.

Rahman, Omar, John Strauss, Paul Gertler, Deanne Ashley, and Kristin Fox. 1994. Gender differences in adult health: An international comparison. *The Gerontologist* 34(4): 463-469.

Rakowski, W. and C. Cryan. 1990. Associations among perceptions of health and health status within three age groups. *Journal of Aging and Health* 2:58-80.

Rawlins, William K. 1992. *Friendship Matters: Communication, Dialectics, and the Life Course*. New York: Aldine de Gruyter.

Ray, Ruth E. 1996. A postmodern perspective on feminist gerontology. *The Gerontologist* 36(5):674-680.

Rees, W. Dewi and Sylvia G. Lutkins. 1967. Mortality of bereavement. *British Medical Journal* 4(Oct.):13-16.

Regan, Mary C. and Helen E. Roland. 1985. Rearranging family and career priorities: Professional women and men of the eighties. *Journal of Marriage and the Family* 47(4):985-992.

Reichard, Suzanne, Florine Livson, and Paul G. Petersen. 1962. *Aging and Personality: A Study of Eighty-Seven Older Men*. New York: John Wiley & Sons.

Reitzes, Donald C., Elizabeth J. Mutran, and Maria E. Fernandez. 1996. Preretirement influences on postretirement self-esteem. *Journal of Gerontology* 51B(5): S242-S249.

Reitzes, Donald C., Elizabeth J. Mutran, and Linda A. Verrill. 1995. Activities and self-esteem: Continuing the development of activity theory. *Research on Aging* 17(3): 260-277.

Remondet, Jacqueline H., Robert O. Hansson, Bonnie Rule, and Glynna Winfrey. 1987. Rehearsal for widowhood. *Journal of Social and Clinical Psychology* 5(3):285-297.

Reno, Virginia P. 1993. The role of pensions in retirement income: Trends and questions. *Social Security Bulletin* 56(1):29-43.

Reskin, Barbara and Irene Padavic. 1994. *Women and Men at Work*. Thousand Oaks, CA: Pine Forge Press.

Reynolds, John R. and Catherine E. Ross. 1998. Social stratification and health: Education's benefit beyond economic status and social origins. *Social Problems* 45(2):221-247.

Richardson, Virginia and Keith M. Kilty. 1991. Adjustment to retirement: Continuity vs. discontinuity. *International Journal of Aging and Human Development* 33(2):151-169.

Riddick, Carol Cutler. 1982. Life satisfaction among aging women: A causal model. In *Women's Retirement: Policy Implications of Recent Research,* edited by Maximiliane Szinovacz (pp. 45-59). Newbury Park, CA: Sage.

Riessman, Catherine Kohler and Naomi Gerstel. 1985. Marital dissolution and health: Do males or females have greater risk? *Social Science and Medicine* 20(6):617-635.

Riger, Stephanie. 1992. Science, social values, and the study of women. *American Psychologist* 47(6):730-740.

Risman, Barbara J. 1987. Intimate relationships from a microstructural perspective: Men who mother. *Gender & Society* 1(1):6-32.

Roberto, Karen A. and Priscilla J. Kimboko. 1989. Friendships in later life: Definitions and maintenance patterns. *International Journal of Aging and Human Development* 28(1):9-19.

Roberts, Greg. 1999. Age effects and health appraisal: A meta-analysis. *Journal of Gerontology* 54B(1):S24-S30.

Rodeheaver, Dean. 1990. Labor market progeria: On the life expectancy of presentability among older women. *Generations* 14(3):53-58.

Rodgers, Roy H. 1973. *Family Interaction and Transaction: The Developmental Approach.* Englewood Cliffs, NJ: Prentice-Hall.

Rollins, Judith. 1985. *Between Women: Domestics and Their Employers.* Philadelphia, PA: Temple University Press.

Rook, Karen S. 1984. The negative side of social interaction: Impact on psychological well-being. *Journal of Personality and Social Psychology* 46(5):1097-1108.

Rosaldo, Michelle. 1980. The uses and abuses of anthropology. *Signs: Journal of Women in Culture and Society* 5(3):389-417.

Rosenfield, Sarah. 1989. The effects of women's employment: Personal control and sex differences in mental health. *Journal of Health and Social Behavior* 30(1):77-91.

Rosenmayr, Leopold. 1981. Objective and subjective perspectives of life span research. *Ageing and Society* 1(1):29-49.

Rosow, Irving. 1963. Adjustment of the normal aged. In *Processes of Aging: Social and Psychological Perspectives, Volume II,* edited by Richard H. Williams, Clark Tibbitts, and Wilma Donahue (pp. 195-223). New York: Atherton Press.

Rosow, Irving. 1978. What is a cohort and why? *Human Development* 21(2):65-75.

Rothman, Robert A. 1993. *Inequality and Stratification: Class, Color, and Gender.* 2nd ed. Englewood Cliffs, NJ: Prentice Hall.

Rowe, John W. and Robert L. Kahn. 1987. Human aging: Usual and successful. *Science* 237(4811):143-149.

Rowe, John W. and Robert L. Kahn. 1997. Successful aging. *The Gerontologist* 37(4): 433-440.

Rowland, Kay F. 1977. Environmental events predicting death for the elderly. *Psychological Bulletin* 84(2):349-372.

Rozzini, Renzo, Angelo Bianchetti, Corrado Carabellese, Mariarosa Inzoli, and Marco Trabucchi. 1988. Depression, life events, and somatic symptoms. *The Gerontologist* 28(2):229-232.

Rubin, Beth. 1996. *Shifts in the Social Contract: Understanding Change in American Society.* Thousand Oaks, CA: Sage.

Rubin, Lillian. 1985. *Just Friends.* New York: Harper & Row.

Rubinstein, Robert L. 1986. *Singular Paths: Old Men Living Alone.* New York: Columbia University Press.

Ruhm, Christopher J. 1989. Why older Americans stop working. *The Gerontologist* 29(3):294-299.

Rushing, Beth, Christian Ritter, and Russell P. D. Burton. 1992. Race differences in the effects of multiple roles on health: Longitudinal evidence from a national sample of older men. *Journal of Health and Social Behavior* 33(2):126-139.

Rybash, John W., Paul A. Roodin, and John W. Santrock. 1991. *Adult Development and Aging.* 2nd ed. Dubuque, IA: William C. Brown.

Ryder, Norman B. 1965. The cohort as a concept in the study of social change. *American Sociological Review* 30(6):843-861.

Sable, Pat. 1991. Attachment, loss of spouse, and grief in elderly adults. *Omega: The Journal of Death and Dying* 23(2):129-142.

Sagy, Shifra and Aaron Antonovsky. 1992. The family sense of coherence and the retirement transition. *Journal of Marriage and the Family* 54(4):983-993.

Sanchez, Laura and Elizabeth Thomson. 1997. Becoming mothers and fathers: Parenthood, gender, and the division of labor. *Gender & Society* 11(6):747-772.

Sanders, Catherine M. 1989. *Grief: The Mourning After.* New York: John Wiley & Sons.

Schaie, K. Warner. 1965. A general model for the study of developmental problems. *Psychological Bulletin* 64(2):92-107.

Schoenbaum, Michael and Timothy Waidmann. 1997. Race, socioeconomic status, and health: Accounting for race differences in health. *Journals of Gerontology* 52B(Special Issue):61-73.

Schone, Barbara Steinberg and Robin M. Weinick. 1998. Health-related behaviors and the benefits of marriage for elderly persons. *The Gerontologist* 38(5):618-627.

Schulz, James H. 1990. Mother, apple pie, and Social Security—It's not time to change. *Journal of Aging and Social Policy* 2(1):69-81.

Schulz, James H. 1995. *The Economics of Aging.* 6th ed. Westport, CT: Auburn House.

Seccombe, Karen. 1992. Employment, the family, and employer-based policies. In *Gender, Families, and Elder Care,* edited by Jeffrey W. Dwyer and Raymond T. Coward (pp. 165-180). Newbury Park, CA: Sage.

Seccombe, Karen and Gary R. Lee. 1986. Gender differences in retirement satisfaction and its antecedents. *Research on Aging* 8(3):426-440.

Settersten, Richard A., Jr. and Gunhild O. Hägestad. 1996. What's the latest? Cultural age deadlines for family transitions. *The Gerontologist* 36(2):178-188.

Shanas, Ethel. 1970. Health and adjustment in retirement. *The Gerontologist* 10(1):19-21.

Shanas, Ethel, Peter Townsend, Dorothy Wedderburn, Henning Friis, Poul Milhoj, and Jan Stehouwer. 1968. *Old People in Three Industrial Societies.* New York: Atherton Press.

Sheppard, Harold L. 1976. Work and retirement. In *Handbook of Aging and the Social Sciences,* edited by R. H. Binstock and E. Shanas (pp. 286-309). New York: Van Nostrand.

Shuchter, Stephen R. and Sidney Zisook. 1987. A multidimensional model of spousal bereavement. In *Biopsychosocial Aspects of Bereavement,* edited by Sidney Zisook (pp. 37-47). Washington, DC: American Psychiatric Press.

Shuchter, Stephen R. and Sidney Zisook. 1993. The course of normal grief. In *Handbook of Bereavement: Theory, Research, and Intervention,* edited by Margaret S. Stroebe,

Wolfgang Stroebe, and Robert O. Hansson (pp. 23-43). Cambridge: Cambridge University Press.

Simpson, Ida Harper, Kurt W. Back, and John C. McKinney. 1966. Attributes of work, involvement in society, and self-evaluation in retirement. In *Social Aspects of Aging,* edited by Ida Harper Simpson and John C. McKinney (pp. 55-74). New York: Van Nostrand.

Sinnott, Jan Dynda. 1977. Sex-role inconstancy, biology, and successful aging. *The Gerontologist* 17(5):459-463.

Sinnott, Jan D. 1982. Correlates of sex roles of older adults. *Journal of Gerontology* 37(5):587-594.

Sinnott, Jan Dynda. 1984. Older men, older women: Are their perceived sex roles similar? *Sex Roles* 10(11/12):847-856.

Skoglund, John. 1980. Attitudes toward work and retirement in Sweden: A multigroup, multivariate analysis. *International Journal of Aging and Human Development* 11(2): 147-162.

Slevin, Kathleen F. and C. Ray Wingrove. 1995. Women in retirement: A review and critique of empirical research since 1976. *Sociological Inquiry* 65(1):1-21.

Smith, Dorothy E. 1987. Women's inequality and the family. In *Families and Work,* edited by Naomi Gerstel and Harriet Engel Gross (pp. 23-54). Philadelphia, PA: Temple University Press.

Smith, Ken R. and Norman J. Waitzman. 1994. Double jeopardy: Interaction effects of marital and poverty status on the risk of mortality. *Demography* 31(3): 487-507.

Smith, Ken R. and Cathleen D. Zick. 1986. The incidence of poverty among the recently widowed: Mediating factors in the life course. *Journal of Marriage and the Family* 48(3):619-630.

Smith, Ken R. and Cathleen D. Zick. 1994. Linked lives, dependent demise? Survival analysis of husbands and wives. *Demography* 31(1):81-93.

Smith, Shelley A. and Marta Tienda. 1988. The doubly disadvantaged: Women of color in the U.S. labor force. In *Women Working,* 2nd ed., edited by Ann Helton Stromberg and Shirley Harkess (pp. 61-80). Mountain View, CA: Mayfield.

Social Security Administration. 1995. *Annual Statistical Supplement to the Social Security Bulletin.* Washington, DC: U.S. Government Printing Office.

Sokolovsky, Jay. 1990. Bringing culture back home: Aging, ethnicity, and family support. In *The Cultural Context of Aging: Worldwide Perspectives,* edited by Jay Sokolovsky (pp. 201-211). New York: Bergin & Garvey.

Solomon, Kenneth and Peggy A. Szwabo. 1994. The work-oriented culture: Success and power in elderly men. In *Older Men's Lives,* edited by Edward H. Thompson, Jr. (pp. 42-64). Thousand Oaks, CA: Sage.

Somers, Anne R. 1985. Toward a female gerontocracy? Current social trends. In *The Physical and Mental Health of Aged Women,* edited by Marie R. Haug, Amasa B. Ford, and Marian Sheafor (pp. 16-26). New York: Springer.

South, Scott J. and Katherine Trent. 1988. Sex ratios and women's roles: A cross-national analysis. *American Journal of Sociology* 93(5):1096-1115.

Spanier, Graham B. and Linda Thompson. 1984. *Parting: The Aftermath of Separation and Divorce.* Beverly Hills, CA: Sage.

Spitze, Glenna. 1988. The data on women's labor force participation. In *Women Working,* 2nd ed., edited by Ann Helton Stromberg and Shirley Harkess (pp. 42-60). Mountain View, CA: Mayfield.

Spitze, Glenna and John Logan. 1989. Gender differences in family support: Is there a payoff? *The Gerontologist* 29(1):108-113.

Spitze, Glenna and John R. Logan. 1992. Helping as a component of parent-adult child relations. *Research on Aging* 14(3):291-312.

Srole, Leo and Anita Kassen Fischer. 1980. The Midtown Manhattan Longitudinal Study vs. "The Mental Paradise Lost" doctrine: A controversy joined. *Archives of General Psychiatry* 37(2):209-221.

Stacey, Judith and Barrie Thorne. 1985. The missing feminist revolution in sociology. *Social Problems* 33(4):301-316.

Stahl, Sidney M. and Jacquelyn Rupp Feller. 1990. Old equals sick: An ontogenetic fallacy. In *The Legacy of Longevity: Health and Health Care in Later Life,* edited by S. M. Stahl (pp. 21-34). Newbury Park, CA: Sage.

Steil, Janice M. and Beth A. Turetsky. 1987. Marital influence levels and symptomatology among wives. In *Spouse, Parent, Worker: On Gender and Multiple Roles,* edited by Faye J. Crosby (pp. 74-90). New Haven, CT: Yale University Press.

Steinbach, Ulrike. 1992. Social networks, institutionalization, and mortality among elderly people in the United States. *Journal of Gerontology* 47(4):S183-190.

Steinmetz, George and Erik Olin Wright. 1989. The fall and rise of the petty bourgeoisie: Changing patterns of self-employment in the postwar United States. *American Journal of Sociology* 94(5):973-1018.

Stevens, Nan. 1995. Gender and adaptation to widowhood. *Ageing and Society* 15(1): 37-52.

Stevens-Long, Judith. 1988. *Adult Life.* 3rd ed. Mountain View, CA: Mayfield.

Stokes, Randall G. and George L. Maddox. 1967. Some social factors on retirement adaptation. *Journal of Gerontology* 22(3):329-344.

Stolar, G. Elaine, Michael I. MacEntee, and Patricia Hill. 1995. Seniors' assessment of their health and life satisfaction: The case for contextual evaluation. In *Health and Health Care Utilization in Later Life,* edited by Jon Hendricks (pp. 145-157). Amityville, NY: Baywood.

Stoller, Eleanor Palo and Rose Campbell Gibson. 1994. Advantages of using the life course framework in studying aging. In *Worlds of Differences: Inequality in the Aging Experience,* edited by Eleanor Palo Stoller and Rose Campbell Gibson (pp. 3-13). Thousand Oaks: Pine Forge Press.

Stoller, Eleanor Palo and Karen L. Pugliesi. 1989. Other roles of caregivers: Competing responsibilities or supportive resources. *Journal of Gerontology* 44(6):S231-238.

Stone, Robyn, Gail Lee Cafferata, and Judith Sangl. 1987. Caregivers of the frail elderly: A national profile. *The Gerontologist* 27(5):616-626.

Strain, Laurel A. and Neena L. Chappell. 1982. Confidants: Do they make a difference in quality of life? *Research on Aging* 4(4):479-502.

Streib, Gordon F. and C. J. Schneider. 1971. *Retirement in American Society: Impact and Process.* Ithaca, NY: Cornell University Press.

Stroebe, Margaret S., Robert O. Hansson, and Wolfgang Stroebe. 1993. Contemporary themes and controversies in bereavement research. In *Handbook of*

Bereavement: Theory, Research, and Intervention, edited by Margaret S. Stroebe, Wolfgang Streoebe, and Robert O. Hansson (pp. 457-475). Cambridge: Cambridge University Press.

Stroebe, Margaret S. and Wolfgang Stroebe. 1983. Who suffers more? Sex differences in health risks of the widowed. *Psychological Bulletin* 93(2):279-301.

Stroebe, Margaret S. and Wolfgang Stroebe. 1993a. The mortality of bereavement: A review. In *Handbook of Bereavement: Theory, Research, and Intervention,* edited by Margaret S. Stroebe, Wolfgang Stroebe, and Robert O. Hansson (pp. 175-195). Cambridge: Cambridge University Press.

Stroebe, Wolfgang and Margaret S. Stroebe. 1987. *Bereavement and Health: The Psychological and Physical Consequences of Partner Loss.* Cambridge: Cambridge University Press.

Stroebe, Wolfgang and Margaret S. Stroebe. 1993b. Determinants of adjustment to bereavement in younger widows and widowers. In *Handbook of Bereavement: Theory, Research, and Intervention,* edited by Margaret S. Stroebe, Wolfgang Stroebe, and Robert O. Hansson (pp. 208-226). Cambridge: Cambridge University Press.

Stryker, Sheldon. 1980. *Symbolic Interactionism: A Social Structural Version.* Menlo Park, CA: Benjamin/Cummings Publishing Company.

Stuart-Hamilton, Ian. 1994. *The Psychology of Aging: An Introduction.* 2nd ed. London: Jessica Kingsley.

Swain, Scott. 1989. Covert intimacy: Closeness in men's friendships. In *Gender in Intimate Relationships: A Microstructural Approach,* edited by Barbara J. Risman and Pepper Schwartz (pp. 71-86). Belmont, CA: Wadsworth.

Sweet, James A. and Larry L. Bumpass. 1987. *American Families and Households.* New York: Russell Sage Foundation.

Szinovacz, Maximiliane. 1982a. Research on women's retirement. In *Women's Retirement: Policy Implications of Recent Research,* edited by Maximiliane Szinovacz (pp. 13-21). Beverly Hills, CA: Sage.

Szinovacz, Maximiliane. 1982b. Retirement plans and retirement adjustment. In *Women's Retirement: Policy Implications of Recent Research,* edited by Maximiliane Szinovacz (pp. 139-152). Beverly Hills, CA: Sage.

Szinovacz, Maximiliane. 1983. Beyond the hearth: Older women and retirement. In *Older Women: Issues and Prospects,* edited by E. W. Markson (pp. 93-120). Lexington, MA: Lexington Books.

Szinovacz, Maximiliane. 1986/87. Preferred retirement timing and retirement satisfaction in women. *International Journal of Aging and Human Development* 24(4): 301-317.

Szinovacz, Maximiliane. 1989a. Decision-making on retirement timing. In *Dyadic Decision Making,* edited by David Brinberg and James Jaccard (pp. 286-310). New York: Springer.

Szinovacz, Maximiliane. 1989b. Retirement, couples, and household work. In *Aging and the Family,* edited by Stephen J. Bahr and Evan T. Peterson (pp. 33-58). Lexington, MA: Lexington Books.

Szinovacz, Maximiliane. 1992. Social activities and retirement adaptation: Gender and family variations. In *Families and Retirement,* edited by Maximiliane Szinovacz, David J. Ekerdt, and Barbara H. Vinick (pp. 236-253). Newbury Park, CA: Sage.

Szinovacz, Maximiliane. 1996. Couples' employment/retirement patterns and perceptions of marital quality. *Research on Aging* 18(2):243-268.

Szinovacz, Maximiliane and Stanley DeViney. 1999. The retiree identity: Gender and race differences. *Journal of Gerontology* 54B(4):S207-S218.

Szinovacz, Maximiliane and Christine Washo. 1992. Gender differences in exposure to life events and adaptation to retirement. *Journal of Gerontology* 47(4):S191-196.

Tausig, Mark. 1986. Prior history of illness in the basic model. In *Social Support, Life Events, and Depression,* edited by Nan Lin, Alfred Dean, and Walter M. Ensel (pp. 267-280). Orlando, FL: Academic Press.

Tavris, Carol. 1992. *The Mismeasure of Woman.* New York: Simon & Schuster.

Taylor, Marylee C. and Judith A. Hall. 1982. Psychological androgyny: Theories, methods, and conclusions. *Psychological Bulletin* 92(2):347-366.

Taylor, Robert Joseph. 1986. Religious participation among elderly blacks. *The Gerontologist* 26(6):630-636.

Teachman, Jay D. 1991. Contributions to children by divorced fathers. *Social Problems* 38(3):358-371.

Teitelman, Jodi L. 1987. Homosexuality. In *The Encyclopedia of Aging,* edited by George L. Maddox (pp. 329-330). New York: Springer.

Thoits, Peggy A. 1986. Multiple identities: Examining gender and marital status differences in distress. *American Sociological Review* 51(2):259-272.

Thoits, Peggy A. 1987a. Negotiating roles. In *Spouse, Parent, Worker: On Gender and Multiple Roles,* edited by Faye J. Crosby (pp. 11-22). New Haven, CT: Yale University Press.

Thoits, Peggy A. 1987b. Gender and marital status differences in control and distress: Common stress versus unique stress explanations. *Journal of Health and Social Behavior* 28(1):7-22.

Thomas, Alexander and Samuel Sillen. 1991. *Racism and Psychiatry.* New York: Carol Publishing Group.

Thomas, Jeanne L. 1994. Older men as fathers and grandfathers. In *Older Men's Lives,* edited by Edward H. Thompson, Jr. (pp. 197-217). Thousand Oaks, CA: Sage.

Thomas, William I. and Florian Znaniecki. 1918. *The Polish Peasant in Europe and America.* Chicago, IL: University of Chicago Press.

Thomas, William I. and Dorothy Swaine Thomas. 1928. *The Child in America.* New York: Alfred A. Knopf.

Thompson, Edward H., Jr. 1994. Older men as invisible men in contemporary society. In *Older Men's Lives,* edited by Edward H. Thompson, Jr. (pp. 1-21). Thousand Oaks, CA: Sage.

Thompson, Larry W., James N. Breckenridge, Dolores Gallagher, and James Peterson. 1984. Effects of bereavement on self-perceptions of physical health in elderly widows and widowers. *Journal of Gerontology* 39(3):309-314.

Thompson, Larry W., Dolores Gallagher, Heidi Cover, Michael Gilewski, and James Peterson. 1989. Effects of bereavement on symptoms of psychopathology in older men and women. In *Older Bereaved Spouses: Research With Practical Implications,* edited by Dale A. Lund (pp. 17-24). New York: Hemisphere.

Thompson, Linda. 1992. Feminist methodology for family studies. *Journal of Marriage and the Family* 54(1):3-18.

Thompson, Linda. 1993. Conceptualizing gender in marriage: The case of marital care. *Journal of Marriage and the Family* 55(3):557-569.

Thompson, Linda and Alexis J. Walker. 1995. The place of feminism in family studies. *Journal of Marriage and the Family* 57(4):847-865.

Thompson, Wayne E. 1958. Pre-retirement anticipation and adjustment in retirement. *The Journal of Social Issues* 14(2):35-45.

Thompson, Wayne E. and Gordon F. Streib. 1958. Situational determinants: Health and economic deprivation in retirement. *The Journal of Social Issues* 14(2):18-34.

Thompson, Wayne E., Gordon F. Streib, and John Kosa. 1960. The effect of retirement on personal adjustment: A panel analysis. *Journal of Gerontology* 15(2): 165-169.

Thornborrow, Nancy M. and Marianne B. Sheldon. 1995. Women in the labor force. In *Women: A Feminist Perspective*, 5th ed., edited by Jo Freeman (pp. 197-219). Mountain View, CA: Mayfield.

Thorson, James A. 1995. *Old Age in a Changing Society*. Belmont, CA: Wadsworth.

Thurnher, Majda. 1974. Goals, values, and life evaluations at the preretirement stage. *Journal of Gerontology* 29(1):85-96.

Tissue, Thomas L. 1968. A Guttman scale of disengagement potential. *Journal of Gerontology* 23(4):513-516.

Tobin, Sheldon S. and Bernice L. Neugarten. 1961. Life satisfaction and social interaction in the aging. *Journal of Gerontology* 16:344-346.

Tornstam, Lars. 1992. The quo vadis of gerontology: On the scientific paradigm of gerontology. *The Gerontologist* 32(3):318-326.

Torres-Gil, Fernando. 1986. An examination of factors affecting future cohorts of elderly Hispanics. *The Gerontologist* 26(2):140-146.

Truitner, Ken and Nga Truitner. 1993. Death and dying in Buddhism. In *Ethnic variations in dying, death, and grief*, edited by Donald P. Irish, Kathleen F. Lundquist, and Vivian Jenkins Nelsen (pp. 125-136). Washington, DC: Taylor & Francis.

Tuckman, Jacob and Irving Lorge. 1953. *Retirement and the Industrial Worker: Prospect and Reality*. New York: Columbia University.

Turner, Barbara F. 1979. The self-concepts of older women. *Research on Aging* 1(4): 464-480.

Turner, Barbara F. 1982. Sex-related differences in aging. In *Handbook of Developmental Psychology*, edited by Benjamin B. Wolman (pp. 912-936). Englewood Cliffs, NJ: Prentice-Hall.

Turner, Barbara F. 1994. Introduction. In *Women Growing Older: Psychological Perspectives*, edited by Barbara F. Turner and Lillian E. Troll (pp. 1-34). Thousand Oaks, CA: Sage.

Turner, Barbara F. and Lillian E. Troll, eds. 1994. *Women Growing Older: Psychological Perspectives*. Thousand Oaks, CA: Sage.

Turner, Jonathan H. 1991. *The Structure of Sociological Theory*. 5th ed. Belmont, CA: Wadsworth.

Turner, Ralph H. 1970. *Family Interaction*. New York: Wiley.

Turner, Ralph H. and Doug Abbott. 1990. Role change. In *Annual Review of Sociology*, edited by W. Richard Scott and Judith Blake (pp. 87-110). Palo Alto, CA: Annual Reviews, Inc.

Uhlenberg, Peter. 1988. Aging and the societal significance of cohorts. In *Emergent Theories of Aging,* edited by James E. Birren and Vern L. Bengtson (pp. 405-425). New York: Springer.

Uhlenberg, Peter, Teresa Cooney, and Robert Boyd. 1990. Divorce for women after midlife. *Journal of Gerontology* 45(1):S3-11.

Uhlenberg, Peter. 1996. Mutual attraction: Demography and life-course analysis. *The Gerontologist* 36(2):226-229.

Umberson, Debra, Camille B. Wortman, and Ronald C. Kessler. 1992. Widowhood and depression: Explaining long-term gender differences in vulnerability. *Journal of Health and Social Behavior* 33(1):10-24.

U.S. Bureau of the Census. 1996a. *65+ in the United States.* Current Population Reports, Special Studies, P23-190. Washington, DC: U.S. Government Printing Office.

U.S. Bureau of the Census. 1996b. *Population Projections of the United States by Age, Sex, Race, and Hispanic Origin: 1995 to 2050.* Current Population Reports, P25-1130. Washington, DC: U.S. Government Printing Office.

U.S. Bureau of the Census. 1998. Statistical Abstract of the United States. Washington, DC: U.S. Government Printing Office.

U.S. Senate, Report of the Special Committee on Aging. 1992. *Developments in Aging: 1991, Vol. 1.* Washington, DC: U.S. Government Printing Office.

U.S. Senate, Report of the Special Committee on Aging. 1994. *Developments in Aging: 1993, Vol. 1.* Washington, DC: U.S. Government Printing Office.

U.S. Senate, Report of the Special Committee on Aging. 1997. *Developments in Aging: 1996, Vol. 1.* Washington, DC: U.S. Government Printing Office.

Vachon, M. L. S., A. R. Sheldon, W. J. Lancee, W. A. L. Lyall, J. Rogers, and S. J. J. Freeman. 1982. Correlates of enduring distress patterns following bereavement: Social network, life situation and personality. *Psychological Medicine* 12:783-788.

Van Zandt, Sally, Roberta Mou, and Doug Abbott. 1989. Mental and physical health of rural bereaved and nonbereaved elders: A longitudinal study. In *Older Bereaved Spouses: Research With Practical Implications,* edited by Dale A. Lund (pp. 25-35). New York: Hemisphere.

Vanek, Joann. 1984. Housewives as workers. In *Work & Family: Changing Roles of Men and Women,* edited by Patricia Voydanoff (pp. 89-103). Palo Alto, CA: Mayfield.

Verbrugge, Lois M. 1985. An epidemiological profile of older women. In *The Physical and Mental Health of Aged Women,* edited by Marie R. Haug, Amasa B. Ford, and Marian Sheafor (pp. 41-64). New York: Springer.

Verbrugge, Lois M. 1989. Gender, aging, and health. In *Aging and Health: Perspectives on Gender, Race, Ethnicity, and Class,* edited by Kyriakos S. Markides (pp. 23-78). Newbury Park, CA.: Sage.

Verbrugge, Lois M. 1990. The twain meet: Empirical explanations of sex differences in health and mortality. In *Gender, Health, and Longevity: Multidisciplinary Perspectives,* edited by Marcia G. Ory and Huber R. Warner (pp. 159-199). New York: Springer.

Vinick, Barbara H. and David J. Ekerdt. 1992. Couples view retirement activities: Expectation versus experience. In *Families and Retirement,* edited by Maximiliane Szinovacz, David J. Ekerdt, and Barbara H. Vinick (pp. 129-144). Newbury Park, CA: Sage.

Waehrer, Keith and Stephen Crystal. 1995. The impact of coresidence on economic well-being of elderly widows. *Journal of Gerontology* 50B(4):S250-S258.

Walker, Alexis J. 1992. Conceptual perspectives on gender and family caregiving. In *Gender, Families, and Elder Care,* edited by Jeffrey W. Dwyer and Raymond T. Coward (pp. 34-46). Newbury Park, CA: Sage.

Walker, Karen. 1994. Men, women, and friendship; What they say, what they do. *Gender & Society* 8(2):246-265.

Wallace, Steven P. 1991. The political economy of health care for elderly blacks. In *Critical Perspectives on Aging: Toward a Political and Moral Economy of Growing Old,* edited by Meredith Minkler and Carroll L. Estes (pp. 253-270). Amityville, NY: Baywood.

Wallace, Steven P., John B. Williamson, Rita Gaston Lung, and Lawrence A. Powell. 1991. A lamb in wolf's clothing? The reality of senior power and social policy. In *Critical Perspectives on Aging: Toward a Political and Moral Economy of Growing Old,* edited by M. Minkler and C. L. Estes (pp. 95-114). Amityville, NY: Baywood.

Wan, Thomas T. H. 1982. *Stressful Life Events, Social Support Networks, and Gerontological Health: A Prospective Study.* Lexington, MA: Lexington Books.

Wan, Thomas T. H. 1984. Health consequences of major role losses in later life: A panel study. *Research on Aging* 6(4):469-489.

Wan, Thomas T. H. and Barbara Gill Odell. 1983. Major role losses and social participation of older males. *Research on Aging* 5(2):173-196.

Ward, Audrey W. M. 1976. Mortality of bereavement. *British Medical Journal* 1(Mar.):700-702.

Ward, Russell A., Susan R. Sherman, and Mark LaGory. 1984. Subjective networks assessments and subjective well-being. *Journal of Gerontology* 39(1):93-101.

Watkins, Susan Cotts. 1980. On measuring transitions and turning points. *Historical Methods* 13(3):181-187.

Watson, Wilbur H. 1986. Crystal ball gazing: Notes on today's middle aged blacks with implications for their aging in the 21st century. *The Gerontologist* 26(2):136-139.

Weber, Max. 1946. *The Theory of Social and Economic Organization,* Translated by A.M. Henderson and Talcott Parsons. New York: Free Press.

Weiss, Lawrence J. 1983. Intimacy and adaptation. In *Sexuality in the Later Years: Roles and Behavior,* edited by Ruth B. Weg (pp. 147-166). New York: Academic Press.

Weiss, Robert S. 1993. Loss and recovery. In *Handbook of Bereavement: Theory, Research, and Intervention,* edited by Margaret S. Stroebe, Wolfgang Stroebe, and Robert O. Hansson (pp. 271-284). Cambridge: Cambridge University Press.

Weissman, M. M. and J. K. Myers. 1978. Rates and risks of depressive symptoms in a United States urban community. *Acta Psychiatrica Scandinavica* 57:219-231.

West, Candace and Sarah Fenstermaker. 1995. Doing difference. *Gender and Society* 9(1): 8-37.

West, Candace and Don H. Zimmerman. 1987. Doing gender. *Gender and Society* 1(2): 125-151.

Wheaton, Blair. 1990. Life transitions, role histories, and mental health. *American Sociological Review* 55(2):209-223.

White-Means, Shelley I. and Michael C. Thornton. 1990. Labor market choices and home health care provision among employed ethnic caregivers. *The Gerontologist* 30(6): 769-775.

Whitley, Bernard E., Jr. 1984. Sex-role orientation and psychological well-being: Two meta-analyses. *Sex Roles* 12(1/2):207-225.

Wilkinson, Ian F., David N. Darby, and Andre Mant. 1987. Self-care and self-medication: An evaluation of individuals' health care decisions. *Medical Care* 25(10):965-978.

Williams, David R. 1992. Social structure and the health behaviors of Blacks. In *Aging, Health Behaviors, and Health Outcomes*, edited by K. Warner Schaie, Dan Blazer, and James S. House (pp. 59-64). Hillsdale, NJ: Lawrence Erlbaum.

Williams, David R., David T. Takeuchi, and Russell K. Adair. 1992. Marital status and psychiatric disorders among Blacks and Whites. *Journal of Health and Social Behavior* 33(2):140-157.

Williams, Dorie Giles. 1985. Gender, masculinity-femininity, and emotional intimacy in same-sex friendship. *Sex Roles* 12(5/6):587-600.

Wilson, Gail. 1995. "I'm the eyes and she's the arms": Changes in gender roles in advanced old age. In *Connecting Gender & Ageing: A Sociological Approach,* edited by Sara Arber and Jay Ginn (pp. 98-113). Buckingham, England: Open University Press.

Windle, Michael. 1986. Sex role orientation, cognitive flexibility, and life satisfaction among older adults. *Psychology of Women Quarterly* 10(3):263-273.

Wingard, Deborah L. 1984. The sex differential in morbidity, mortality, and lifestyle. *Annual Review of Public Health* 5:433-458.

Wolf, Douglas A. 1984. Kin availability and the living arrangements of older women. *Social Science Research* 13(1):72-89.

Wolinsky, Fredric D. and Robert J. Johnson. 1992. Widowhood, health status, and the use of health services by older adults: A cross-sectional and prospective approach. *Journal of Gerontology* 47(1):8-16.

Wood, Wendy, Nancy Rhodes, and Melanie Whelan. 1989. Sex differences in positive well-being: A consideration of emotional style and marital status. *Psychological Bulletin* 106(2):249-264.

Wortman, Camille B. and Roxane Cohen Silver. 1990. Successful mastery of bereavement and widowhood: A life-course perspective. In *Successful Aging: Perspectives from the Behavioral Sciences,* edited by Paul B. Baltes and Margret M. Baltes (pp. 225-264). Cambridge: Cambridge University Press.

Wortman, Camille B., Roxane Cohen Silver, and Ronald C. Kessler. 1993. The meaning of loss and adjustment to bereavement. In *Handbook of Bereavement: Theory, Research, and Intervention,* edited by Margaret S. Stroebe, Wolfgang Stroebe, and Robert O. Hansson (pp. 349-366). Cambridge: Cambridge University Press.

Wright, Paul H. 1989. Gender differences in adults' same- and cross-gender friendships. In *Older Adult Friendship: Structure and Process,* edited by Rebecca G. Adams and Rosemary Blieszner (pp. 197-221). Newbury Park, CA: Sage.

Wright, Paul H. and Mary Beth Scanlon. 1991. Gender role orientations and friendship: Some attenuation, but gender differerences abound. *Sex Roles* 24(9/10):551-566.

Young, Frank W. and Nina Glasgow. 1998. Voluntary social participation and health. *Research on Aging* 20(3):339-362.

Young, Michael, Bernard Benjamin, and Chris Walls. 1963. The mortality of widowers. *The Lancet* 2:454-456.

Younoszai, Barbara. 1993. Mexican American perspectives related to death. In *Ethnic Variations in Dying, Death, and Grief: Diversity in Universality,* edited by Donald P. Irish, Kathleen F. Lundquist, and Vivian Jenkins Nelsen (pp. 67-78). Washington, DC: Taylor & Francis.

Zautra, Alex J., John W. Reich, and Jason T. Newsom. 1995. Autonomy and sense of control among older adults: An examination of their effects on mental health. In *Promoting Successful and Productive Aging,* edited by Lynne A. Bond, Stephen J. Cutler, and Armi Grams (pp. 153-170). Thousand Oaks, CA: Sage.

Zick, Cathleen D. and Ken R. Smith. 1986. Immediate and delayed effects of widowhood on poverty: Patterns from the 1970s. *The Gerontologist* 26(6):669-675.

Zick, Cathleen D. and Ken R. Smith. 1988. Recent widowhood, remarriage, and changes in economic well-being. *Journal of Marriage and the Family* 50(1):233-244.

Zick, Cathleen D. and Ken R. Smith. 1991. Patterns of economic change surrounding the death of a spouse. *Journal of Gerontology* 46(6):S310-320.

Zisook, Sidney. 1987. Unresolved grief. In *Biopsychosocial Aspects of Bereavement,* edited by Sidney Zisook (pp. 23-34). Washington, DC: American Psychiatric Press.

Zisook, Sidney, Stephen R. Shuchter, and Lucy E. Lyons. 1987. Adjustment to widowhood. In *Biopsychosocial Aspects of Bereavement,* edited by Sidney Zisook (pp. 51-74). Washington, DC: American Psychiatric Press.

Zollar, Ann Creighton and J. Sherwood Williams. 1987. The contribution of marriage to the life satisfaction of black adults. *Journal of Marriage and the Family* 49(1):87-92.

Zsembik, Barbara A. 1993. Determinants of living alone among older Hispanics. *Research on Aging* 15(4):449-464.

Zsembik, Barbara A. and Audrey Singer. 1990. The problem of defining retirement among minorities: The Mexican Americans. *The Gerontologist* 30(6):749-757.

Author Index

Subject Index

253

ISBN 0-89503-210-4

9 780895 032102 >